HISTORY
OF THE
OLD TOWNSHIP
OF DUNSTABLE

HISTORY

OF THE

OLD TOWNSHIP
OF DUNSTABLE

INCLUDING

NASHUA, NASHVILLE, HOLLIS, HUDSON,
LITCHFIELD, AND MERRIMAC, N. II.:
DUNSTABLE AND TYNGSBOROUGH,

MASS.

BY CHARLES J. FOX.

NASHUA:
CHARLES T. GILL, PUBLISHER.
1846

NASHUA:
Murray & Kimball,
PRINTERS.

ISBN: 978-1-6673-0569-1 paperback
ISBN: 978-1-6673-0570-7 hardcover

NOTICE

A few pages only of this volume were in type, when its author was called away by death, from the community who esteemed and the friends who loved him. As arrangements had been made for the publication of the work, a large subscription obtained, and the promise of its appearance given to the public, it was thought best that no delay should take place. The history, as prepared by Mr. Fox, extended to the year 1840, during which the greater part of it was written. He had however, when undertaking its publication, procured information from various sources, as to transactions since that period, especially with regard to the present state of business in the village of Nashua. To condense this information, and incorporate it with what had been previously written, — to collect such additional facts as seemed desirable to be preserved in a volume of this kind, and to superintend the mechanical execution of the work, has been the task of the author's friends, — a task of some delicacy and difficulty, but rendered interesting not only by the nature of the work itself, but by its connection with one, who left so many claims to the affectionate remembrance of those who knew him. If under such circumstances, mistakes should be found to have passed uncorrected, which the eye of the author would have discovered, — or if the information given should seem deficient on any point where the further researches of the writer would have supplied it, the indulgence of the reader is requested.

Of the Author himself, a brief notice in this place will doubtless be expected by those who are acquainted with the circumstances under which the work is published. It is hoped that before long, a more full account of his character, labors and influence will be presented to the world by one who knew him intimately, and who is in every respect eminently suited to the task.

Charles James Fox was born at Antrim, N. H., in the month of October, 1811. He received his preparatory education at Dartmouth College, where he was graduated in 1831. He pursued the study of law, at first in the law school of Yale College, and afterwards with Daniel Abbot, Esq., of Nashua (now Nashville,) N. H. With this gentleman he subsequently entered into partnership. Having been chosen in 1837 a member of the State Legislature, he was appointed in connection with Judge Parker and Mr. Bell, to prepare for publication the Revised Statutes of New Hampshire. The great labor which he encountered in the fulfilment of this duty, added to that of an extensive legal practice, it is believed laid the foundation of that disease which at so early a period, deprived the community of his valuable life.

In 1841, Mr. Fox, in connection with Rev. Samuel Osgood, then pastor of the Unitarian Church in Nashua, prepared and published the "New Hampshire Book," a collection of pieces in prose and verse, from the writings of natives and adopted citizens of this state.

While a member of the Legislature, Mr. Fox took a deep interest in the establishment of the State Lunatic Asylum, of which he was appointed one of the Directors.

On the third of June, 1840, Mr. Fox was united in marriage to Miss Catherine P. Abbot, the daughter of his partner.

In the year 1843, Mr. Fox, in consequence of his declining health, took a voyage to the Mediterranean, visiting the interesting countries which surround that sea, and extending his travels as far as Egypt.

This voyage not having accomplished the restoration of his health, in the following autumn he sailed for the West Indies, accompanied by Mrs. Fox. Notwithstanding his feeble state of body, he looked on the scenes around him with an observant eye, and treasured up many interesting and instructive reminiscences, which were in part given to the world after his return, in a series of letters, published in the Nashua Gazette.

During this visit to the West Indies, the subject of slavery especially engaged his attention. He viewed it with the feelings of a philanthropist, united with the calm judgment of a lawyer; and had his health permitted him to complete his first design in the letters above referred to, his it testimony on this subject would have possessed a peculiar value. Enough however is contained in the letters which he was able to write and publish, to show his deep and enlightened interest in whatever concerned the rights and the welfare of his fellow beings.

From this journey he returned in a state of great feebleness, in June, 1845. During the succeeding fall and winter, he gradually sunk, though with intervals of apparent improvement, until his death, which took place February 17th.

1846. Industrious to the last, the hours when such exertion was possible, were devoted to the revision of the History which is now presented to the public, and to poetical compositions, chiefly on religious subjects.

The character of Mr. Fox had always, it is believed, been marked by purity and uprightness. As early as 1838, he became a member of the Unitarian Church in Nashua; he was an efficient teacher in the Sunday School, and a firm supporter of religious institutions and enterprises, until sickness compelled him to retire from public action. His views in the anticipation of death were calm ; he seemed to be without fear, and to rest on the assurances of his Heavenly Father's love. Only when he spoke of the greatness of the blessings which that love had provided, did his voice falter, and his dying words seem too weak to express his overflowing gratitude. With such ties to life as few possess, beloved and honored by the community, dear to the Church of Christ, and cherished as a son, a husband and a father, he surrendered himself with calm faith to the will of his Creator.

CONTENTS

HISTORY
OF THE OLD TOWNSHIP
OF DUNSTABLE

PREFACE

The following work was undertaken in consequence of a Vote passed at the Annual Meeting of the New Hampshire Historical Society, June 1840, appointing the Author Chairman of the Committee upon *Histories of Towns*. It was remarked that great deficiencies existed, and that materials should be speedily collected while so many of the immediate descendants of the first settlers were yet living. Attention was thus turned to the subject: – an examination of ancient records made and a collection of materials commenced, and the result is the compilation which is now submitted to the public.

It would be inconvenient and burdensome to cite the authority for every statement that is made, but the reader may be assured that no fact is stated as such without what is deemed to he good authority. The value of a work like this depends in a great measure upon the accuracy of its details, and to this the writer confidently lays claim. A large portion is extracted from the Town and Proprietary Records of Dunstable, which are in a good state of preservation, excepting a few years between 1694 and 1710. Much has been derived from the Town, Military, Ecclesiastical, Pecuniary, and Legislative Records of the Commonwealth of Massachusetts, prior to 1741, in the office of the Secretary of State, at Boston. For many accommodations in examining and copying the Records I am indebted to Rev. Joseph B. Felt, who has been employed for many years by the State in arranging and binding them. The materials for minute and accurate history there collected and arranged by Mr. Felt, are very curious and valuable. A similar collection of papers, belonging to a period subsequent to 1741, and including the French and Revolutionary wars, is found in the office of the Secretary of this State, at Concord, to which free access has been granted.

Frequent reference has also been had to the American, Massachusetts, and New Hampshire Historical Societies; to Farmer's and Moore's Historical Collections, Farmer's Notes to Belknap's New Hampshire; to the various Indian publications of Mr. Samuel E. Drake, the N. H. Gazetteer, and to all the Town and State Histories from which any thing could be gleaned. For much information we are indebted to the old inhabitants of the Town, and to the descendants of the early settlers.

Much time and labor have been devoted to the work. It may not he of general interest, hut it is hoped that its object will be appreciated by those for whom especially it was designed. The History of the settlement and growth of our Towns is deservedly attracting increased attention. As our old men pass away, and records are destroyed, and traditions forgotten, these collections thus preserved from destruction, humble and useless though they may appear to some, will become more and more valuable. Desirous of doing what he may for the home of his adoption, and fondly believing that the subject will he intrinsically interesting to every inhabitant of "Old Dunstable," this work has been prepared and is submitted by the Author.

* * *

Since the above was written, (1841,) five years have elapsed, and the work is unpublished, partly owing to the pressure of other labors, and partly to severe and long protracted sickness. An interval of comparative ease and the request of friends have now induced its preparation for the press, and it is offered to the indulgence of the public. It has been revised, enlarged and brought down to the present time. An effort has been made to obtain full and accurate statistics of the condition of the Village, hut under the circumstances, errors, omissions and imperfections must occur. For these charity is craved.

That this and some other portions of the work will not he so interesting to the general reader as the more romantic incidents is very evident, but there are few local Histories that contain so many of the latter as the present. Besides, the former are absolutely necessary to the complete history of a town, especially of a manufacturing town. To the kindness of friends the Author is so greatly indebted for assistance in such various forms, that he will only say, God bless them nil!

INTRODUCTION

IT was a remark of Edmund Burke, no superficial observer, that "they who never look back to their ancestors, will never look forward to posterity." There is great truth and beauty in the remark. Those who "build the tombs of the prophets," do not always, indeed, heed their precepts or follow their example, but those who care nothing for the past, its actors or its story, will care little for the welfare of the future. It is natural and commendable to care for those who have gone before us. "They have labored, and we have entered into their labors." The men who settled this region, and "hewed the ancient woods away," were such as the world had rarely seen. They were ready to do all, and dare all, and suffer all for the sake of conscience. They 0000000"called no man master," and the germ *of* freedom which they planted in the wilderness, became the noble "Liberty Tree" of the Revolution.

Of such descent we may well be proud. We wish to know who they were, and when, and where, and how they lived. Their toils and privations and sufferings, their opinions and peculiarities to us should be important. From them is derived all that is peculiar to the New England character; its energy, its ingenuity, its perseverance, and its hatred of tyranny in all its forms and manifestations. An insight into their every day life would be most valuable, but they have passed away, and the story of the *first settlers of Dunstable,* with its startling romance and stem realities, has nearly perished with them. A few materials yet exist, scattered and imperfect, in cotemporary journals and musty records, in ancient burial grounds or in uncertain traditions, only to be gathered with great labor and antiquarian zeal and patience. These perishing memorials have been sought out and embodied with filial regard, by one who is proud of a descent from the first settlers, trusting that the simple story of Indian perils and Revolutionary patriotism, of toil and perseverance, of enterprise and success will not prove entirely destitute of interest or of instruction.

CHAPTER I.
THE FIRST SETTLERS
OF DUNSTABLE

THE landing of the Pilgrims at Plymouth in December, 1620, is an epoch in the world's history. "On this bleak New England shore," in the wilderness, with the snows of winter around them and a few wretched dwellings to protect them, and wild beasts and wilder men, they established a Colony which is destined to solve a problem for the human race. Its motto and its basis was "freedom to worship God." Persecuted in the old world alike by Catholic and Episcopalian for opinion's sake, driven from their homes, they came to this "wilderness world" with gladsome hearts, "singing the songs of Zion," even in this "strange land," for that "here they could worship God according to the dictates of their consciences in peace."

The Plymouth settlers were but pioneers, and soon crowds flocked hither, ready to dare all and to endure all for the priceless boon of a free conscience and free speech. Boston, Salem, Portsmouth and Dover were settled, and every where, with each little band of brethren, the "man of God" went forth to cheer them in toil, in peril, and in death. As the fame of this new asylum for the oppressed began to spread abroad more widely, greater crowds of emigrants came, until the older settlements became too populous. Adventurous spirits went forth into the wilderness upon every side to found new plantations, and at a very early period, not long after the settlement of Boston, attention was turned towards the valleys of the Merrimac and the Nashua. In August, 1652, (1) the valley of the Merrimac as far northward as the outlet of Lake Winnipisiogee, was surveyed by Capt. Simon Willard and Capt. Edward Johnson, and its rich basins and valuable fishing stations were laid open to to the eager gaze of the adventurers.

The valleys of the Merrimac and Nashua are of alluvial formation. That they have undergone great changes is very evident. Their general appearance, the shape of their basins, their outlets, their different levels, and the stratified character of the soil, all show that at some remote period the greater portion of these valleys must have been covered with water in the form of Lakes or large Ponds. Geologists find the same characteristics upon all our Rivers, and some even refer their origin to the Deluge. But whenever and however their origin may have been, it is evident that the valley of the Merrimac was once a succession of Lakes, one ending at Pawtucket Falls and another at Amoskeag Falls, through whose rocky basins the waters at length burst their way, and formed their present lower channel, leaving their former beds dry.

The same is equally true of the valley of the Nashua, one outlet being at Mine Falls, and another at the high bluff near the Nashua Corporation, through which the river has forced a passage, and left large basins exposed for cultivation. In corroboration of this theory we know that logs have often been found here, buried in the earth at a great depth. When the excavation for the foundation of the Locks near the Merrimac was being made in 1825, at a spot about one hundred feet from the River, and at a depth of many feet below the surface, the workmen found several logs, a quantity of charcoal, as if the remains of a fire, and a *toad*, which, on being exposed to the sun and air, revived and hopped away. Such discoveries are not of unfrequent occurrence, but as to the time and mode of their deposit we are left only to theory and conjecture.

The valley of the Merrimac was not an object of desire to the English alone. From the earliest periods it seems to have been looked upon by the Indian as almost a Paradise. The *Winnipisiogee*, or "the very pleasant place where there is but little land," was deeply beloved. (1.) The Merrimac with its numerous *Naamkeeks*, or fishing stations, and its rich planting fields for maize, was still more dear. So far, indeed, had its fame extended, that in 1604, years before the Landing at Plymouth, a French Jesuit, writing from Canada to France, could say: "*The Indians tell us of a beautiful River lying far to the South, which they call Merrimac.*" (2.)

The Indians who inhabited the more southerly portions of the valley were of a mild disposition, and invited intercourse with the whites. In 1655 the settlements had extended as far North as Chelmsford and Groton. From 1655 to 1665 was a period of unwonted activity and prosperity. There was peace with the Indians, and the tide of population rolled onwards rapidly. The Indians had planting fields all along the valleys of the Merrimac, the

Souhegan, and the Nashua, and these were objects of eager desire to the settler. About 1655, grants of land in this vicinity were made to those who belonged to the exploring company of Johnson and Willard. In 1656 the lands upon both sides of the Merrimac, extending on the west side from Naticook brook (1.) to a line about a mile south of Penichuck brook, and including the greater part of Litchfield, were granted to William Brenton, and called "Brenton's Farm." (2.) Nearly all the interval lands about Naticook were granted not long after.

In 1659 and 1660 large tracts of land were granted upon the Souhegan river, (3.) at a place called by the Indians *Quohquinna-pashessan- anagnog*, being the meadows in Amherst which lie at the mouth of the small brook, which, arising in Mont Vernon, and flowing around the plain in Amherst, runs into the Souhegan in the South part of the town. Five hundred acres were granted to Capt. William Davis of Boston and Capt. Isaac Johnson of Roxbury; (1.) 500 acres to Mrs. Anna Lane; and 300 acres to John Wilson of Boston. 1000 acres were also granted to the town of Charlestown for a "School Farm," lying upon the Souhegan, in Milford, about four or five miles westerly of the first grants, "at a great hill called Dramcap hill," and 500 acres to Mrs. Anna Cole "adjoining thereto." (2.)

About the same time a grant of 400 acres, lying at the mouth of Salmon Brook, was made to John Whiting. It was bounded on the north "by the upland," and extended up the brook about a mile and a half, embracing the southerly part of Nashua Village. Several hundred acres, also, were granted at Penichuck Pond, and so down Penichuck Brook, in Merrimac and Nashville.

About 1662, 500 acres upon the easterly side of the Merrimac, in Litchfield, "at Nacook," were granted to the town of Billerica for a "School Farm," and 300 acres adjoining, to "Phinehas Pratt and others for straights and hardships endured by them in planting at Plymouth *of which he was one.*" (3.)

Four hundred acres were granted to Gov. Endicott, "lying in the westerly part of Pelham," about six miles north of Pawtucket Fails, and one mile west of Beaver Brook, at a great hill called *Masha-shathuck,* (4.) "lying between two other great hills, and adjoining southerly on a great Pond called *Pimmo-milli-quonnil.*"

About this period, but at what date is uncertain, a grant of a large tract in Hudson and Pelham was made to Henry Kimball, and called *"Henry Kimball's Farm."* Samuel Scarlet had a farm also, on the north side of Merrimac River, perhaps in Tyngsborough; Lieut. Joseph Wheeler, and his father Capt. Thomas Wheeler, had a farm upon the Merrimac, in Nashua, a little south of Salmon Brook, and several others whose names are not preserved.

In September, 1673, a grant of 1000 acres, lying in Nashville, was made to the "Ancient and Honorable Artillery Company" of Boston. It was bounded East by the Merrimac, south by the Nashua, West by Spectacle Brook, (1.) and extended about one mile northerly of Nashua River. This embraced the whole of the village of

Nashville, and was called the *"Artillery Farm."* From this circumstance the little Pond in the north part of the village was called *"Artillery Pond."*

At this period, 14,000 acres, lying along the Merrimac, upon both sides, between Souhegan River and Chelmsford, had been granted to various individuals, but as yet few settlements had been made. It became necessary, therefore, for their mutual benefit, to consolidate all the grants into one *plantation,* and to secure to the inhabitants all the privileges and immunities of an incorporated Township. Accordingly, in September, 1673, the proprietors of the farms already laid out, and others who were disposed to settle here, presented a Petition to the General Assembly, of which the following is a copy. (2.)

"To the Honored Governor, Deputy Governor, with the Magistrates and Deputies now assembled in the General Court at Boston, Sept. 19, 1673.

"The Petition of the Proprietors of the farms that are laid out upon Merrimac River, and places adjacent, with others who desire to joyn with them in the settlement of a plantation there –

"HUMBLY SHEWETH

"That whereas there is a considerable tract of the Country's land that is invironed with the proprieties of particular persons and towns, viz: by the line of the town of Chelmsford, and by Groton line, and by Mr. Brenton's farm, by Souhegan farms, and beyond Merrimac River by the outermost line of Henry Kimball's farm, and so to Chelmsford line again – All which is in little capacity of doing the country any service except the farms bordering upon it be adjoined to said land, to make a plantation there; and there being a considerable number of persons who are of a sober and orderly conversation, who do stand in great need of accommodations, who are willing and ready to make present improvement of the said vacant lands: And the Proprietors of the said farms are therefore willing to join with and give encouragement to those that shall improve the said lands: – the farms of those that are within the tract of land before described, being about 14,-000 acres at the least:——

"Your Petitioners therefore humbly request the favour of the Honorable Court that they will please to grant the said tract of land to your Petitioners, and to such as will join with them in the settlement of the lands before mentioned, so that those who have improved their farms there, and others who speedily intend to do the same, may be in a way for the support of the public ordinances of God, for without which the greatest part of the year they will he deprived of, the farms lying so far remote from any towns: and farther that the Honorable Court will please grant the like immunities to this plantation, as they in their favours have formerly granted to other new Plantations: – So shall your Petitioners be ever engaged to pray:——

"1. Thomas Brattle.

2. Jonathan Tyng.

3. Joseph Wheeler.

4. James Parkerson.

5. Robert Gibbs.

6. John Turner.

7. Sampson Sheafe.

8. Samuel Scarlet.

9. William Lakin.

10. Abraham Parker.

11. James Knapp.

12. Robert Proctor.

13. Simon Willard, Jr.

14. Thomas Edwards.

15. Thomas Wheeler, Sen.

16. Peter Bulkely.

17. Joseph Parker.

18. John Morse, Sen.

19. Samuel Combs.

20. James Parker, Jr.

21. John Parker.

22. Josiah Parker.

23. Nathaniel Blood.

24. Robert Parris.

25. John Jolliffe.

26. Zachariah Long."

The Petition was granted upon conditions which were then universally inserted in the Charters; that the Grantees should *"settle"* the Plantation, procure a minister within three years, and reserve a farm for the use of the Colony. By *setiling* the Plantation was understood procuring a competent number of *actual settlers,* (twenty or more,) who should build houses capable of defence, at least *eighteen feet square,* and who should live upon and improve their lands: and also, the erection of a Meeting House. The following is a copy of the original Charter, dated October 15, 1673, (corresponding with October 26th, New Style.) which includes all the above grants. (1.)

"At a General Court held at Boston ye 15th (26th) October, 1673.

In answer to the Petition of Thomas Brattle, Jonathan Tyng, James Parker and William Lakin, in behalf of themselves and others joyning in their humble Petition to desire the favor of this Court to grant them liberty to settle a plantation with their ffarmes, and a considerable tract of land belonging to ye country being invironed with the proprieties of particular persons and towns; as by ye line of Chelmsford, and by Groton line, and by Mr. Brenton's ffarm, by Souhegan ffarmes, and beyoud Merrimac River by ye utmost line of Henry Kimbo's farme, and so to Chelmsford line again, as also such other immunities to the plantation as this Court hath formerly granted to other new plantations: –

The Court judgeth it meet to grant their request provided a farme of five hundred acres of upland and medo he laid out of this tract for the country's use, and that they shall in settling the plantation endeavor so as to finish it once (I.) within three years, and procure an able and othordox minister amongst them.

That this is a true copy taken and compared with the original records, *Attest*

EDWARD RAWSON, Secretary."

MAP OF OLD DUNSTABLE.

In May, 1674, the new Plantation was surveyed by Jonathan Danforth, and its boundaries are thus described: (2.)

"It lieth upon both sides Merrimac River on the Na-sha- way River. It is bounded on the South by Chelmsford, by Groton line, and partly by country land. The Westerly line runs due North until you come to Souhegan River to a hill called dram cup bill to a great pine near to ye said River at the N. W. comer of Charlestown School farm; bounded by Souhegan River on the North; and on the East side Merrimac it begins at a great stone which was supposed to be near the North East corner of Mr. Brenton's land; and from thence it runs Sou. south east six miles to a pine tree marked:F: standing within sight of Beaver Brook; thence it runs two degrees West of South four miles and a quarter which reaehed to the south side of Henry Kimble's farm at Jeremie's Hill; thence from ye South east angell of said farm it runs two degrees and a quarter westward of the south near to the head of the Long Pond which lieth at ye head of Edward Colburn's farm. – And thus it is bounded by ye said Pond and the head of said Colburn's farm; taking in Captain Scarlett's farm so as to close again; all which is sufficiently bounded and described.

Dunstable, 3d. mo. (May) 1674." (3.)

The Township of Dunstable embraced a very large tract, probably *more than two hundred square miles,* including the Towns of Nashua, Nashville, Hudson, Hollis. Dunstable and Tyngsborough. besides portions of the towns of Amherst, Milford, Merrimac, Litchfield, Londonderry, Pelham, Brookline, Pepperell, and Townsend, and formed a part of the County of Middlesex. At this late day it is extremely difficult to define its boundaries accurately, but by a perambulation of lines made in 1734, an approximation may he made. The north eastern corner was a very large and high rock now standing about three miles north easterly of the mouth of Souhegan River in Londonderry. The south east corner was " at the corner of Methuen and Dracuf." in sight of Beaver Brook." The north west corner was at" dram cup hill" on the Souhegan, in the westerly part of Milford, and the westerly line which ran *"due South"* passed " near the west end of Muscatanapus Pond," in Brookline. (1.) It extended ten or twelve miles west of Merrimac River, and from three to five miles east of it, and its average length north and south was from twelve to fourteen miles. The present Township of Nashua and Nashville occupies very nearly the centre of the original Township.

In 1674, because there was "very little medo left except what is already granted to the ffarmes." the easterly line of the township was extended to Beaver Brook, by an additional grant from the General Court, and the Town was called DuNstable. It received its name in compliment to Mrs. Mary Tyirg, wife of Hon. Edward Tyng, one of the Magistrates of the Commonwealth of Massachusetts, who came from Dunstable, England.

Among the original Proprietors we find the names of many of the leading men in the Colony, some of whom, with the children and friends of others, removed here and took up their abode at an early period. Of this number we find Gov. Dudley, who married a daughter of Hon. Edward Tyng of this town, Rev. Thomas Weld, who was the first minister, and married another daughter, Thomas Brattle, Peter Bulkely, Heze- kiah Usher, Elisha Hutchinson, Francis Cook, and others who were Assistants and Magistrates. Many of the first settlers belonged to Boston and its vicinity, a circumstance which gave strength and influence to the infant plantation.

At what time and by whom Dunstable was first settled is uncertain, but it must have been considerably earlier than the date of the charter in 1673. In the Charter farms are mentioned as then existing, and some of "the farmers" were among the Petitioners. Of this number were Scarlett, Wheeler, and others. In 1675. *orchards* are mentioned as then in existence, which must have been the growth of years. In 1674, *"the house of Lt. Wheeler"* is designated as a place of holding a meeting of the Proprietors, and we have some reason to suppose that he may have been the earliest settler. (1.) Wheeler and Bren- ton were fur traders among the Indians. In 1657, the trade with the Indians was regulated by the General Court, and the exclusive right of this trade upon Merrimac river was sold to " Maj. (Simon.) Willard, Mr. (William,) Brenton, Ensign (Thomas.) Wheeler, and Thomas Henchman," for £25. The sale bears date July 1, 1657. (1.)

For the purpose of trafficking with the Indians more conveniently, it was customary to establish trading houses beyond the settlements, and at places to which they could easily resort. It is not impossible that Wheeler may have resided here for such a purpose, at an early date after his grant, as Henchman resided a little farther south in Chelmsford. About 1665, John Cromwell, an Indian trader also, resided at Tyngsborough, hut soon after removed to Merrimac, where he built a trading house, about two miles above the mouth of Penichuck brook, at the falls which now bear his name. (2.) According to the custom of the time, it is said that he used his foot as *a pound weight* in the purchase of furs, until the Indians, beginning to suspect him of cheating them, drove him away and burned his house, the cellar of which still is or was recently visible. It is stated by Farmer, (3.) whose authority is unquestionable, that the ancient settlement" was within the limits of Nashua, and as grants of land here were made in 1659, and farms existed here before 1673, and as Chelmsford was settled in 1655, we may reasonably conclude that some, who stood "in great need of accommodations," found their way to the rich intervals upon our rivers, at a period not much later than the date of the grants.

It has often been remarked that, in the settlement of New England, we may discover the hand of an overruling Providence. The Plague, which swept off the Indian tribes in and around Plymouth and Piscataqua, in 1612 and 1613, prepared the way for the coming of the forefathers, and similar providential events occurred as population moved westward. The valleys of the Merrimac and the Nashua were inhabited by numerous small tribes, or branches of tribes of Indians, who lived in villages containing one hundred or two hundred souls, and subsisted chiefly by fishing and hunting. The Nashaways had their head quarters at. Lancaster; the Nashobas at Littleton; the Pawtuckets at Pawtucket Falls: the Wamesits at Wamesit Falls, at the mouth of Concord river; the Naticooks in this vicinity; and the Penacooks around Penacook, now Concord, N. H. They were all, however, subject to Passaconoway. The Mohawks, or Maquas, a fierce and savage tribe from New York, were the hereditary enemies of them all. The Indian tribes which dwelt nearest to the English settlements, and especially the Pawtuckets and Wamesits, from their weakness, and their fears both of the Mohawks and the English, craved the friendship and protection of the latter. They served as guides and sentinels for the exposed frontiers, and were often of great service. The Penacooks, however, were a more hold, warlike, and dangerous race, who refused all attempts to christianize them, although their dread of the English was generally sufficient to keep them from open hostility.

In the spring of 1669, a portion of the Penacooks, fearing an attack from the Mohawks, moved down the Merrimac to the Pawtucket, and built a fort there for their protection. Their neighborhood was a cause of alarm to the settlers, some of whom shut themselves up in garrisons; but in the succeeding autumn they joined in an expedition against the Mohawks, by whom they were overpowered, and almost entirely destroyed. (1.) The greater part of the Indians in this vicinity, especially the more turbulent and dangerous to the number of *six or seven hundred,* united in this expedition, and nearly the whole of them perished, with more than *fifty* chiefs. The remnant, dispirited and powerless, united with the Wamesits, and became *"praying Indians."*

At this time, Passaconaway (2.) was sachem of the Penacooks and held rule over all the Indians from the Piscataqua to the Connecticut, and all down the Merrimac. He resided at Penacook, and the Naticooks, Pawtuckets and Wamesits were subject to his power. He had been a great warrior, and was the greatest and "most noted powow and sorcerer of all the country." (3.) He died before 1670, at the great age of one hundred and twenty. "In 1660, not long before his death, at a great feast and dance, he made his farewell speech to his people. In this he urged them, as a dying man, to take heed how they quarrelled with their English neighbors, for though they might do them some harm, yet it would prove the means of their own destruction. He told them that he had been a bitter enemy to the English, and had tried all the arts of sorcery to prevent their settlement, but could by no means succeed." (4.)

This declaration made a great impression, for we find that Wannalancet, his second son and successor, after the eldest son with the more restless part of the tribe had removed into Maine, was always after a friend to the whites. He resided generally at Wamesit falls, and was proprietor, with his tribe, of all the lands in this vicinity. About 1663, the eldest son of Passacona- way was thrown into jail for a debt of £45, due to John Tinker by one of his tribe, and which he had promised verbally should be paid. To relieve him from his imprisonment, his brother Wannalancet and others who owned Wicasuck Island, (I.) sold it and paid the debt.

Soon after, the General Court granted him one hundred acres of land "on a great hill about twelve miles west of Chelmsford," and probably in Pepperell, because he had "a great many children and no planting grounds." In 1665, he petitioned the General Court that this island might be restored to him and his brethren, the original owners, and the original petition, signed by him with the others, in a fair, bold hand, is now on file at the Secretary's office. His request was granted, and the Island purchased and restored By the colony. (2.)

About 1675, during the war with King Philip, he left Wamesit, and resided in Canada and various other places, lest he should be drawn into the contest. During these wanderings he warned the whites of many intended attacks and averted others. When Wannalancet returned to Pawtucket, after the death of Philip, he called upon Rev. Mr. Fiske, of Chelmsford, and inquired what disasters had befallen the town during the war. Mr. Fiske replied that they had been highly favored, for which he desired " to thank God." "*Me next,*" said the shrewd Sagamore, who claimed his share of the merit. Thus providentially was all this region freed from hostile indians, and the way opened for the coming of our fathers in comparative safety.

The valleys of the Naticook, of Salmon brook and the Nashua, (or Watananock as it is called in the Court Records.) especially near their mouths, were favorite resorts and abodes of the Indians. There, memorials of their residence have often been discovered. Such spots, combining a rich and easily wrought alluvial soil with productive fisheries, were always chosen: and the choice was a wise and beautiful one. The Indian was the child of Nature, and gazed upon her charms with filial admiration. With a true sense of the sublime, to him " the mountains were God's altars," and he looked up to their clond-capped summits with deep awe, as the dwelling place of "the Great Spirit."'

With a sense of the beautiful equally true, their homes were grouped together in some sheltered valley, girt round with hills, and woods, and water falls; or by the border of some quiet lake, or upon the rich alluvium of the river; but whether for convenience or beauty, they were ever by the water-side. And truly, when these spots were covered with the grand old woods, their primal vesture, when the white man's steps had not yet profaned the solitude, few scenes could have been found more lovely than the valleys of the Merrimac, of Salmon brook, and the Nashua.

The Chiefs who dwelt in those valleys did not generally live in a style of much greater magnifi- cence than their subjects, though they enjoyed greater abundance. Their confederacy was a great democracy, where danger, conflict and toil and privation were shared alike by all, the leader being distinguished only by greater exertions and braver daring. But on great occasions they exhibited a rude splendor and profusion befitting the dignity of the tribe and its rulers, Sachems, and to which all contributed. Whittier, in his " Bridal of Penacook," has given us a graphic picture of a wedding and dance given by Passaccnaway on the marriage of his daughter, Weta- moo, to Winnepurkit, Sachem of Saugus, Maine.

He has most beautifully and happily introduced the sweet and flowing Indian names, (how barbarous the taste which substituted most of our modern ones !) which abound along the Merrimac and its tributaries, and the whole scene is delightful as a specimen of Indian domestic life. For this reason, and as a portion of the luxuries were furnished by our own streams and hillsides, it is thought that its insertion here will not be inappropriate: –

THE BASHABA'S (J.) FEAST.

"With pipes of peace and bows unstrung,
Glowing with paint, came old and young,
In wampum, and furs and feathers arrayed,
To the dance and feast Bashaba made.

Bird of the of and beast of the field,
All which the woods and waters yield,
On dishes of birch and hemlock piled,
Garnished and graced that banquet wild.

Steaks of the brown bear fat and large,
From the rocky slopes of the Kearsarge;
Delicate trout from Babhoosuck brook,
And salmon spear'd in the Contooccok;

Squirrels which fed where nuts fell thick,
In the gravelly bed of the Otternic,
And small wild hens in reed-snares caught,
From the banks of Sondagardee brought.

Pike and perch from the Suncook taken,
Nuts from the trees of the Black Hills shaken,
Cranberries picked in the Squamscot bog,
And grapes from the vines of Piscataquog.

And drawn from that great stone vase which stands
In the river scooped by a spirit's hands, (1.)
In white parched pile, or thick suppawn,
Stood the birchen dishes of smoking corn.

Thus bird of the air and beast of the field,
All which the woods and water yield,
Furnished in that olden day,
The bridal feast of the Bashaba.

And merrily when that feast was done,
On the fire-lit green, the dance begun;
With the squaws' shrill stave, and deeper hum
Of old men beating the Indian drum.

Painted and plumed, with scalp locks flowing,
And red arms tossing, and black eyes glowing;
Now in the light and now in the shade,
Around the fires the dancers played.

The step was quicker, the song more shrill,
And the beat of the small drums louder still,
Whenever within the circle drew,
The Saugus Sachem and Weetamoo."

Among the first settlers of Dunstable we find the names of Rev. Mr. Thomas Weld, Joseph Wheeler, John Blanchard, Jonathan Tyng, Cornelius Waldo, Samuel Warner, Obadiah Perry, Samuel French, Robert Parris, Thomas Cummings, Isaac Cummings, Joseph Hassell, Christopher Temple, John Goold, Samuel Coold, John Lollendine, Christopher Reed, Thomas Lund, Daniel Waldo, Andrew Cook, Samuel Whiting, John Love well. John Acres, John Waldo, William Beale, Samuel Beale, John Cummings, Robert Usher, Henry Farwell, Robert Proctor, Joseph Lovewell, John Lovewell, jr. The earliest compact settlements were made near the month of Salmon brook, between its mouth and the main road, and so down the Merrimac, upon the spots deserted by the Indians.

The land which lay between Salmon brook and the Merrimac was called "The Neck," and for greater security the "housne-lotts" (*house lots*) of the first settlers were laid out adjoining each other, and "within the neck." The lots which lay nearest Salmon brook ran from Salmon brook to the Merrimac, and were generally from thirty to forty rods in width upon each stream. After the first six or eight lots, the west line of the lots was bounded upon "Long Hill." In the rear of the school house in the Harbor district in Nashua, and the north and east edges of the Mill Pond, several cellar holes are still visible, and within a few years an ancient well was open. Apple trees are there standing, hollow, splintered, covered with moss and almost entirely decayed, bearing marks of very great antiquity. The early settlers came from the south eastern part of England, where cider and perry were manufactured in great quantities, and they brought with them the same tastes and habits. Orchards are spoken of in our town records as early as 1675, and these shattered relics of an age that is past may possibly have been the original stock, or at least their immediate descendants.

About fifty rods north east of the school house, near a small cluster of oaks, stood the "OLD FORT," or garrison, in which the inhabitants dwelt in seasons of imminent danger, and to which they often retired at night. There was a well in the fort which was open until within a few years. South of this spot, on the north hank of Salmon brook, and just in rear of the house of Miss Allds, were the houses of Hassell, Temple, and Perry, the cellar holes of which are still visible. The field adjoining was owned by Perry, and is still known as the "Perry Field."

After the Charter was obtained in 1673, the inhabitants increased rapidly. The proprietors made liberal grants to actual settlers, and upon the following conditions, which have been selected from their articles of agreement drawn up Oct. 15, 1673.

"Every one yt (1.) is received (as an inhabitant,) shall have 10 acres for his person, and one acre more added thereto for every £20 estate, and none shall have above 30 acres in yr house Ions, nor none under 10 acres, and yt all after divisions of land shall be proportioned according to their home lotts, and so shall all yr public charges be, both as to church and town.

"All ye inhabitants yt are received into this town shall make improvements of ye lotts yt they take up, by building upon them, by fencing and by breaking up land, by the time prefixed by the General Court, wb. is by Oct. 1676, and they shall live, each inhabitant upon his own lott, or else put such inhabitant upon it as the town accepts.

"To the intent yt we may live in love and peace together we do agree, yt whatever fence we do make, either about cornfields, orchards or gardens, shall be a sufficient *four rail* fence, or yt which is equivalent, whether hedge, ditch, or stone wall, or of loggs, and if any person sustain damage through the deficiency of their own fences not being according to order, he shall bear his own damage. – And if any man's cattle he unruly he shall do his best endeavour to restrain them from doing himself or his neighbour (any harm.)"

These conditions, which evince much foresight, combined with the local advantages, were readily accepted, for May 11th, 1674, a meeting was holden at "the house of Lt. Joseph Wheeler," and a written agreement made between the proprietors and settlers. In this agreement it is provided, that "the meeting house which is to be erected shall stand between Salmon brook and the house of Lt. Wheeler, as convenient as may be for the accommodation of both." As a meeting house in those perilous times, when men toiled and worshipped with their rifles by their side, would not be very likely to be erected beyond the settlement, we may reasonably suppose that the settlement at Salmon brook had already commenced, and that at that date there were a considerable number of inhabitants.

FOOTNOTES

(1)   This survey was made by order of the General Assembly of Massachusetts to determine the Northerly bound of the Colony, and an inscription was made upon a large stone in Winnipisiogee River, at a point *"three miles North of the head of Merrimac River,"* to designate the spot. The Colony of Massachusetts then claimed all the land lying "three miles" North and East of the Merrimac from its mouth to this point, and thence due West to New York. This stone was discovered a few years since, and gave rise to many conjectures as to its origin. For an account of it, see 4 N. *H. Historical Collections,* 194.

(1.) The Indians are also said to have called it, "The smile of the Great Spirit." The name is *Winni-pecsi-okhe,* and should be pronounced *Win-ni-pis-saw'-key,* with the accent on the last syllable but one.

(2.) Sieur De Monts. Relations of the Jesuits, 1604. Merrimac means *Sturgeon.* There is also a *Merrimac* which flows into the Missouri river.

(1.) *Naticook* is the little brook just above Thornton's Ferry, in Merrimac.

(2.) The Indian name of Litchfield and Merrimac was *Naticook.* Sometimes the land East of the river was called *Nacook.* – *Belknap,* 224. N. H. Gazetteer. Litchfield.

(3.) This was anciently written *Souhegenack,* and means, it is said, *crooked.* – 5 N. H. Hist. Coll., 87.

(1.) Capt. Johnson was killed at the great Narragansct Swamp Fight, Dec. 19, 1675.

(2.) These grants were ail made by Massachusetts. For an account of them see *Assembly Records,* 1659, 1600, in the office of the Secretary of the Common wealth, at Boston, *pages* 327, 357, 358, 359, 364, 404.

(3.) Drake's Book of the Indians, page 35. Mass. Assembly Records, 1662, 1665.

(4.) *Massa-attuck* means *Deer-hill. Pimmo-mitti-quonnit* signifies *a Long Pond.*

(1.) The little brook about a mile Westerly of the village, which runs through the farm now owned by Hiram Woods. – *Mass. Assembly Records,* 1673: *page* 729.

(2.). *Mass. Assembly Records,* 1673. The original Petition is on file, and the ancient spelling has been preserved.

(1.) *Mass. Assembly Records,* **1673,** *Page* **730.** *Records of Towns,* 1673. **In** order to **make** the dates which are previous to *A.* D. **1751,** compared with our present reckoning, *eleven days* should in all cases be added.

(1.) The meaning of this is obscure: perhaps it is that the number of settlers necessary to make or "finish" a settlement shall he procured within three years.

(2.) *Town and Proprietary Records, Page 1.*

(3.) Before A. D. 1751, the year began March 25th., and the months were often numbered thus: March, or first month; April, second month; May, third month, &c. In 1751 they began to reckon the year from the first day of January. At that time, in consequence of having reckoned only 365 days to a year, *eleven days* had been gained, which were, then struck out of the calendar. Dales prior to 1751 are called Old Style; subsequent, New Style.

(1.) This Pond is situated near the Meeting House, and is still called *"Tan opus Pond." Musca-tanapus* signifies *Bear Pond.* – *Mass. Records. Towns.* 1734. *Page* 63.

(1.) Lt. Wheeler left town in Philip's War, 1675, and did not return. His father, Capt. Thomas Wheeler, of Groton, the noted Indian fighter, for a time resided with him. – 2 *N. H. Hisl. Coll.* 5.

(1.) *Mass. Assembly Records,* 1657, *page* 293. The trade of "Nashuway river" was sold at the same lime for £3.

(2.) The Indian name of Cromwell's Falls was *Nesenkeag,* and, as was generally the case, as at Naticook, Amoskeag, &c., the land for some distance around received the same name.

(3.) *Belknap, 117, note by Farmer, and his manuscript records.* In his Catechism of the History of New Hampshire," he says: – "This town had been settled several years before the date of the Charter. *Page* 23.

(1.) *Book of the Indians, 45. Allen's History of Chelmsford, 140 to 161.*

(2.) *Gookin's History of the Christian Indians. 2 Am. Antliq. Collections.*

(3.) *Hubbard's Indian Wars.*

(4.) *Gookin. Hubbard. 4 N. H. Hist. Coll. 23.*

(1.) Wicasuck is the small island in Merrimac river, near Wicassee falls, in Tyngsborough.

(2.) *Assembly Records, Mass., \ bfö,-pagc 106.*

(1.) The name given to two or three principal chiefs.

(1.) There are rocks in the river at the Falls of Amoskeag, in the cavities of which, tradition says, the Indians formerly stored and concealed their corn.

(1.) I have preserved the original spelling, in which yr, yt, ye, are written for their, that, and the.

CHAPTER II.
THE INDIAN WAR
OF 1675

In the summer of 1675 the war with Philip, the powerful and wily Sachem of the Wampanoags, commenced, which involved nearly all the Indians in New England. It was not without a hitter struggle that the red men left their pleasant valleys, where they had roamed in childhood, and where the bones of their fathers rested. Township after township had been occupied by the white men. and they had been crowded from their ancient hunting fields and fishing stations. At length they were surrounded by settlements, and mutual aggressions and heart-burnings ensued. The red man and the white man could not longer live together, and the annihilation of one party or the other seemed the only alternative. The Indians combined for a war of extermination, and all throughout New England were burning and massacre and devastation. Lancaster, Groton and Chelmsford were destroyed, and hundreds killed or carried into captivity.

At such a period, with a war of extermination raging all around them, the settlers of Dunstable were indeed in a perilous situation. Scarcely as yet were the forests cleared away, and their dwellings erected. Even their meeting-house was not yet finished. To increase their alarm. Wannalancet withdrew from Wamesit, and surprise magnified it into a proof of hostility. When the news of the first bloodshed came to Dunstable, in 1675, "seven Indians, belonging to Narragansett, Long Island and Pequod, who had been at work for seven weeks with one Mr. Jonathan Tyng, of Dunstable, on Merrimac river, hearing of the war they reckoned with their master, and getting their wages, conveyed themselves away without his privity, and being afraid, marched secretly through the woods, designing to go to their own country. (1.) At Quaboag, (now Brookfield, Mass.,) however, they were discovered by some friendly Indians, arrested and sent to Boston, where they were confined fora considerable time, but nothing being proved against them, they were at length discharged."

The settlers petitioned for relief from the Colony, in their distresses, and Capt. Samuel Mose- ly, just on his march to the fight at Bloody Brook, thus writes: "Nasa-wok, alias Lancaster, August 18, 1678. According to my orders from Maj. Gen. Denison, I sent to Dunstable *eighteen* men for to enlarge their garrison, and to Chelmsford twelve men, and to Groton twelve men." (2.) – This force was continued for their protection during the whole of the year, and an attack prevented.

Sept. 8, 1675, instructions were given by the Governor and Council (3.) to Capt. Thomas Brattle and Lt. Thomas Henchman, to take various measures for the better security of the settlement. They were ordered,

First: To draft fifty men and form garrisons at Dunstable, Groton, and Lancaster.

Second: To appoint a Guardian over the friendly Indians, at each of their towns, who should oversee them, and prevent all difficulties or dangers which might occur upon either side:

Third: To "send a runner or two to Wannalancet, Sachem of Naamkeak, (J.) who had withdrawn into the woods from fear," and to persuade him "to come in again" and live at Wamesit:

Fourth: To inform the Indians at Penacook and Naticook that if they will live quietly and peaceably, they shall not be harmed by the English.

These instructions were immediately and strictly obeyed. The garrison at Dunstable was strengthened. Lt. Henchman took charge of the Indians at Wamesit. Runners were sent out to Wannalancet, but they did not prevail upon him to return until the close of the war the next summer. Capt. Mosely, with his choice company of *one hundred* men, making Dunstable his place of rendezvous, marched up to Naticook and Penacook to disperse the hostile Indians who were said to be gathered there for the purpose of mischief. "When the English drew nigh, whereof they had intelligence by scouts, they left their fort, and withdrew into the woods and swamps, where they had advantage and opportunity enough in ambushment to have slain many of the English soldiers, without any great harm to themselves, and several of the young Indians inclined to it, but the Sachem, Wannalancet, by his authority and wisdom restrained his men, and suffered not an Indian to appear or shoot a gun. They were very near the English, and yet though they were provoked by the English, who burned their wigwams and destroyed some dried fish, yet not one gun was shot at any English-man."(1.) Wannalancet is said to have been restrained by the dying speech of Passaconaway, his father.

The Indians who dwelt at Naticook (2.) were alarmed at their hostile movements, and gathering their corn hast-ily, prepared to leave their homes. This created new sus-picion and alarm among the settlers, and nearly all of them deserted the town, although companies of scouts were constantly traversing the wilderness for the protec-tion of the frontiers.

The winter of 1675 was a time of fear and of trial. Nev-er had "the Indian enemy" been more active or dreaded. Even the "Christian Indians" had communications with their hostile brethren, and the whiles began to suspect *them* of treachery. The alarm increased to such a degree that every settler left Dunstable except Jonathan Tyng.(3.) With a resolution which is worthy of all praise, and of which we with difficulty conceive, he fortified his house; and although "obliged to send to Boston for his food," sat himself down in the midst of his savage enemies, alone, in the wilderness, to defend his home. Deeming his posi-tion an important one for the defence of the frontiers, in Feb. 1676, he petitioned the Colony for aid.(4.)

"The Petition of Jonathan Tyng Humbly sheweth:

That yr Petitioner living in the uppermost house on Merrimac river, lying open to ye enemy, yet being so seated that it is as it were a watch house to the neighbouring towns, from whence we can easily give them notice of the approach of the enemy, and may also be of use to the publique in many respects; also are near unto the place of the Indian's ffishing, from which in the season thereof they have great supplies, which I doubt not but we may be a great means of preventing them thereof; there being never an inhabitant left in the town but myself: –

Wherefore your Petitioner doth humbly request that your Honors would be pleased to order him *three or four men* to help garrison his said house, which he has been at great charge to ffortify, and may be of service to the publique: your favour therein shall further oblige me as in duly bound to pray for a blessing on your Councils, and remain Your Honorables' humble servant,

JONATHAN TYNG."

Dunstable, Feb. 3, 1675-'6.(1.)

This petition was granted immediately, and a guard of several men despatched to his relief, which remained during the war. This plantation was never deserted, and he thus became *the earliest permanent settler* within the limits of Dunstable.

February 25, 1675-'6, an attack was made by the Indians upon Chelmsford, and several buildings were burned. Colburn's garrison on the east side of the Merrimac was strengthened, but nearly all the outer settlements were deserted. A few days later, March 20, another attack was made, and Joseph Parker wounded. (2.) There was no surgeon in the vicinity, and an express was sent to Boston to obtain one. The Council ordered Dr. David Middleton to repair forthwith to Chelmsford, from whence he writes, "We expect the Indians to attack us every hour," and he asks that troops may be sent for their defence without delay, lest they should be cut off by the enemy. (1) Such is a specimen of life upon the frontiers during the heat of an Indian war.

A small garrison had been maintained at Lieut. Henchman's house from August, 1675, but in April, 1676, for the greater security of the frontiers, the Governor and Council ordered a fort to be built at Pawtucket falls, (2.) which was immediately done, and placed under the command of Lieut. James Richardson. In May, 1676, an additional force was stationed at the fort, under the command of Capt. Henchman, on account of "intelligence of the approach of the enemy." This was an effectual check to the incursions of the Indians; and the death of Philip, which occurred soon after, (August, 1676,) with the destruction of the greater part of his forces, put an end to the war. (3.) The settlers returned to their deserted homes, and the settlement received new life and vigor.

The General Court still retained their guardianship of the Indians, and in the summer of 1676, ordered those "that relate, to Wannalancet," or Pawtuckets, or Wamesits, to remove to a place "near Mr. Jonathan Tyng's, at Dunstable." This was, perhaps, near Wicasuck falls and island, which were their property. Here they were placed, "with Mr. Tyng's consent, and under his inspection when at home, and in his absence," says Gookin, "the care of them is under one Robert Parris, who is Mr. Tyng's vail." The whole number thus removed to Dunstable was about ten men and fifty women and children – "fifteen men and fifty women and children" having been "removed elsewhere," to various places, and "bound out to service." For Indians who had ever been so true and friendly to the English, this would seem to he no very grateful or even kindly treatment.

These were Christian or "praying" Indians, and Dunstable was one of the *"six places"* at which they had a church and religious teachers. Here, says Gookin, one of their unvarying friends, who visited and comforted them, "they meet together to worship God, and keep the Sabbath." (1.) Some of their teachers were Indians, their own brethren, who had been educated by Eliot, and here their prayers and praises went up to the common Father of the red man and the white man, who "hath made of one blood all nations of men for to dwell upon the face of the earth." Here, too, came Eliot, the noble "Apostle of the Indians," who had been their teacher at Wamesit, and who did not desert them when they were scattered abroad. Where his feet have trodden and his prayers ascended, we may "call it holy ground."

The treatment of the Indians by "our forefathers generally, and of Wannalancet especially, was not Christian, and scarcely humane. They were ordered to move and remove at their will, imprisoned on the most unfounded suspicions, their hunting fields taken away, their fishing places and corn-fields encroached on with impunity, yet Wannalancet remained friendly to the end. They seemed to consider the Indians as "children of the devil," and that they, like the Jews* were raised up to destroy them. Even in their Covenant of Faith, the same feeling exhibits itself, since they promise "not to lay a stumbling block before any, no, *not even the Indians*

As a farther illustration of the spirit of those days, we quote the following from Dr. Increase Mather, the leading minister of the time. Speaking of *"the efficacy of prayer"* he says: "Nor could they cease praying to the Lord against Philip, until they had prayed the bullet into his heart." Again he adds, "We have heard of twenty-two Indian *captives* slain together all of them, and brought down to hell in one day." (1.)

A garrison was maintained at Mr. Tyng's, by a part of Capt. Mosely's famous company, and at the expense of the Colony, until August, 1676. The General Court allowed him £100 (2.) for his disbursements, as he was "put to great expense, being obliged to buy his food in Boston," and after the departure of the Indians in 1683, granted him Wicasuck island in payment therefor. (3.) They also granted him a considerable sum for damage done by the Indians during the war, and also to "Thomas Wheeler and son, the latter of whom was wounded." (4.)

The war with the Narragansets was indeed ended, but the settlers had not escaped all danger or alarm. March 22, 1677, (5.) a party of Mohawks, always the enemy of the English, suddenly appeared in Dunstable, at the mouth of the Souhegan. Their appearance is thus described in a letter from "James Parker," at "Mr. Hinchmanne's farme ner Meremack," and forwarded "to the Honred Govner and Council at Bostown, HAST, POST HAST." (1.)

"Sagamore Wanalancet come this morning to informe ine, and then went to Mr. Tyng's to informe him, that his *sod* being one ye other sid of Meremack river over against Souhegan upon the 22 day of this instant, about tene of the clock in the morning, he discovered 35 Indians on this sid the River, which he soposed to be Mohokes by ther spech. He called to them; they answered, but he could not understand ther spech; and he having a conow ther in the river, he went to breck his conow that they might not have ani ues of it. In the mean time they shot about thirty guns at him, and he being much frighted fled, and come home forthwith to Nahamcok, wher ther wigowames now stand."

In consequence of this alarm a company of scouts, under Lt. James Richardson, (2.) traversed the valley of the Merrimac during the whole season, to ward off any threatened attack. A garrison was also maintained at the expense of the Colony. But in September 1677 a party of French Mohawks from Quebec suddenly came to Naam-keak (near Pawtucket Falls,) with whom was said to be the brother of Wannalancet, and carried him with all his tribe to Canada. They did no damage to the English, however, although they had suffered so many provocations, and now enjoyed such an opportunity for revenge, "being restrained as is supposed by Wannalancet." (3.)

From this long catalogue of perils, alarms, and disasters, we may now turn to the civil affairs of the town, and to a period when *peace* brought with it its attendant blessings – security and prosperity. The settler no longer feared an ambuscade in every thicket, nor listened in the night watches for the prowling footsteps of a foe. England and France, Charles II. and Louis XIV., were at war no longer. The "Treaty of Nime- guen,"(1.) strange though it be, was the protection of Dunstable. The deserted cabin was again tenanted, the half cleared field was cleared and tilled, and new cabins sent up their smokes all along our rich intervals.

FOOTNOTES

(1.) Gookin's Praying Indians. 2 Am. Antiq. Coll. 443.

(2.) Original letter. *Military Records, Mass.* 1675.

(3.) *Military Records, Mass. 1675, page 252. Gookin, 2 Am. Ant. Coll. 462.*

(1.)Pawtucket falls and vicinity. Amoskeag, properly *Namaskeak,* is the same word. It is said to mean *"the great fishing place"* and was a favorite of the Indians. The Merrimac received this name for some distance around the Falls, as it did other names at other places, or as is quaintly expressed by an Indian in a letter of May 1685 to the Governor: "My place at *Malamake River,* called Pannukkog (Penacook,) and Natukhog (Naticook,) that river great many names." 1 *Belknap, appendix,* 508.

(1.) Gookin, in 2 Am. Antiq. Coll. 463.

(2.) The name given by the Indians to the lands on both sides of the Merrimac, about Naticook brook and pond in Merrimac and in Litchfield.

(3.) Tyng's house probably stood not far from Wicasuck Falls, below Tyngsborough village.

(4.) See original petition. *Mass. Military Records,* 128.

(1.) What was called Feb. 3, 1675, when the year ended in March, is Feb. 3, 1076 if we consider the year as ending in December, and in order lo designate this, all dates occurring in the months of January, February, or March, previous to A. D. 1751, are described in the above manner. The true date is Feb. 3. 1676.

(2.) He was a settler of Dunstable, and constable from 1675 to 1682.

(1.) Mass. Military Records, 1676, page 168.

(2.) Mass. Military Records, page 211.

(3.) 3 N. H. Hist. Coll., 99 – 100. 1 Holmes' Annals, 429.

(1.) Gaokin's Christian Indians. 2 Am. Ant. Coll., 525.

(1.) *Go ok in's History of the Praying Indians. 2 Am. Ant. Coil.*

(2.) Pounds, shillings and pence were the currency of New England until the Revolution, when the Dorlar and our decimal currency were adopted instead. The pound containing twenty shillings was worth 83.33; shillings and pence are still used in reckoning.

(3.) *Mass. Military Records,* 1683.

(4.) *Mass. Military Records, 1676, page* 121.

(5.) *Holmes' Annals,* 429. 1 *Belknap,* 80. *Allen's Chelmsford,* 155.

(1.) 3 *N. H. Hist. Coll.,* 100.

(2.) Mass. *Military Records,* 1677, *page* 519.

(3.) *Gookin. 2 Am. Ant. Coll.* 520.

(1.) July 31, 1678.

CHAPTER III.
HISTORY
FROM 1675 TO 1685

Town meetings were holden in Dunstable as early as 1675, and town officers were then chosen, for in 1682 we find the town voting "yt Joseph Parker have 20 shillings allowed him for his *seven years* services as Constable."(1.) No records, however, of any meeting are preserved of an earlier date than November 28, 1677. This was a meeting of the proprietors as well as of the settlers, and was holden at Woburn, at which place the meetings for the choice of own officers were held for many years, and occasionally as late as 1711. The record is as follows: (2.)

"Nov. 28, 1677. At a Town meeting held at Woburn.

"Capt. Thomas Brattle, Capt. (Elisha) Hutchinson, Capt. (James) Parker, Mr. Jonathan Tinge, and Abraham Parker were chosen Selectmen for the Town of Dunstable for the year ensuinge, and to stand as such till new be chosen. (3.)

"It was also agreed upon and voted yt as soon as may be, a minister be settled in the town of Dunstable. The time and person to be left to the Selectmen; his pay to be *in money*, or if in other pay the rate being to be made as money to add a third part more.

"Likewise yt all public charges relating to the minister and other occasions is always to be levied upon allottments, and every man engages his accommodations, [pledges his farm,] to answer and perform the same.

"It was also voted that the minister the first year shall have fifty *pounds*, [equal to about $300.00 now,] and the overplus of the ffarmes, and never to be abated."

Then follows a vote extending the time for building a meeting house and settling a minister, which was a condition of the grant in 1673, but which had not been complied with, for the space of *three years* longer, for the purpose of saving the forfeited rights of the settlers. They intended, nevertheless, to build at once, for it was "left with Mr. Jonathan Tyng, Capt. Parker and Abraham Parker to agree with John Lollendine, (who was the first house and mill wright in town,) to secure and finish said house," which had been commenced before the desertion of the settlement in 1675.

Several persons were also "admitted as inhabitants," and it was voted "yt the selectmen have power to add other inhabitants, provided that with the present they exceed not the number of *eighty* families."

Before the Revolution of 1689, no person could vote or be elected to any office until he had been admitted a Freeman of the Commonwealth. This might be done by the General Assembly or the County Court, but only upon evidence of his being a member in good standing of some Congregational Church. Before voting every person was required to take "the Freeman's Oath."

This meeting house was finished in 1678, and was probably built of logs. The precise spot where it stood is not known, but probably it was not far distant from the settlement at Salmon brook. As the settlement increased a new meeting house was erected near the old Burying Ground in the south part of Nashua. In the Journal of a scout in 1724, it is said to have stood about *nine miles* distant from Penichook pond. No other church, except those which succeeded this upon the same spot, was erected in the southern part of New Hampshire for more than forty years, and its minister, like another John the Baptist, was "the voice of one crying in the wilderness."

April 22, 1679, William Tyng. son of Jonathan Tyng, was born in this town. This is the first birth which is found upon the records of the town. April, 1680, Sarah, daughter of John Lollendine, was born. It is probable that other births occurred at a much earlier date, since it is known that there were many inhabitants for years previous, and in 1680 "30 families were settled there and a learned orthodox minister ordained among them."(l.)

Before 1679, a lot of land upon Salmon brook was granted by the town, and known as *"the mill lot"* and a saw mill erected. Where it stood is not known, but it is not improbable that it was on the spot where the "Webb

Mill," near the house of J. Bowers, Esq., now stands, since it is known that a mill stood there at a very early period, and it would probably be located as near the settlement as possible. There was originally a beaver dam at that place, and it required but little labor to prepare the site for the mill. Many years ago a mill crank was dug up near the spot, which must have come from its ruins.

As early as May 1, 1679, and perhaps before that time, Rev. Thomas Weld was employed here as a minister. In the settlement of New England, *religion* was at the very foundation. The means of religious instruction ever kept pace with the spread of population, and "he who counted Religion as *twelve*, and the world as *thirteen*, had not the spirit of a true New England man."(I.) In the very charter, therefore, it was provided by the General Court, that the grantees were to "procure and maintain an able and or- thodox minister amongst them." and to build a meeting house "within three years."' This condition could not be complied with on account of Philip's War, which com- pelled them to desert the settlement, yet, as we have seen, at the *first* town meeting which was holden after its re- settlement, the *first vote* was for the choice of Selectmen, and the *next* a provision for the ministry and a pl!ace for public worship, the Selectmen just chosen being appoint- ed agents to carry the vote into effect. A *"thirty acre right,"* as it was called, entitling the owner to about six hundred acres on the subsequent divisions of the common lands, was granted fora "ministerial lot," as a farther encourage- ment to the ministry. Upon this Mr. Weld resided, and it is probably a part of the Fletcher farm now owned by John Little.

As an illustration of the character and manners of the early inhabitants of the town, the laws of the Colony at this period, as an exponent of public opinion, form perhaps the best criterion. In 1651, *"dancing at weddings"* was forbidden, and in 1660, *"William Walker was imprisoned a month for courting a maid without the leave of her parents."* In 1675, because *"there is manifest pride appearing in our streets,"* the wearing of *"long hair or periwigs,"* and also *"superstitious ribands,"* used to tie up and decorate the hair, were forbidden under severe penalties. – Men, too, were forbidden to *"keep Christmas* because it was a Popish custom. In 1677 an act was passed to prevent *"the profaneness"* of *"turning the back upon the public worship before it is finished, and the blessing pronounced."* – Towns were directed to erect *"a cage"* near the meeting house, and in this all offenders against the sanctity of the Sabbath were confined.

At the same time children were directed to be placed in a particular part of the meeting house, apart by themselves, and Tythingmen were ordered to be chosen, whose duty it should be to take care of them. So strict were they in their observance of the Sabbath, that "John Atherton"(1.) a soldier of Col. Tyng's company, was fined by him *"forty shillings"* for *"wetting a piece of an old hat to put into his shoes,"* which' chafed his feet upon the march, and those who neglected to attend meeting for three months were publicly whipped. Even in Harvard College students were *whipped* for grave offences in the chapel, in presence of students and Professors, and prayers were had before and after the infliction of the punishment. As the settlers of Dunstable are described in the Petition as "of sober and orderly conversation." we may suppose that these laws and customs were rigidly observed.

We ought not to wonder at the seeming austerity of the Puritans: still less should we blame or ridicule, for to them does New England owe her peculiar elevation and privileges. Scouted at by the licentious courtiers, whether Episcopalian or Catholic, for their strictness and formality, nicknamed "Crop-ears," ridiculed for their poverty and want of education, they naturally clung tenaciously to those peculiarities for which they had suffered, and prized them most dearly. As naturally did they dislike all which savored of the offensive worship or customs of their persecutors, and strive sedulously to differ from them.

They would have no proud *"Churches"* for "the Church of Christ is a *living* Temple," so in their plain, unsteepled, barn-like "MeetingHouses" they worshipped God with a prouder humility. The Establishment was the mystic "Babylon," and all its forms, rituals and tastes of course anti-Christian. No band or surplice added dignity to the *minister*, for he was but the equal, nay, the servant of all. Long hair or a wig was an abomination, and a crime against all laws human and divine. No sound of bells summoned them to worship, and no organ lifted their prayers and praises to Heaven upon the wings of music. They placed no shrub or flower over the graves of the dead, but instead the plain slab with quaint carving of death's head, or cross bones, or hour-glass, and solemn inscription. All ornament was a vain show, and beauty a Delilah.

They believed their wilderness homes to be "the New Jerusalem," and, taking the Bible as their standard, labored in all things outwardly and inwardly to be "a peculiar people." And they were so. They did really *believe* in God and religion, and they strove to practice what they believed at any sacrifice. The world has seen few such men, and it will be well for New England if she forget not *the principle*, the real, living FAITH, which inspired and exalted the Puritans.

No records exist of any meeting from November 1677, to April 1680, when Joseph Cummings, Jr., was chosen a Selectman in the place of Captain Hutchinson; Joseph Parker, Jr., Constable; "Capt. Parker, Robert Paris, Joseph Parker and John Lollendine a committee to assign lotts." At a subsequent meeting they also "chose these men to run the line between Groton and us." In the Spring of this year lands were improved upon the north side of the Nashua.

June 14, 1681, "Jona. Blansher [Blanchard] and Thomas Lun [Lund] were chose fence few- ers [viewers,] and an order was passed commanding all persons "to take care of & yook yr. hogs on penilty of paing double damiges."

In November 1680, a great comet appeared, at which, says Holmes, "the people were greatly surprised and terrified."(1.) It continued to be visible until February, *1681*, and was "the largest that had ever been seen." So great and general was the alarm excited, that a *"general fast"* was appointed by the Governor and Council, and one reason assigned in the proclamation was, *"that awful, portentous, blazing star, usually foreboding some calamity to the beholders thereof."* This fast was observed with great strictness. We may smile at the ignorant and superstitious terror of even the dignitaries and wise men of the land in those days, but our smile must be checked a little when we remember the alarm excited in 1833, in our own community by a similar cause.

Dec. 28, 1681, died Hon. *Edward Tyng*, aged *81*. Where he settled is unknown, but probably not far from the "Haunted House," so called, in Tyngsborough. He was born in Dunstable in England, in *1600*, settled in Boston as a merchant, *1639*, was Representative 1661 and *1662*, Assistant from *1668* to *1681*, and Colonel of the Suffolk Regiment. It appears that he was elected major general after Leverett, but it is not known that he served in that office. He removed to Dunstable in 1679.

He left *six* children: – *Jonathan*, who settled in this town; (see notice,) *Edward*, who was one of Sir Edmund Andros's Council, 1687, and Governor of Annapolis; (see notice); *Hannah*, who married Habijah Savage, (son of the celebrated Major Thomas Savage, commander in chief in Philip's war,) who afterward married Rev. Thomas Weld, and resided here; *Eunice*, wife of Rev. Samuel Willard, pastor of the old South Church, Boston, and Vice

President of Harvard college; *Rebecca*, wife of Gov. Dudley; and another daughter who married a Searle. He was buried in the family tomb in Tyngsborough, and a monument with an inscription points out the spot.(l.)

In 1682, the inhabitants seem to have increased considerably, and the settlement to have acquired a firm footing. The records assume a new form, and become more numerous and town-like. – "Capt. Brattle, Capt. Parker, Mr. Tinge, Sergeant John Cummings, and Robert Parris were˘ chose Selectmen." Provision was made for the collection of taxes, by ordering that the allotments of such as neglect or refuse to pay their taxes, should "be sould at an outcry on the next public meeting day after such neglect or refus." Even at this early day there were some, to whom "religion was as twelve and the world as thirteen," or even more. Trespasses were committed upon the common lands, and the town found it necessary to order that "every man that felleth any wood or tre in the comon shall pay *fiv shillings* for such offence." The cattle, also, seem to have become equally unruly, for it was found necessary to heighten their fences to a "saffisient *five* raile or equivalent."

May 8, 1682, "at a selectmen's meeting, it was ordered that the hogs of Dunstable of three months ould and upward, be soficiently yoked and rung at or before the twentieth of the present month, and John Ackers be appointed and Imployed to pound, youke and Ringe such hogs; and for so doing it is ordered that the owner of every such hog shal pay to the said Swinyard twelv penc, and John Acres is appointed hoge constable tose this order exsicuted." So early was the necessity for this ancient and respectable office recognized by our wise forefathers, and the trust committed to one who was qualified to "EX-ISCUTE" it.

August 28, 1682, "Mine Islands" were laid out to Hezekiah Usher. (1.) The islands at the foot of "Mine Falls" had acquired this name already, on account of mines which were supposed to.exist there. The rumor was that they had been long worked by the Indians, who obtained from them their supply of lead. The banks of the Nashua, Souhegan and the Merrimac had been carefully explored, and "Mr. Baden, an ingenious miner and assayer, was sent over to New England for this purpose. Lead ore was found, but not plenty, and so intermixed with rock and spar as to be not worth working." (2.)

Usher was an original proprietor, a man of wealth and enterprize, and Uncle of John Usher, Lieutenant Governor of New Hampshire in 1692, He seems to have been a speculator, and to have imbibed the extravagant ideas then prevalent among that class of emigrants, respecting the great mineral wealth of New England. They had read of Mexico and Peru. They had listened to the Indians as they told of "the Great Carbuncle," which dazzled the eyes of the beholder, upon the summit of the White or "Crystal Hills," where no human foot had ever trodden or dared to tread, and the Great Spirit had his home. Visions of gold and silver, lying hidden in the bowels of the hills in untold quantities, floated before their distempered fancies by night and by day Every sparkling rock, every discolored spot of earth was to them an El Dorado, and such, without doubt, were our own *Mine Islands* in the eyes of Usher.

He made excavations there, and found lead and iron, it is said, in small quantities, but the enterprise proved a profitless one, and was abandoned. This was probably not long after they were granted to him, as we find that May 15, 1686, Mason, the proprietor of New Hampshire, "farmed out to Hez. Usher, and his Heirs *all the mines, minerals, and ores* within the limits of New Hampshire, for the term of one thousand years, reserving to himself *one fourth* of the *royal ores,* and *one seventeenth* of all the baser metals."(1.) Of such a character and extent, however, were his explorations at these islands, that they were familiarly called *"the Mines"* in all letters, records, and journals of scouting parties for half a century afterwards.(2.)

Although this was a period of peace, and the Indians were committing no depredations, there was danger from roving and lawless parties, and a small mounted guard was deemed expedient. Daniel Waldo and John Waldo were employed for this purpose. (1.)

Dec. 3, 1682, the town "let out to goodman Akers to cut *ten cords* of wood for *two shillings a cord, country pay,* and Sargt. Cummings is to cart the same for *two shillings a cord,* same paye." This was probably for the minister, Mr. Weld, who was married not long previous, and from it we may learn something of *prices* in those days. – Corn was worth about *two shillings* per bushel in 1683, and the relative price of labor and provisions was nearly the same as at present.

At the same time a committee was appointed, consisting of John Parker, Robert Paris, and John Lollendine, to "lay out a Highway from Groton Meeting House to Dunstable Meeting House." The main *river road*, down the Merrimac, had been laid out long previously, and bridges built over the small streams. This road passed easterly of the present road, crossing Salmon brook at the bridge near Miss Allds' house; thence running northerly near the old Allds' road below Judge Parker's house, and crossing the Nashua at a ford way near its mouth, not far from the Concord railroad bridge.

The Proprietorship of the Township was divided into "thirty acre rights," as they were termed, or *house lots* of that size, with the privilege of an equal share in all subsequent divisions *of* the common lands in the township. Of these there were about *eighty*, and the proportion of each such *right* was about *six hundred acres*. – The market value of these lands at this period may be estimated from the fact, that the proprietors, being indebted to Mr. Tyng in the sum of £23, (about $75.00,) they gave him *three* "thirty acre rights," or about 1800 acres, in full discharge of his claim. (1.)

Of these proprietors, according to a certificate of the selectmen dated November 30, 1682, *twenty-one* persons resided out of town, in Boston, Salem, Marblehead, Cambridge, and Chelmsford, and *fourteen* in Dunstable; viz. "Iona. Tyng, widow Mary Tyng, John Cummings, senior, Thomas Cummings, John Blanchard, Abraham Parker,

Joseph Wright, Samuel Warner, Joseph Parker, senior, John Lollendine, Obadiah Perry, Thomas Lund, Joseph Hassell, and John Acres." Most of the inhabitants were not proprietors.

Oct. 9, 1682, "a 20 acre right" was granted to Rev. Mr. Weld as an additional encouragement to the ministry. At the same time a *tax* was imposed of "twenty shillings in mony" upon every 30 acre right, "toward the building of a meeting house, which is to be built within one year after the date hereof, according to the dimensions of the meeting-house at Groton." A committee was chosen, also, to collect contributions for this purpose "of such as have ffaimes within the town," and "to agree with a purson or pursons for the doing of said work." This meeting house, the second in town, was built probably in 1683, of a larger size and better finish, to accommodate the increasing wants of the inhabitants, and must have cost three or four hundred dollars.

"Money," as specie was called at that day, was difficult to be obtained as in all new settlements, and possessed a comparative value far superior to that of produce or "country pay." It is recorded that "Mr. Weld is not willing to accept of one third advance from those that pay him in money as proposed, but accepts to have *double the sum of such as pay not in money.*"

"In 1683, Major Bulkley, (Hon. Peter Bulkley of Concord, one of of the Council,) Capt. Hutchinson, Mr. Tinge, Jno. Blanchard, Sargeant Cummings, and Robert Parris were chosen selectmen for the year ensuinge. John Lollendine was chosen constable, Christopher Temple and Andro Cooke war chosen veioers of fenses, Sam'l Warner and John Cummings war choes Servaires of Hyways."

The taxes upon each "30 acre right" for the four years together, from 1679 to 1683, were about 36 shillings.

John Cummings seems to have been town clerk for many years previous to 1700, although there is no record of any choice. For several years after 1683 the town officers were nearly the same as in the years preceding, whose names have been recorded. Many of their posterity still dwell here, and it was thought it might not be uninteresting to know who in its days of weakness and peril and suffering were the "fathers of the town."

We have seen how "zealously affected" the proprietors of Dunstable were toward building a meeting house and settling a minister in 1677. – Religious motives, however, were not the only ones which actuated them, since their pecuniary interests were benefited thereby. By an agreement dated May 21, 1684, setting forth their desire for the "increase and flourishing of said plantation, *one chief means whereof, under God, is the settling a pious and able minister thereof."* they therefore bound themselves to pay 155. annually on each 30 acre right for this purpose, till the inhabitants can pay £50 per annum.

In the summer of 1685 the inhabitants were thrown into a new alarm by the suspicions movements of the Penacook Indians, and many retired to the garrisons. The alarm was soon, however, discovered to be unnecessary, the Penacooks themselves fearing an attack from the Mohawks, and taking precautions against it.(1.) Such was the life of the early settler even in time of peace. The inhabitants generally lived in garrisons or fortified houses, and scouts were abroad constantly to detect the approach of the lurking foe. The farmer tilled his fields with his arms ready for self defence, and as the lonely wife heard the frequent story of massacre and captivity, her ear detected, with trembling apprehension, in every unusual sound, the footsteps of the "Indian enemy."

THE PILGRIM'S VISION,
BY OLIVER WENDELL HOLMES.

[Recited at the Pilgrim Dinner
at Plymouth, Dec. 22, 1845.]

In the hour of twilight shadows,
The Puritan looked out –
He thought of the "bloudy Salvages"
That lurked all round about,
Of Wituwawmet's pictured knife
And Pecksuot's whooping shout –
For the baby's flesh was tender,
Though his father's arms were stout.

His home was a freezing cabin,
Too bare for the hungry rat,
Its roof was thatched with ragged grass,
And bald enough of that;
The hole that served for casement

Was glazed with an ancient hat,
And the ice was gently thawing
From the log whereon he sat.

Along the dreary landscape
His eyes went to and fro,
The trees all clad in icicles,
The streams that did not flow –
A sudden thought flashed o'er him –
A dream of long ago –
He smote his leathern jerkin
And murmured, "Even so!"

"Come hither, God-be-Glorified,
And sit upon my knee.
Behold the dream unfolding,
Whereof I spake to thee
By the winter's hearth in Leyden
And on the stormy sea –
True is the dream's beginning – '
So may its ending be !

"I saw in the naked forest
Our scattered remnant cast,
A screen of shivering branches
Between them and the blast;
The snow was falling round them,
The dying fell as fast;
I looked to see them perish,
When lo ! the vision passed.

"Again mine eyes were opened,
The feeble had waxed strong;
The babes had grown to sturdy men
The remnant was a throng;
By shadowed lake and winding stream.
And all the shores along,
The howding demons quaked to hear
The Christian's godly song.

"They slept – the village fathers –
By river, lake and shore,
When far adown the steep of time
The vision rose once more;
I saw along the winter snow
A spectral column pour,
And high above their broken rank
A tattered flag they bore.

"Their Leader rode before them,
Of bearing calm and high.
The light of Heaven's own kindling
Throned in his awful eye;
These were a Nation's champions
Her dread appeal to try;
God for the right! I faltered,
And lo ! the train passed by

"Once more – the strife was ended,
The solemn issue tried,
The Lord of Hosts, his mighty arm
Had helped our Israel's side.

Gray stone and grassy hillock
Told where her martyrs died.
And peace was in her borders
Of Victory's chosen bride,

"A crash – as when some swollen cloud
Cracks o'er the tangled trees!
With side to side, and spar to spar,
Whose smoking decks are these ?
I know Saint George's blood-red cross.
Thou Mis tress of the Seas,
But what is she whose streaming bars
Roll out before the breeze ?

"Ah, well her iron ribs arc knit,
Whose thunders try to quell
The bellowing throats, the blazing lips
That pealed the Armada's knell !
The mist was cleared – a wreath of stars
Rose o'er the crimsoned swell,
And wavering from its haughty peak,
The cross of England fell!

"O, trembling Faith! though dark the morn,
A heavenly torch is thine;
While feebler races melt away,
And paler orbs decline,
Still shall the fiery pillar's ray
Along thy pathway shine.

To light the chosen tribe that sought
This Western Palestine !

"I see the living tide roll on,
It crowns with flaming towers
The icy capes of Labrador,
The Spaniard's 'land of flowers!'
It streams beyond the splintered ridge
That parts the Northern showers,
From eastern rock to sunset wave
The Continent is ours !"

He ceased – the griin old Puritan –
Then softly bent to cheer
The pilgrim-child whose wasting face
Was meekly turned to hear:
And drew his toil worn sleeve across,
To brush the manly tear
From cheeks that never changed in wo.
And never blanched in fear.

The weary pilgrim slumbers*
His resting place unknown:
His bands were crossed, his lids were closed;
The dust was o'er him strown,
The drifting soil, the mouldering leaf,
Along the sod were blown,
His mound has melted into earth,
His memory lives alone.

So let it live unfading,
The memory of the dead,
Long as the pale anemone
Springs where their tears were shed,
Or raining in the summer's wind
In flakes of burning red,
The wild rose sprinkles with its leaves
The turf where once they bled !

Yea when the frowning bulwarks
That guard this holy strand
Have sunk beneath the trampling surge.
In beds of sparkling sand,
While in the waste of ocean,
One hoary rock shall stand.
Be this its latest legend –
HERE WAS THE PILGRIM'S LAND !

FOOTNOTES

(1.) The constable was the collector of taxes also, and the compensation for all his services was about fifty cents per year.

(2.) For this and all other similar references, examine *Dunstable Records* of the date affixed.

(3.) Brattle was of Boston, Hutchinson of Woburn, James Parker of Groton, Tyng of Dunstable, and Abraham Parker of Chelmsford. The latter resided soon after in this town, and is the ancestor of Edmund Parker, Esq.

(1.) Petition in 2 *Province Papers – Towns –* 253, in office of N. H. Secretary of State.

(1.) *Higginson's Election Sermon, 1663.*

(1.) He was of Lancaster, Mass.

(1.) *Holmes' Annals, 451.*

(1.) *Farmer's Genealogical Register*, to which I am largely indebted in this way.

(1.) Usher was somewhat of a wit. The converted Indians were commonly called " praying Indians," but Usher, having heard of some outrage said to have been committed by them, called them [11] *preying Indians.*"

In 1685, he was hunting for mines, in Deerfield. – *Mass. Records, 4685, page 485.*

(2.) 2 *Douglass' Summary*, 108. 5 *N. H. Hist. Coll.* 83. *Lead* ore, containing a minute proportion of silver, has been discovered at Mine Falls by Dr. Jackson, in his geological survey of the State.

(1.) 1 *Belknap* 116. *Royal ores* were gold and silver. These were reserved to the Crown.

(2.) See original journals of Fairbanks, Blanchard, and others, 1700 to 1725 in "Journals of Scouts." Mass. Records.

(1.) They were inhabitants of the town, and sons of Dea. Cornelius Waldo, the aneestor of nearly all the Waldos in New England. *Farmer's Genealogical Register.*

(1.) These rights include the greater part of the town of Tyngsborough, and are still in the possession of the family.

(1.) 1 Belknap, 115.

CHAPTER IV.
HISTORY FROM 1685
TO THE DEATH OF REV.
MR. WELD IN 1702.

Up to this period Mr. Weld had been preaching here but had never been ordained. In 1684, however, a new meeting house was erected, and having consented to settle, he was ordained, December 16, 1685. At the same time a church was formed, consisting of *seven* male members, viz. Jonathan Tyng, John Cummings, senior, John Blanchard, Cornelius Waldo, Samuel Warner, Obadiah Perry, and Samuel French. John Blanchard and Cornelius Waldo were chosen the first Deacons.

The following is the Covenant which was adopted in the neighboring churches at that period, and which undoubtedly was adopted here. It is substantially the same as that which was framed for the First Church in Salem, by the associated Churches of the Colony, in 1629, and promulgated by the General Assembly in 1680, for the use of the Colony.(1.)

"We covenant with our Lord and with one another, and we do bind ourselves in the presence of God, to walk

together in all his ways according as he is pleased to re-
veal himself unto us, in his blessed word of truth, and do
explicitly profess to walk as followeth, through the power and grace of our Lord Jesus Christ.

"We avouch the Lord to be our God, and ourselves
to be his people in the truth and simplicity of our spirits.

"We give ourselves to the Lord Jesus Christ and the
word of his grace for teaching, ruling and sanctifying of us
in matters of worship and conversation, resolving to cleave
unto him alone for life and glory, and to reject all contrary
ways, canons, and constitutions of men in his worship.

"We promise to walk with our brethren with all
watchfulness and tenderness, avoiding jealousies, suspicions, backbitings, censnrings, provocations, secret ris-
ings of spirit against them; but in all cases to follow the
rule of our Lord Jesus Christ to bear and forbear, to give
and forgive, as he hath taught us.

"In public or in private we will willingly do nothing
to the offence of the church; but will be willing to take advice for ourselves and ours as occasion may be presented.

"We will not in the congregation be forward either to
shew our own gifts and parts in speaking, or scrupling, or
there discover the weakness and failings of our brethren,
but attend an orderly call thereto, knowing how much
the Lord may he dishonored, and his Gospel and the pro-
fession of it slighted, by our distempers and weakness in
public.

"We bind ourselves to study the advancement of
the Gospel in all truth and peace, both in regard to those

that are within and without; no ways slighting our sister churches, but using their counsels as need shall be; not laying a stumbling block before any, no, not the Indians, whose good we desire to promote; and so to converse that we may avoid the very appearance of evil.

"We do hereby promise to carry ourselves in all lawful obedience to those that are over us in Church or Commonwealth, knowing how well pleasing it will be to the Lord, that they should have encouragement in their places, by our not grieving their spirits through our irregularities.

"We resolve to approve ourselves to the Lord in our particular callings, shunning idleness as the bane of any State, nor will we deal hardly or oppressively with any, wherein we are the Lord's stewards.

"Promising also unto our best ability to teach our children the knowledge of God, and of his holy will, that they may serve him also; and all this not by any strength of our own, but by the Lord Jesus Christ, whose blood we desire may sprinkle this our Covenant made in his name."

At this date there were but four churches and four ministers within the present limits of New Hampshire. (1.) It was during this year that Cranfield, the royal Governor of this State, issued his arbitrary decree against the Congregational Clergy, ordering their "dues to be withheld," and threatening them "with six months' imprisonment for not administering the sacraments according to the Church of England." – But this decree did not affect Dunstable, which was still supposed to lie within the hounds of Massachusetts.

In 1686 the Indians at Wamesit and Naticook sold all the lands within the limits of Dunstable to Jonathan Tyng and others, together with all their possessions in this neighborhood, and nearly all of them removed from the vicinity.(2.) How much was paid for this purchase of Dunstable, or rather release of their claims, is unknown, but probably about £20, as we find that this sum was assessed upon the proprietors soon After, for the purpose of "paying for lands bought of the Indians."(3.)

In 1687 the town raised £1 12s. 3d. towards our proportion of the expense of "building the great bridge" over the Concord river in Billerica. This was done by order of the General Assembly, and for many years afterwards, it was rebuilt and kept in repair from time to time, as occasion required, by the joint contributions of Dunstable, Dracut, Groton, Chelmsford, and Billerica, the towns more immediately benefited.

May 21, 1688, "Samuel Goold is chosen dog WHIPPER FOR THE MEETING HOUSE." What Were the duties of this functionary we are not informed, except so far as is implied in the name. (1.) It stands alone without precedent or imitation. The choice is recorded with all gravity, among other dignitaries of the town, and the office was doubtless in those days a serious and real one, and no sinecure, unless we suspect our grave forefathers of a practical joke.

In 1688 occurred the revolution in England which in December drove James II. from the throne and kingdom, and abolished forever the Catholic supremacy in that country. It was followed immediately by a revolution in New England. Sir Edmund Andros, the royal Governor, who had become exceedingly unpopular by his arbitrary measures, was deposed, and a popular government instituted upon the basis of the ancient charters. This was done even before the news of the revolution in England had reached Boston.

The different towns in the colony were invited to choose delegates to meet in convention at Boston, and assume the government. This convention met accordingly in May, 1689, almost every town being represented. Dunstable was among the number. In May, 1689, John Waldo was a delegate from this town; in June, 1689, Cornelius Waldo; and in December, 1689, Robert Parris.(2.) This was a popular assertion of "inalienable rights," and a foreboding and precedent of the revolution of 1776.

But the settlement was not destined to be always so fortunate as it had been during the preceding years. There had been occasional alarms and trifling injuries, indeed, but it was comparatively a season of peace and quiet. In 1689, the war with the French, known as *King Willia's War*, broke out between France and England. It was occasioned by the Revolution, of which we have just spoken, (the French taking up arms for King James,) and lasted until 1698. (1.) The French excited, by means of the

Jesuits, nearly all the Indian tribes to arm against the English, and the history of the frontier during this period,
the darkest and bloodiest in our annals, is but a succession
of devastations and massacres. In these bloody scenes the
Pen- acooks were not idle. Almost every settlement upon
the frontiers was attacked, some of them repeatedly; and
several hundred men, women and children were either
killed or carried into captivity.

The war was commenced by an attack upon Dover,
June 28, 1689, in which Major Waldron and more than
fifty others were killed or taken prisoners. (2.) It was a
perfect surprise, as no warning of hostility had been giv-
en. An attack upon Dunstable, by the same party and
at the same time, was plotted, but it was providentially
discovered by two friendly Indians, who informed Major
Henchman, the commander of the fort at Pawtucket falls,
of their intention. He aroused the settlement at once to
a sense of their imminent danger, by the fearful news;
"Julimatt fears that his chief will quickly be done at Dunstable." (3.)

"*Quickly!*" How little do we appreciate the startling
import of such a message ! With a foe to deal with who
gave no alarm, even then the warning might be too late.
Even then the attack might be planned and the ambuscade laid. But Providence watched over them.

The inhabitants retired to the garrisons which were
fortified, and preparations for defence were made. A
messenger was also despatched to warn Major Waldron
of his danger, but he was detained on the way and did
not arrive until after the massacre.

In consequence of this news, the Assembly ordered two parties of mounted troopers, consisting of twenty men each, to Dunstable and Lancaster, "for the relief and succor of those places, and to scout about the heads of those towns and other places adjacent, to discover the enemies' motions, and to take, surprise, or destroy them as they shall have opportunity." (1.) July, 5, 1689, another company of 50 men was sent to Dunstable and Lancaster as a reinforcement, and twenty men to Major Henchman at Pawtucket, as a guard for the settlers.

The timely warning to Maj. Henchman probably saved the settlement from a fate similar to that of the unfortunate Waldron, for in another letter of Maj. Henchman to the Governor and Council, dated July 12, 1689, (2) he says, after mentioning "the great and imminent danger we are in (at Chelmsford,) upon account of the enemy, the town being threatened the next week to be assaulted." "And also at Dunstable, on Thursday night last towards morning, appeared within view of Mr. Waldo's garrison *four* Indians, who showed themselves as spies, and it is judged, (though not visible) that all the garrisons in said town were viewed by the enemy; and that by reason thereof their cattle and other creatures were put into a strange affright.

"Wherefore, Honorable and Worshipful, I judge it highly needful and necessary that we have relief, and that speedily of about *twenty* men or more for the repulsing the enemy and guarding some out places, which are considerable on each side Merrimac, as Messrs. Howard, Yarnum, Coburn, &c. (1) who must otherwise come in to us, and leave what they have to the enemy, or be exposed to the merciless cruelty of bloody and barbarous men. I have ordered of those troops which are made up of towns which are in danger, *forty* at a time, to be out upon scout until the latter end of next week, concerning whom I think it needful and necessary that they be then released to go home to guard the several towns they belong to." But imminent as was the danger it passed away without attack, the Fort at Pawtucket Falls, the mounted scouts, the garrisons, the precautions of the settlers, baffling all the wiles of the savages.

In 1690 Christopher Reed was chosen *Ty- thingman*, the earliest records of the choice of such an officer in the town.

During this year it is not known that any attack was made by the Indians upon this town, although they ravaged the settlements from Salmon Falls to Amesbury, burning a great number of houses , and killing and capturing nearly two hundred persons. (2.) Two companies of scouts, consisting of *seventy* men each, under the command of Capt. Thomas Chandler, and Lieut. Simon Davis, were ranging the wilderness constantly for the prevention of damage to the frontiers. (1) But Nov. 29, 1690 a truce was agreed upon with them until the first of May, which was strictly observed, and the inhabitants passed the winter in security.

In the summer of 169 L the war was renewed, and the Indian ravages recommenced. Small scouting parties attacked many of the neighboring settlements. Like beasts of prey, they came without warning, and retired without detection. On the evening of Sept. 2, 1691, they suddenly appeared in this town, and attacked the house of Joseph Hassell, senior. Hassell, his wife Anna Hassell, their son Benjamin Hassell, and Mary Marks, daughter of Patrick Marks, were slain.|(2) There is a tradition that Mary Marks was killed between the Hollis road and the canal about a quarter of a mile above the Nashua Corporation.

They were all buried upon the little knoll where Hassell's house stood, and a rough stone without inscription points out the spot. A second stone stood there until within a few years, having been preserved for so long a period as raised to the dead, but at length falling into the hands of a new proprietor, and standing in the way of his plough, it was taken up and thrown into the cellar by their side which is not yet quite filled up.

On the morning of the 28th Sept. the Indians made another attempt, and killed Obadiah Perry and Christopher Temple. There is a rock in the channel of Nashua river now covered by the flowage of the water, about 30 rods above the upper mill of the Nashua Corporation, which was called "Temple's Rock," and was reputed to he near the spot of his murder. It is said that they were also buried upon the spot just described. – Perry was one of the founders of the Church, and a son in law of Hassell. All of these are original settlers, active, useful and influential men,and all of them town officers, chosen but a few weeks previous.

The actors in those scenes have passed away and even tradition has been forgotten. The only record which exists of the circumstances of the massacre, is the following scrap, noted down probably by the Rev. Mr. Weld, not long after it, occurred.

"Anno Domini 1691. JOSEPH HASSELL, senior, ANNA HASSELL, his wife, BENJ'. HASSELL, their son, } were slain by our Indian enemies on Sept. 2nd in the evening.

MARY MARKS, the daughter of Patrick Marks, was slain by the Indians also on Sept. 2nd. in the evening.

OBADIAH PERRY and CHRISTOPHER TEMPLE dyed by the hand of our Indian enemies September the twenty eighth day, in the morning."

At this time there were several garrisons in Dunstable, and a number of soldiers stationed there by the colony, as appears by a return of their condition which is as follows, "Dunstable town, seven men; Mr Tyng's garrison, six men; Nathaniel Howard's, three men; Edward Colburn's, (probably at Holden's brook) four men; and at Sargeant Varnum's four men." These continued in the pay and service of the country until Nov. 17 1692, and perhaps still longer. (1)

In June 1692, Mr Jonathan Tyng and Major Thomas Henchman were representatives of Dunstable. (2) With the exception of the years 1689 and 1692, no other mention is made of Representatives from this town for many years. At this time no one was allowed the right of suffrage who did not possess a freehold estate of the value of forty shillings per annum, or personal property of the value of £ 20.

In March 1694 a law was enacted by the General Court, "that every settler who deserted a town for fear of the Indians, should forfeit all his rights therein." So general had the alarm become that this severe and unusual statute was necessary. Yet neither the statute, nor the natural courage of the settlers which had never quailed, was sufficient to withstand the protracted and incessant peril which menaced Dunstable, and in 1696 the Selectmen affirmed, that "near two thirds of the inhabitants have removed themselves with their rateable estates out of the town." The town, harassed and poor, prayed an abatement of £ 50, part of their state tax, due by those who had left town, and this request was granted accordingly. (1) Troops were kept here for the protection of the settlers who remained, and all the garrisons were placed under the supervision of Jonathan Tyng, who had previously been named in the Royal Charter as one of the Royal Council of the province.

In consequence of this desertion of so large a portion of the inhabitants, the support of the ministry became very burdensome. In June 1696 the General Court granted "£ 30, for the support of the ministry at the Garrison in Dunstable for the year ensuing." (2) In June 1697, £ 20 were allowed, and in 1698, £12 per annum for two years ensuing, and for the same purpose.

In 1696 and 1697, Wannalancet, who had returned to Wamesit, was again placed under the care of Jonathan Tyng, and the General Court allowed £20 for "keeping him."(l.) In June, 1698, there was a garrison of eight men at Dunstable, and a scouting party of forty men, one half of whom were ordered to scout from Dunstable to Lancaster, and the other half from Dunstable to Amesbury, constantly.(2.)

The war lasted till 1698, when a treaty of peace was concluded between France and England, at Ryswick. Immediately after, a treaty was entered into with the Indians at Casco, and peace declared, which lasted until 1703. During the remainder of this war, there is no authentic record of any attack upon the inhabitants, although there were occasional alarms. At this time, and for fifty years after its settlement, Dunstable was a frontier town, and during a greater portion of the time the country was involved in an Indian war. With nothing hut a dense wilderness between the "barbarous savages" and the inhabitants, they were constantly exposed to surprise and massacre.

Dunstable must have been peculiarly fortunate to have escaped scatheless, while Dover, Portsmouth, Exeter, Durham, Haverhill, Andover, Billerica, Lancaster, and Groton, upon both sides of us and even in the interior, were ravaged almost yearly. This is not at all probable, and though most of the private and local history of that day is forgotten, we find vague hints in ancient chronicles and records, and vaguer traditions, nameless and dateless, which indicate that the story of the first half century of Dunstable, if fully told, would be a thrilling romance.

It is to the latter part of this war that we must assign the capture of Joe English, a friendly Indian who resided at Dunstable. He was a grandson of Masconnomet, sagamon of Agawam, (Ipswich, Mass.) and as such possessed no small note and influence.(1.) "He was much distinguished," says Belknap, "for his attachment to the white inhabitants. In a preceding war (to that of 1703,) he had been taken prisoner in the vicinity of Dunstable, and carried to Canada, from whence, by his shrewdness and sagacity, he effected his escape and returned to his friends at Dunstable."

Joe English was quite a hero in these regions and in those days, and a hill in New Boston, very abrupt on one side, and a pond in Amherst, are still called by his name. A tradition is current that Joe was once pursued by an Indian on this hill, and finding it impossible to escape otherwise, he allowed his pursuer to approach him very closely, and then ran directly towards the precipice, threw himself suddenly down upon a ledge with which he was familiar, while his pursuer, unable to arrest his course, and unconscious of danger, was dashed in pieces at the bottom. Numerous other anecdotes are related of Joe, but we will not repeat them, or vouch for their truth.

The story of the capture and escape of Joe English is told at greater length by the compiler of "Indian Anecdotes." "A party of English were attacked by the Indians on Penichuck brook, in the north part of Dunstable, and were all killed except four persons, one of whom was Joe English, a friendly Indian, who had rendered himself peculiarly serviceable to the English. Him they took prisoner and sent to Canada, where he pretended to be highly exasperated against the white men, and said he meant hereafter to be a good Indian; that the whites had deceived him and he would not trust them in future.

"After these professions of fidelity to their interests, he told them that if they would let him have the command of a party of Indians, he would go and surprise Deerfield, one of the frontier towns of Massachusetts. They accordingly furnished him with a party, and he soon commenced his march. He also persuaded the Indians to let one of the English prisoners accompany him. On their arrival at the mountains which surrounded Deerfield, Joe told them that he was afraid that they had not provisions enough for the expedition, and that previous to the attack it would be better to hunt one day. To this the company assented. Joe told them they must go around the mountain, and drive the deer towards where they were, and that he and the Englishman would remain where they were, and kill them as they approached.

"Joe had purposely taken his station at a place where he could reach the town, and sent the Indians around the mountain so that he knew he should not be interrupted in his attempt to join the English. The Indians having gone in pursuance of his directions, he and his comrade fled to the settlement and apprised the inhabitants of Deerfield of their danger. The Indians soon discovered the deception of their commander, by the firing of guns and beating of drums which were heard from the town, and the attempt was abandoned.

He soon after returned to his duty as a soldier at Dunstable, in which employment he took much pleasure, and felt no little pride in the performance of it. The Indians of course felt an inveterate hostility against him, and determined upon securing him. They therefore waylaid all the places where they should be likely to take him, but still he escaped their stratagems."(1.)

Whether this story be authentic or not I cannot say; "I tell the tale as 'twas told to me." That he was captured, however, and that he escaped from captivity, we do know, but how or where no record discloses. It appears from a grant made by the General Court of Massachusetts, June 14, 1698, to "Joseph English an Indian escaping from French Captivity," that he had just returned, and the sum of £6 was allowed him as a "recompense for his services" in "giving intelligence of the motions of the enemy with intent to do mischief upon the frontiers at this time." (2)

It was also during this war, in 1697, that the celebrated Mrs. Duston was captured at Have r- hill, and escaped by killing her captors, ten in number, at the mouth of the Contocook river in Concord, N. H. This was considered as one of the most remarkable and heroic exploits on record. In her lonely wanderings down the Merrimac homeward, the first house she reached was that of old John Lovewell, father of "worthy Capt. Lovewell," which stood on the north side of Salmon brook a few feet northeast of the Allds bridge. The cellar is still visible.

Although Dunstable suffered little during the war from actual injuries, yet the continual exposure to the tomahawk and scalping knife, and the frequent alarms prevented its growth. Such was its effect, indeed, that though as early as 1680 there were *thirty* families or more in the town, in 1701 the number did not exceed twenty-five families. (1.) The settlement had more than once been nearly deserted, and very few improvements were made. A saw mill had been erected at the earliest settlement, and others followed at "Mine Falls" and on Salmon brook, but no grist mill had been built, the inhabitants resorting to Chelmsford. In 1695, Daniel Waldo set up a grist mill at the mouth of Stony Brook, several miles down the Merrimac, and was "to grind the corn and *malt* of the inhabitants of Chelmsford, *except on the fourth day of each week which is appropriated to the use of Dunstable.*" He agreed to grind "according to turn as much as may be."(2.)

Oct. 4, 1697, every inhabitant was ordered "*to bring half a cord of wood* to Mr. Weld by the first of November, or forfeit *five shillings* for each neglect." This was in addition to his salary.

As silver was then worth ten shillings an ounce, five shillings would be equal to half an ounce of silver, or 50 cents of our currency. This would make the value of wood about a dollar a cord.

In 1698 the town joined with other towns in rebuilding Billerica bridge, and raised for that purpose and other town expenses, £6 7s. Of course it could not have been a very splendid or expensive structure.

June 29, 1699, it was voted that John Lollendine "build a sufficient cross bridge over Salmon brook, near Mr. Thos. Clark's ffarm house, *provided that the cost thereof do not exceed the sum of* forty shillings." The town was to pay one half and Mr. Clark the other. The bridge was to be *warranted* "to stand a twelvemonth) and if the water carry it away, he is to rebuild it at his own cost."

In 1699 the "woodrate" was increased, and assessed according to the ability of the inhabitants, who were required to furnish him *nineteen* cords. The "minister rate" assessed upon the proprietors of Dunstable, including inhabitants, Was £17 2s. *2d.* (perhaps $50.00,) and was probably the amount of his salary.

It is a singular and instructive fact, and one that might lead to useful reflections, that Mr. Weld was assessed, like any other inhabitant, both to the wood-rate and minister's rate, – to the former one cord and to the latter eleven shillings. I had supposed that the respect paid the pastor in those days was so great, as to exempt him from all such burdens, but it seems that the principle of equality was carried into rigorous practice. Nor did the "minister" receive any title except that of *Mr.*, not even that of *Rev.*, for this was an "innovation of vanity" upon puritan simplicity, of a much later date. D. D. and S. T. D., and such like, are quite of modern introduction. It should be remembered, however, that even the title *Mr.* was not in 1699 applied to "common people."

The following is a list of all the inhabitants who were heads of families and contributed to the woodrate in 1699. The number of inhabitants did not probably exceed 125.

"Maj. Jonathan Tyng, John Lollendine,
Mr. Thomas Weld, Robert Usher,
Robert Parris, Nath'l Cummings,
Nathaniel Blanchard, Abraham Cummings,
Joseph Blanchard, John Cummings,
Thomas Cummings, John Lovewell,
Thomas Blanchard, Joseph Hassell,
Mr. Samuel Searle, Mr. Samuel Whiting,
Samuel Ffrench, William Harwood,
Tho's Lunn, [Lund,] Daniel Galeusha."

In 1700, the town voted that they would *"glaze the meeting house"* which was done accordingly, at a cost of £1 1s. 6d. Probably it had never been glazed before, and from this we may learn the narrow means of the settlers, and how different were the rude houses in which they worshipped from the costly edifices which now occupy their places. The windows could have been neither very large nor very numerous.

In 1701, the selectmen of the town prayed the General Court for further assistance in the support of the ministry, and set forth, as was customary, their condition and sufferings, at considerable length. As showing the situation of the town at this period, and the customs of the times, the petition is inserted entire.(1.)

"To his Majesty's most Honorable Council and Representatives in the Great and General Court now assembled in Boston by adjournment.

The Petition of the Selectmen of Dunstable in behalf of the inhabitants there settled, Humbly Sheweth: – that whereas the wise God, (who settleth the bounds of all our Habitations,) hath disposed ours, but an handful of his people, not exceeding the number of *twenty-five families*, in an outside plantation of this wilderness, which was much depopulated in the late war, and two third parts of them, though living upon husbandry, yet being but new beginners, and their crops of grain much failing of wonted increase, are in such low circumstances, as to be necessitated to buy their bread corn out of town for the support of their own families, whence it comes to pass that they are capable of doing very little or nothing towards the maintenance of a minister here settled: and our Non-resident Proprietors being far dispersed asunder, some in England, and some in several remote places of this country, and making no improvement of their interest here, most of them for divers years past have afforded nothing of assistance to us in so pious a work; there having also in some years past been some considerable allowances for our help herein out of the Public Treasury, (for which we return our thankful acknowledgments,) the continuance whereof was never more needful than at this time:

These things being duly considered we think it needful hereby to apply ourselves to your Honors. Humbly to request the grant of such an annual Pension out of the Country Treasury, for the support of the ministry in this place, as to yourselves may seem most needful, until our better circumstances may render the same needless.

Moreover having been lately informed, by a Representative from a neighboring town, that Dunstable's proportion in the Country rate newly emitted was £6, coining from the multiplication of 20s. six times, but finding by the printed paper lately come to us that we, the *smallest town in the Province*, are assessed £9, being £3 beyond Stow which we deem in respect of the number of inhabitants may exceed us at least one third part: We humbly hereupon desire that the original assessment may be revised, and if there be any mistake found in the proportion assigned to us, (as we judge there may be,) that it may be rectified; and we shall remain your Honors' Humble Servants,

ever to pray for you.

Joseph Farwell,
Robert Parris.
William Tyng."

Dunstable, July 28, 1701.

In answer to this petition the sum of £12 was allowed from the Treasury in September, 1701.

June 9, 1702, died Rev. Thomas Weld, first minister of the town, aged 50 years. A tradition has long been current that he was killed by the Indians in an attack upon his garrison.(1.) But this must be a mistake, for "In the year 1702," says Penhallow, who lived at this time and wrote the history of the war, "the whole body of the Indians were in a tolerable good frame and temper," and there is no mention of any attack until August, 1703.(2.)

Mr. Weld was a native of Roxbury, Mass., and grandson of Rev. Thomas Weld, the first minister of Roxbury, who came from England in 1632, and was one of the most distinguished among the eminent men of that day. He was one of the three who made the famous first "translation of the Psalms into metre for the use of the churches of New England," which has been the occasion of no little merriment; the translators being selected, not because they possessed any poetic genius whatever, but because they were the "most pious and godly men."

Mr. Weld graduated at Harvard College in 1671, and probably studied divinity with his uncle, Rev. Samuel Danforth, a celebrated minister, and came to Dunstable in 1678 or 1679. Nov. 9, 1681, he married Elizabeth, daughter of Rev. John Wilson, of Medfield, son of the first minister of Boston, and both of them very eminent men. She died July 29, 1687, aged 31, and is buried in the old burying ground near the southerly line of Nashua, where a large horizontal slab of granite records her death. Some years afterwards he married widow Hannah Savage, daughter of Hon. Edward Tyng, who was admitted an inhabitant in 1677. She survived him many years, and died at the house of their son, Rev. Habijah Weld, in Attleborough, Mass., in 1731.(1.)

But little is known respecting the character of Mr. Weld. He was much beloved by his people, and is said by Farmer to have been a distinguished man.(2.) Alden says that Mr. Weld "was esteemed in his day a man of great piety, an exemplary Christian, and a very respectable clergyman." (3.) He is supposed to be the author of the verses in Mather's Magnolia, upon the death of his uncle, Rev. Samuel Danforth, who died in 1674.(4.) He is buried beside his wife, and over his grave is a granite slab similar to that of his wife, but without any inscription.

FOOTNOTES

(1.) *Mass. Assembly Records, 1680, page 281. Allen's Chelmsford, 103.*

(1.) *Portsmouth, Dover, Exeter, and Hampton,* all organized in *1638.*

(2.) *Allen's Chelmsford,* 151. I *Belknap.*

(3.) *Proprietary Records of Dunstable.*

(1.) That such an officer was a necessary one we may infer from the fact, that in Beverly a fine of sixpence was imposed on every person whose dog came into the Meeting house during divine service. *Stone's History of Beverly.*

(2.) Mass. *Records,* 1689, *page* 81, 89.

(1.) 1 Belknap, 224.

(2.) 1 Belknap, 129.

(3.) 1 *N. H. Hist. Coll.,* 223.

(1) *Allen's Chelmsford,* 149,

(2) *Mass. Military Records,* 1689, *page* 56.

(1.) Some of these were in Dunstable, (now Tyngsborough,) and some in Chelmsford.

(2) 1 *Belknap* 132, 144.

(1.) *Mass Military Records* 1690, *page* 141.

(2.) Hassell's house stood on the north hank of Salmon Brook, on a small knoll just in rear of Miss Allds' house, where the cellar and grave stones may still be seen.

(1.) *Mass. Military Records, 1692.*

(2.) *Mass. Legislative Records, 1692 page* 219.

(1) *Mass Assembly Records* 1696.

(2.) *Mass. Legislative Records, 463, 562, 609.*

(1.) *Mass. Military Records, 1697, page 530.*

(2.) *Mass. Military Records, 1698.*

(1.) 1 *Belknap*, 173, *note.*

(1.) *Indian Anecdotes*, 161.

(2.) *Mass. Military Records, 1698 Journals, 590.*

(1.) *Petition 1701 supra.*

(2.) *Allen's Chelmsford, 30.*

(1.) Mass. **Ecclesiastical Records**, 1701.

(1.) N. H. *Gazeteer, Dunstable.*

(2.) *Penhallow's Indian War.* 1 *N. H. Hist. Coll. 20, 23.*

(1.) *N. H. Historical Collections, 57 – 64. Farmer's Genealogical Register. Alden's Epitaph: Dr. Alden was a descendant of Mr. Weld.*

(2.) *Historical Catechism.*

(3.) *Alden's Collections, 111.*

(4.) *Mather's Magnolia.*

CHAPTER V.
INDIAN WARS FROM
1703 TO 1713

In the summer of 1702, it was proposed by the General Court to build a trading house for the Indians, and a fortified garrison "at *Wadaa*nuck,"(1.) as the settlement at Salmon brook was then called, hut owing to the lateness of the season the intention was not accomplished.

Oct. 24, 1702. Governor Dudley informed the House that he was going to Dunstable on Monday, to meet several of the Penacook Indians there, "who were come down to speak with him." He was absent until Oct. 29th., but the results of his interview, whatever they might be, did not allay the fears of the General Court. Believing from the movements of the Indians that preparations for the defence of the frontiers should be made, they passed the following order: (2.)

"November 10, 1702. The winter being too far advanced for the erecting of a trading house for the supply of the Indians at Penacook, and for fortifying the garrison at Wataanuck in the county of Middlesex – Resolved, that a convenient house next adjoining thereto, such as his Excellency shall direct, be fitted up and fortified for that purpose with hewn timber and a suitable garrison posted there for the defence thereof; the fortification not to exceed forty feet square."

This was probably the old fort, or "Queen's Garrison,"(1.) as it was called, which stood about sixty rods easterly of Main street, in Nashua, and about as far northerly of Salmon brook, near a cluster of oaks. Some traces of the fort were to be seen until within a few years. Here a small garrison was posted, as appears by the following return to the Governor and Council, dated Dec. 25, 1702, which contains the list of the soldiers then at the garrison.(2.)

"William Tyng, Lieutenant; John Bowers, Sergeant: Joseph Butterfield, Drummer; John Spalding, John Cummings, Joseph Hassell, Ebenezer Spalding, Daniel Galusba, Paul Fletcher, Samuel French, Thomas Lund."

"Jonathan Tyng, Lt. Colonel."

In 1703 war was renewed between France and England. It lasted until 1713, and was called "Queen Anne's War." The Indians, as usual, took part with the French, and in August 1703 a general attack was made upon all the frontier settlements. Terror and devastation reigned every where. Within a few weeks more than two hundred whites were either killed or captured. – The General Assembly being sensibly affected by these massacres, offered a bounty of £40 for every Indian scalp. "Captain Tyng was the first who embraced the tender. He went in the depth of winter, (1703-4.) to their head quarters, [at Pequawkett,] and got *five*, for which he received *two hundred pounds."* (1.)

He afterwards became a Major, and it is said "was a true lover of his country, and very often distinguished himself as a gentleman of good valor and conduct." (2.) The Indians did not forget the slaughter of their friends, or their national law of blood for blood, although its execution might be long delayed. In 1710 he was waylaid by them between Concord and Groton, and so severely wounded that he soon after died.(3.)

It was probably soon after the commencement of this war that the garrison of Robert Parris was surprised, and himself and family massacred. – He lived in the southerly part of Nashua, on the Main road, on the farm which adjoined that of Rev. Mr. Weld on the north. (4.) He was a large landed proprietor, and had been selectman and representative of the town. "The Indians in one of their predatory excursions attacked his house, and killed him, his wife, and oldest daughter. – Two small girls who composed the rest of his family, ran down cellar, and crawled under an empty hogshead. The savages plundered the house, struck with their tomahawks upon the hogshead, but neglected to examine it, and departed leaving the house unburned, probably fearing that the flames would alarm the neighbors. The orphan girls were sent to Charlestown, Mass., and there brought up. One of them married a Richardson, and the other a Goffe, father of the celebrated Col. Goffe, whose posterity are numerous in this vicinity."(5.)

In March. 1704, the town was again compelled to seek aid from the Colonial Treasury for the support of the ministry, and for defence against their enemy, and presented the following moving petition. Upon the consideration of the petition the sum of £20 was granted to the town for these purposes.(1.)

"To the General Court in session, 8 March 1703.(2.)

The most humble Petition of the inhabitants of the Town of Dunstable in the County of Middlesex, *Shewrth:*

That whereas your distressed Petitioners, through the calamities of the several Indian rebellions and depredations, are much reduced in our estates, and lessened in our numbers, (notwithstanding the addition of many desirable families when there was a prospect of a settled peace,) so that we are not capable wholly to support the ministry of the Gospel, after which Ark of God's presence our souls lament. and the want of which, more than all other great hardships, and hazards, doth discourage us. and threaten the ruin of this desirable plantation, but the enjoyment of such a rich mercy will animale us still to stand, (as we have long done,) in the front of danger:

"Inasmuch also as his Excellency, in his great wisdom and providence for the security of this eminently frontier place, and of this part of the Provincs so much exposed to the invasion of the bloody salvages, hath been pleased to post a considerable force of soldiers here, the great advantage whereof hath been experienced in these parts, but they can never hear a sermon without travelling more than *twelve miles* from their principal post, which is to them no small discouragement: (3.)

"We are therefore humbly bold to lay before the wise and compassionate consideration of this Great and General Assembly the sorrowful circumstances of her Majesty's good subjects in said town, and; do most humbly implore that such a supply may be ordered, out of the Treasury of the Province, towards the support of the ministry in Dunstable, as to your great wisdom and candor shall appear meet, we being found, (as we are in duty bound,) to contribute to such a service for our souls to the uttermost of our ability, and much beyond the proportion of others in greater congregations for the ordinances of God's worship among themselves; – And your poor Petitioners are the more encouraged thus to pray in hope, since their former applications of this kind have ever been compassionately regarded and bountifully answered by former Great and General Assemblies of this Province."

"Your obedient and humble servants.

SAMUEL WHITING, WILLIAM TYNG, JOSEPH BLANCHARD,}
Selectmen in behalf of of the Town."

In 1704 a block house was erected somewhere in town by Col. Tyng, by the direction and at the expense of the colony, but the place of its location is not designated.(1.)

It may be a matter of some interest and curiosity, as illustrating the manners and customs of the times, to insert the following account of the expenses of the funeral of James Blanchard, who died in 1704. He was a farmer in tolerable circumstances.

"Paid for a winding sheet,	£0 – 18s. – 0d.
Paid for a coffin,	0 " 10 " 0
Paid for digging grave,	0 " 7 " 6
Paid for the use of the pall,	0 " 5 " 0
Paid for gloves (to distribute at the funeral,)	1 " 1 " 0
Paid for wine, segars, and spice (at the funeral,)	1 " 5 " 9
Paid for attendance, expenses, &c.	1 " 17 " 5
	£6 " 19 " 5"

In January 1706, "the trading house at Wataanuck in Dunstable, being now useless, they [the House of Representatives,] were not willing to continue to support a garrison there. To which his Excellency returned answer, that he made no further use thereof than as a convenient post for lodging some of the persons being under pay and at hand for the relief of Groton and the near parts upon an attack, and for scouting, and not as a fortress or garrison."(1.) From this circumstance, at this time probably little danger was anticipated.

In April 1706 the sum of £10 was granted, by the General Assembly, to Samuel Butterfield who had been "taken captive by the Indians, cruelly treated, and stripped of all, having killed one of them, and knocked down two others, after they had seized him." (2.) No hint is given of the time or place of capture.

Early in the summer of 1706, Col. Schuyler of Albany gave notice to Governor Dudley of New Hampshire, that a party of Mohawks, 270 in number, were marching to attack Piscataqua. – "Their first descent was at Dunstable, July 3, 1706, where they fell 011 a house that had twenty troopers posted in it, who by their negligence and folly, keeping no watch, suffered them to enter, which tended to the destruction of one half their number."(3.) This was, it is said, at "the Weld garrison."

A more particular account of this attack has been preserved, which is as follows. These troopers, who were mounted scouts, "had been ranging the woods in the vicinity, and came towards night to this garrison. Apprehending no danger, they turned their horses loose upon the interval, piled their arms and harness in the house, and began a carousal to exhilarate their spirits after the fatigues of the day. A party of Indians had lately arrived in the vicinity, and on that day had designed to attack both Weld's and Galusha's garrisons. One of their number had been stationed to watch each of these garrisons, to see that no assistance approached and no alarm was given. A short time previous to the approach of the cavalry the Indian stationed at Weld's had retired to his party, and reported that all was safe.

"At sunset a Mr. Cummings and his wife went out to milk their cows, and left the gate open. – The Indians who had advanced undiscovered, started up, shot Mrs. Cummings dead upon the spot, and wounded her husband. They then rushed through the open gate into the house with all the horrible yells of conquering savages, but started with amazement on finding the room filled with soldiers merrily feasting. Both parties were completely amazed, and neither acted with much propriety. The soldiers, so suddenly interrupted in their jovial entertainment, found themselves called to fight when entirely destitute of arms, and incapable of obtaining them.

"The greater part were panic struck and unable to fight or fly. Fortunately all were not in this sad condition. Some six or seven courageous souls, with chairs, clubs, or whatever they could seize upon, furiously attacked the advancing foe. The Indians, who were as much surprised as the soidiers, had but little more courage than they, and immediately took to their heels for safety; thus quitting the house defeated by one quarter their number of unarmed men. The trumpeter, who was in the upper part of the house when the attack commenced, seized his trumpet and began sounding an alarm, when he was shot dead by an Indian upon the stairway. He was the only one of the party killed.

"Cummings who was wounded had his arm broken, but was so fortunate as to reach the woods while the Indians were engaged in the house. That night he lay in a swamp in the northerly part of Tyngsborough, about a quarter of a mile west of the great road, and a few rods south of the state line. The next day he arrived at the garrison near Tyngsborough village."(1.)

There were several of these garrisons in town to which the inhabitants fled in times of danger like the present, and where they usually spent their nights. "They were environed by a strong wall of stone on of hewn timber built up to the eaves of the houses, through which was a gate fastened by bars and bolts of iron. They were lined either with brick or plank. Some of them had port holes for the discharge of musketry." They were generally built of logs, and had the upper story projecting three or four feet beyond the lower story walls, for the purpose of greater security.(2.)

This last account of the attack contradicts that of Penhallow in some particulars, but as Penhallow, who wrote the history of the Indian wars of that period, was an officer, and a cotemporary, his statement that half the number of troopers were destroyed is most probably correct. The circumstances of the surprise corroborate it. In a cotemporary Journal of Rev. John Pike of Dover, the attack is thus mentioned: "July 3rd, 1706, Capt. Pearson of Rowley marching with his troops to Dunstable, and being posted with part of his troops at one Blanchard's house, while they were at supper in the chamber, the enemy had slyly turned Blanchard's sheep into his corn, which he and his wife going out to restore, were both slain. The doors and gates being open, the enemy entered the house, killed Pearson's trumpeter with *three other troopers,* and wounded *five more.* At last they were driven out of the house with the loss of one Indian. Pearson was much blamed for not setting his sentinels out." (1.)

There is discrepancy and confusion in these accounts, probably arising from the fact that two attacks are blended together. Penhallow is probably correct in his statement that the conflict with the troopers, and the death of Mrs. Cummings occurred at Cummings's house. Blanchard's garrison was at some distance from this scene, and he with most of his family, and others not mentioned by Penhallow or Pike, were killed at the same time, as appears by the following extracts from the ancient records of the town. From these it would seem that the garrisons were attacked *"at night."*

"Nathaniel Blanchard dyed on July the 3rd at night 1706. Lydia Blanchard, wife of Nathaniel Blanchard, and Susannah Blanchard, daughter Nath'l Blanchard, dyed on July 3rd at night in the year 1706.

"Mrs. Hannah Blanchard dyed on July the 3rd at night in the year 1706.

"Goody Cummings, the wife of John Cummings died on July the third at night, 1706.

"Rachel Galusha died on July the 3rd, 1706."

"After that," on the same day, says Penhallow, "a small party attacked Daniel Galusha's house, who held them in play for some time till the old man's courage failed, when on surrendering himself he informed them of the state of the garrison; how that one man was killed and only two men and a boy left, which caused them to rally anew and with greater courage than-before. Upon which one man and the boy got on the outside, leaving only Jacob [Galusha] to fight the battle, who for some time defended himself with much bravery, but overpowered with force and finding none to assist him, was obliged to quit and make the best escape he could. But before he got far the enemy laid hold of him once and again, and yet by much struggling he rescued himself. Upon this they burned the house, and next day fell on Amesbury."(1.)

Galusha's garrison was about two miles west of Weld's garrison, on Salmon brook, at a place formerly called Glasgow, where Henry Turrell now lives. Pike mentions the attack, but in a manner to show that our accounts are very imperfect. "Near about the same time, or soon after, they assaulted another house belonging to Jacob Galusha, a Dutchman. The house was burned, some persons were killed and some escaped. The whole number said to have been slain in Dunstable at this time was nine persons."(2.)

In a note to "Penballow's Indian Wars," by John Farmer, Esq., the following more particular account of this attack is given: "The savages disappointed in this part of their plan, (the attack on Weld's garrison) immediately proceeded to Galusha's, two miles distant, took possession of and burned it. One woman only escaped. Had the company at Weld's armed and immediately pursued, they might probably have prevented this disaster; but they spent so much time in arming and getting their horses, that the enemy had an opportunity to perpetrate the mischief, and escaped uninjured.

"The woman above mentioned, when the Indians attacked the house, sought refuge in the cellar, and concealed herself under a dry cask. After hastily plundering the house, and murdering, as they supposed, all who were within it, the Indians set it on fire, and immediately retired. The woman, in this critical situation, attempted to escape by the window, but found it too small. She however succeeded in loosening the stones, till she had opened a hole sufficient to admit of her passage, and with the house in flames over her head, she forced herself out and crawled into the bushes, not daring to rise for fear she should be discovered. In the bushes she lay concealed until the next day, when she reached one of the neighboring garrisons." (1.)

In the Records of the General Court of Massachusetts, mention is made several times of these conflicts. The sum of £4 was granted to "Robert Rogers, of Rowley," who was "one of Capt. Peirson's company when attacked by the Indians at Dunstable, and was wounded by a spear run into his breast." (2.) The sum of £10 was also allowed to Capt. Peirson, "for the scalp of an Indian enemy slain the last summer by him and his company at Dunstable, to be by him distributed and paid to such of his troops, and the inhabitants of said town, that were at the garrison when and where the Indian was slain."

In 1712 we find the following petition of Daniel Gallusha, in which he states, "that about six years past, when the Indians attacked and took the house of Daniel Gallusha, his father in Dunstable, he being posted there under her Majesty's pay, and serving there with his own arms, while running hastily to take his own gun, by mistake took one of the public arms, and the enemy pressing sure upon him, he was forced to make his escape, the house being burned by the enemy, with his gun and others therein. Upon which Col. (Jonathan) Tyng stops forty shillings of his wages for the said gun." (1.) This is perhaps the person called by Penhallow, Jacob Galusha.

The Indians still remained in the vicinity, and a few days afterwards this company of "troopers" fell into an ambuscade, and lost several of their number. The only circumstances now known are contained in the following brief notice: "Joseph Kidder and Jeremiah Nelson, of Rowley, were killed 10th July, 1706, and John Pickard mortally wounded, and died at Billerica on the 5th August following." (2.)

Within a few days the Indians again made their appearance. "July 27th. Lt. Butterfield and his wife, riding between Dunstable and another town, (Chelmsford,) had their horse shot down by the enemy. The man escaped, the woman was taken, and Joe English, a friendly Indian, in company with them at the time, was slain." (3.) This attack is said to have taken place at Holden's Brook, a little south of the State line.

After the escape of Joe English from the Indians and the deception he had practised upon them, they determined upon revenge. This ambuscade was the consequence, and the story is thus told more at length as handed down by tradition: "After his return to Dunstable, Joe with another soldier was appointed to guard Captain Butterfield and his wife on a visit to some of their friends in the upper part of Chelmsford. They were mounted on horseback preceded by Joe, with his gun loaded, and the other soldier following in the rear.

"In passing Holden's Brook, now in Tyngsborough, a party of Indians discovered them, who immediately fired after they crossed the brook, killed the horse on which Capt. Butterfield and wife were riding, and then rushed on to kill their prey. Joe had gone too far from the brook to effect his retreat, and he being the principal object they wished to secure, they pursued him. Capt. Butterfield and the other soldier made their escape, but Mrs. Butterfield was taken prisoner.

"Joe espying on his left a considerable thicket of woods, ran towards it with all possible haste, but he found the Indians gained upon him. He, therefore, turned round, faced them, and presented his gun, upon which they fell immediately to to the ground. This gave Joe some advantage, and after taking breath he set out again for the thicket. This he repeated several times, when the Indians, finding he was likely to escape by his near approach to the woods, with which they knew he was perfectly acquainted, and where he could easily conceal himself, one of them fired, and the ball entered the arm with which he carried his gun, which he was immediately compelled to drop, and ran with greater speed than before. He was just on the point of entering the thicket, when a second ball entered his thigh and brought him to the ground.

"The Indians were highly elated with the prospect of taking vengeance on Joe, and they had already in their minds, prepared the keenest and most excruciating tortures for their victim. Joe was not ignorant of the suffering that awaited him, and wished to provoke them so much that they might despatch him at once. They soon came up to him, and vented their feelings in all the expressions of savage triumph and pleasure. – "Now Joe," said they, "we've got you." Joe immediately made them a gesture and a reply of such insulting scorn, that they were highly irritated. His purpose was answered, for they despatched him with their tomahawks without further ceremony." (1.)

Joe English was a grandson of Masconnomet, chief Sagamore of Agawam, (Ipswich, Mass.) As one of his heirs he owned an interest in large tracts of land lying in that vicinity and upon the Merrimac, which he conveyed by various deeds in 1701 and 1702. (2.) Many are the stories which are related of his courage, his fidelity, his adventures, and his hair breadth escapes. His death was lamented as a public loss. The General Assembly made a grant to his widow and two children *"because he died in the service of his country."* (3.) And his memory, although humble, was long cherished as one who fell by the hands of his own brethren, on account of his friendship for the whites.

We find no further mention of damage done by the Indians in Dunstable for many years, although they made frequent and bloody attacks upon other neighboring and frontier towns. There were incursions, indeed, and alarms, for in March, 1710, it was "voted and agreed upon by the inhabitants that the selectmen should take care in order to obtain some help and assistance from the country, by a petition to the General Court." This was done only in cases of great emergency. A company of "snow men" were kept scouting, and ordered here for the protection of the settlement, under Col. Tyng, and garrisons established at several places at which the settlers dwelt. The history of the frontiers until the close of the war, in 1713, is but a series of attacks, burnings, captivity, and massacre. "From 1675 to 1714 it is estimated that Massachusetts and New Hampshire lost 6000 young men and male children, including those killed and those who were made captives without ever being recovered."

In November, 1711, the inhabitants still lived principally in garrison houses, where soldiers under the pay of the Colony were stationed constantly for their defence. From a return of the number, location, and situation of these garrisons made to the General Court at that time, it appears that there were *seven* garrisons, containing thirteen families and eighty-six persons, in this town. This perhaps did not include the whole number of families in town. If it did, the number had diminished more than one half since 1680 – a striking proof of the dangers and sufferings of the early settlers.

The following is a list of the garrisons, number of families, number of male inhabitants in each garrison, number of soldiers stationed in each garrison, and the whole number of inhabitants in each garrison. The "Queen's Garrison" was probably Wataanuck, at Salmon Brook. (1.)

	Names of Garrisons.	No. of families.	No. of male inhab.	No. of Soldiers.	Total.
1	Col. (Jonathan) Tyng's	1	1	6	8
2	Mr. Henry Farwell's,	3	3	2	28
3	Mr. (John) Cummings'	2	2	2	21
4	Col. (Sam'l) Whiting's,	3	0	1	8
5	Mr. (Thomas) Lund's,	1			
6	Queen's Garrison,	2	1	4	21
7	Mr. (John) Lollendine's,	1	0	4	
	Total,	13	7	19	86

In June, 1713, a grant of £10 was made to Samuel Whiling, who had been "taken captive and carried to Canada" during the war, but had escaped, and who, in consequence of wounds and sufferings, was still under the doctor's care and unable to labor. (2)

It was probably some time during this war that Richard Hassell, (a son of Joseph Hassell killed in 1691,) was taken captive by Indians on Long Hill in the south part of the town and carried to Canada.

Thus feeble and suffering had been the condition of the settlement for many years. Fear and desolation reigned every where. Compelled to dwell in garrisons, and to labor at the constant peril of life, how could the settlers thrive? Dunstable was scarcely more advanced in 1714 than it was in 1680, so disastrous had been the effects of the long and bloody wars. Many of the most useful inhabitants had been slain or taken captive, heads of families especially. Some had removed to places more secure from Indian depredation, and deserted all. Few, very few emigrated to what might well be termed "the dark and bloody ground," and it was no time for marriage feasts when the bridal procession might at every step become a funeral one, and the merry laugh be drowned by the rifle and the war whoop.

"The war on the part of the Indians," says Bancroft, "was one of ambushes and surprises. They never once met the English in open field; but always, even if eight fold in number, fled timorously before infantry. But they were secret as beasts of prey, skilful marksmen, and in part provided with fire arms, fleet of foot, conversant with all the paths of the forest, patient of fatigue, and mad with a passion for rapine, vengeance, and destruction; retreating into swamps for their fastnesses, or hiding in the greenwood thickets, where the leaves muffled the eyes of the pursuer.

"By the rapidity of their descent they seemed omnipresent among the scattered villages, which they ravaged like a passing storm, and for years they kept all New England in a state of alarm and excitement. The exploring party was waylaid and cut off, and the mangled carcasses and disjointed limbs of the dead were hung upon the trees to terrify pursuers. The laborer in the field, the reapers as they went forth to the harvest, men as they went to mill, the shepherd's boy among the sheep, were shot down by skulking foes whose approach was invisible.

"Who can tell the heavy hours of woman ? – The mother if left alone in the house feared the tomahawk for herself and children. On the sudden attack the husband would fly with one child, the wife with another, and perhaps one only escape. The village cavalcade making its way to meeting on Sunday, in files on horseback, the farmer holding his bridle in one hand and a child in the other, his wife sealed on a pillion behind him, it may be with a child in her lap as was the fashion in those days, could not proceed safely, but at the moment when least expected bullets would come whizzing by them, discharged with fatal aim from an ambuscade by the wayside. – The forest that protected the ambush of the Indians secured their retreat. They hung upon the skirts of the English villages ' like the lightning on the edge of the cloud.'" (1.)

"Did they surprise a garrison? Quickly," writes Mary Rowlandson of Lancaster, "it was the dolefullest day that ever mine eyes saw. Now the dreadful hour is come. Some in our house were fighting for their lives: others wallowing in blood: the house on fire over our heads, and the bloody heathen ready to knock us on the head if we stirred out. I took my children to go forth, but the Indians shot so thick that the bullets rattled against the house as if they had thrown a handful of stones. We had six stout dogs but not one of them would stir.

"The bullets flying thick, one went through my side, and through my poor child in my arms." The brutalities of an Indian massacre followed. "There remained nothing to me," she continues being in captivity, "but one poor wounded babe. Down I must sit in the snow with my sick child, the picture of death, in my lap. Not the least crumb of refreshing came within either our mouths from Wednesday night till Saturday night, excepting only a little cold water. One Indian, and then a second, and then a third would come and tell me: 'Your master will quickly knock your child on the head.' This was the comfort I had from them; miserable comforters were they all." (1.)

Such was the life of the early settlers of Dunstable, and could our plains unfold the bloody scenes and heart touching events which have here taken place, their story would be as strange and thrilling as that of Mary Rowlandson. These scenes have indeed passed away, and their actors are well nigh forgotten, but we ought never to forget that our soil has been sprinkled with their blood, and that to them we owe most of the blessings which we enjoy.

NOTES:

(1.) This name, nr rather *Watana'nuck,* was the one given by the Indians to the Falls in the Merrimac, near "Taylor's Falls Bridge;" to the little pond in Hudson about a mile easterly *of* these Falls; to Salmon brook and Sandy pond; and to the whole plain upon which Nashua Village in Nashua now stands. It is the same word as Outanic.

(2.) *Military Records,* 1702, *page* 336.

(1.) Queen Anne.

(2.) *Mass. Military Records, 1702.*

(1.) *Pdnhallow.* 1 N. H. Hist. Coll. 27. This was Capt. John Tyng, eldest son of Col. Jonathan Tyng of this town.

(2.) *Penhallow. 1 N. H. Hist. Coll. 60.*

(3.) Allen's Chelmsford, 35.

(4.) Proprietary Records of Dunstable.

(5.) 2 Farmer & Moore's Historical Collections, 306. Parris is not improbably the same name as Pierce, since, January 8, 1702, we find recorded the marriage of "Jane Pierce, alias Parris." *– Town Records.*

(1.) *Mass. Ecclesiastical Records,* 1704, *page* 191.

(2.) This was 8th. March, 1703-4, or 1704.

(3.) This garrison was at Salmon brook, and the nearest meeting house, (except in town,) was at Chelmsford, then twelve miles distant.

(1.) *Mass. Military Records,* 1704.

(1.) Mass. Military Records, 1706.

(2.) *Mass. Military Records,* 1706.

(3.) Penhallow. 1 N. H. Hist. Coll., 48, 49.

(1.) 1 *N. H. Hist. Coll.* 133.

(2.) *Allen's Chelmsfood,* 148.

(1.) Pike's Journal. 3 N. H. Hist. Coll. 56.

(1.) 1 *N. H. Hist. Coll.* 49.

(2.) Pike's Journal. 3 N. H. Hist. Coll. 56. His name *was* Daniel.

(1.) 1 N. *H. Hist. Coll.* 133: *note.* 1 *Belknap,* 173: *note.*

(2.) *Mass. Military Records.* May 26, 1707.

(1.) *Mass. Military Records,* 1712, *page* 225.

(2.) 1 *Belknap,* 173: *note.*

(3.) *Pike's Journal. 3 N. H. Hist. Coll.* 57.

(1.) *Indian Anecdotes,* 161. *Farmer's Historical Catechism,* 24.

(2.) *Mass. Military Records,* 1706.

(3.) His signature was a bow with the arrow drawn to its head. History of Rowley, 373, 381.

(1.) *Mass. Military Records,* 1711.

(2.) *Mass. Military Records,* 1713.

(1.) 2 *Bancroft's United States,* 102.

CHAPTER VI.
ECCLESIASTICAL HISTORY
FROM 1702 TO 1737

For many years after the death of Rev. Mr. Weld the ecclesiastical affairs of the the town are involved in much obscurity. No minister was settled here during the war, and no records remain of the proceedings of the town until 1710. Yet during this long struggle, although the settlement was nearly deserted, the public services of the church were not neglected in their distress and care for self-preservation. In June, 1705, the General Court granted £26 to the town for the support of the ministry for the year ensuing.(1.) Who was the minister at this period is not known certainly, but probably it was Rev. Samuel Hunt, as in September, 1706, he was desired by the Governor and Council to *continue* at Dunstable, by the following order: (2.)

"Boston, Sept. 4th. 1706. I am ordered by his Excellency the Governor and Council to acquaint you that your service as minister at Dunstable is acceptable to them, and desire a continuance thereof, and they will endeavor to promote yr. encouragement by the General Assembly as formerly, and hope they will be prevailed with to make it better: I am sir,

your humble servant,

Isaac Addington, Sec'y."

"Mr. Samuel Hunt, Clerk."

Mr. Hunt continued his ministry at Dunstable until the spring of 1707, when he was ordered to accompany the expedition against Port Royal as Chaplain of the forces, as appears by the following petition, (1.) upon which the sum of £18 was allowed:

"The Petition of Samuel Hunt, Clerk, sheweth:

"That your petitioner has served as minister at Dunstable ever since the fourth of Sept. 1706, having received a signification from this Honorable Board, under the hand of Mr. Secretary Addington, that the same was desired by your Excellency and Honorables; intimating withal that your petitioner should have the same encouragement as formerly, (or better,) which your petitioner understood to be the same as he had at Casco Bay, which was fifty-two pounds per annum, and his board. And on the 23d April last past, yr. petitioner was dismissed from that service in order to go to Port Royal, when he had served 33 weeks at Dunstable aforesaid, for which your petitioner has not yet received any salary – aud yr. petitioner prays that the same may be allowed as aforesaid. *Samuel Hunt.*"

Bufford & Co's Lith. Bostun

CHURCH AND CEMETERY NASHVILLE

"Dec. 5, 1707."

As early as the 1st of October, 1708, Rev. Samuel Parris commenced preaching in Dunstable, and the General Court granted him £20 per annum for three years or more, toward his support. (2.) He remained here until the winter of 1711 or the spring of 1712, but how much longer is unknown. Mr. Parris was previously settled at Salem viilage, (or Danvers) and in his society and in his family, it is said, commenced the famous "Salem Witchcraft" delusion of 1691, which led to the death of so many innocent persons, and which filled New England with alarm, sorrow, and shame. (3.)

"Sept. 12, 1711. [It was] agreed upon to repayr the meeting house, it being left to the selectmen to let out the work, and take care for the boards and nails."

After Mr. Parris left Dunstable, public worship still continued, and the pulpit was supplied constantly, for in June 1712, the General Court granted "£10 to Dunstable for the support of the ministry the last half year," and in June 1713, £10 more "for the year past." This is the last record of any assistance granted to the town by the colony. With the return of peace, prosperity smiled upon the settlement. New settlers thronged in, farms were extended, and the inhabitants were enabled to bear their own burdens.

In 1713, Rev. Ames Cheever, who graduated at Harvard in 1707, was preaching in Dunstable. Nov. 20th, 1713, it was voted, "that the resident proprietors of Dunstable pay Mr. Cheever £40 a year." How much earlier Mr Cheever commenced his labors is uncertain, but he continued preaching here until June, 1715, at which time he received a call. "At a General Town meeting of the Inhabitants legally warned, at Dunstable, on June the 6th, 1715, Then voted and agreed, that Joseph Blanchard is to pay to Mr. Cheever his money that is due him, and upon discoursing with him, if he seems to incline to settle with us, then to declare to him, that the Town at a meeting voted that they would readily consent that he should come and settle with us, and have the same encouragements as to *settlement* and *salary* as was voted him at our last meeting concerning him. Also, voted that Joseph Blanchard shall deliver a letter to Mr. Short, (Rev. Matthew, who graduated at Harvard, 1707) or some other minister, to come and preach with us for some time."

In those days, ministers were settled for life. and it was customary for the Town to give them a ministerial *farm, or* a certain sum of money by way of deficit, which was called a *settlement.* – He received an annual salary in addition. This settlement was usually, in a town like Dunstable, from £80 to £100 in value, while the salary ranged from £50 to £100 per annum.

Mr. Cheever, however, did not accept the call to settle, and soon after a Mr Treat was preaching here. "Nov. 2d, 1715, it was voted for to desier Mr. Treat to continue with us sum time longer, and to give him as before, which was 20 shillings a Sabbath. Also, voted that Sarg't Cumings should be looking out for a minister in order for settlement."

"January 16th, 1717, voted that Henry Farwell and Savg't Cummings are to endever to get a minister as soon as they can, and to see after Mr. Weld's place (the old parsonage) to by it if it he to be had. Also, Joseph French is to entertain the minister." French lived at the first house on the main road northerly of the State line.

"1st May, 1717, voted that there be a day of last kept sum time this instant May. Voted that ye 15th day of this instant May, be the day appointed to be kept as a day of Fast. At the same time Decon Cumings was chosen for to discourse Mr. Stoder (Rev. Samson Stoddard, of Chelms-

ford,) concerning the Fast." This was a fast ordained by
Gov. Shate, (1.) and was, probably, in consequence of the
alarming threats and depredations which were made at
this time, by some of the Indian tribes against the frontier
settlements. (2.)

"Sept. 26th, 1717, voted that the Rev. Jona. Pare-
point [Peirpoint, of Reading, Mass., grad. Harvard, 1714,]
should have a call in order for settlement. Also, voted that
the minister should have £80 a year salary, and *one hundred* pounds for his settlement. Voted that Major Eleazer
Tyng and Ensign Farwell should acquaint Rev. Mr. Pair-
pont with what is voted at this meeting."

This call was equally unsuccessful with the former,
and "Sept. 2d, 1718, chose a committee to go to discourse
with Mr. Coffin [Enoch, grad. Harvard, 1714,] in order for
a settlement." It is stated by Mr. Farmer, so noted for his
accuracy, that the Rev. Mr. Prentice was settled here this
year. This is a mistake, and the same error occurs in all
other notices of Dunstable. (1.)

"Dec. 1st, 1718, voted that the Rev. Enoch Coffin
should have £80 a year salary *in money*. Also, voted to
give him land which cost the town £80, and ten acres of
meadow for his settlement; and also 200 acres of the common lands." Both the church and the town unanimously
agreed "to give Rev. Mr. Enoch Coffin a call to be our
settled minister."

It would seem that Mr. Coffin accepted the call, for
May 18th, 1719, "a committee was chosen with Mr. Coffin to lay out his meadows," which were offered him

in case of settlement, and during this year, in the records of land laid out, he is styled the *present minister* of
said Town. – Something, however, occurred to prevent
his legal ordination at that time, as nearly a year after,
March 7th, 1720, a committee was chosen "to go to our
neighboring ministers, and to discourse them all in order for the ordination of Rev. Mr. Coffin." But he was
not settled at all, for May 20th, 1720, "a committy was
chosen to compound matters with Mr. Coffin, concerning the Town's settlement money, and Mr. Coffin's offer
to the Town concerning his place."

Mr. Coffin resided here for some time with his family, and Nov. 5th, 1719, a daughter, Mehitabel, was born.
He left town June. 1720, and returned to his native place,
Newbury, Mass. – He afterwards went as chaplain with
the first band of settlers to Concord, N. H., and settled
there May, 1726, where he died August 17th, 1727. aged
32. (1.)

The. Ecclesiastical affairs of the town were for many
years involved in so much confusion and difficulty, as
almost to warrant the facetious remark of Col. Taylor to
Gov. Burnet. The Governor. who was no friend to long
graces before meals, on his first journey from New York
to take upon him the government of Massachusetts and
New Hampshire, enquired of Col. Taylor when the graces
would shorten. He replied, "The graces will increase in
length until you come to Boston: after that they will short-
en until you come to your government of New Hampshire, when your Excellency will find no grace at all." (2.)

In June, 1720, Rev. Nathaniel Prentice began to preach here. Aug. 20th, 1720, the town gave Mr. Prentice a call, with the offer of £100 settlement, and £80 a year salary; but warned by their premature grants of land to Mr. Coffin before ordination, they prudently inserted a *proviso,* that he was "not to enter upon said £80 salary till *after* he is our ordained minister."

Mr. Prentice accepted the call, and was probably ordained during the fall of 1720. He probably claimed a larger salary, as Nov. 13th, 1720, it was voted, "That when Mr. Prentice comes to keep house and have a family, and stands in need of a larger supply, then to ad Reasonable Aditions to his salary, if our abilities will afford it." They also voted, Dec. 8th, 1720. "That Mr. Prentice after marriage should have *a sufficient supply of wood, or ten pounds of passable money in lew thereof yearly.*" He was soon after married to Mary Tyng, of Dunstable, and died here, according to Mr. Farmer, Feb. 27th, 1737. (1.) He was buried, it is said, in the old south burying ground, beside his children, but there is no monument or inscription to mark the place of his interment.

Of the character and talents of Mr Prentice, we have little information. "It is said of him," says Mr. Sperry, "that he was a man of wit and a good sermonizer." That he was popular we may conjecture from the fact that the people here were contented under his preaching for so many years, and additions from time to time after his settlement, were made to his salary. In 1730, and perhaps earlier, £90 were raised for him: in 1731 the *non resident taxes* added: in 1732 he received £105 and the non resident taxes: and in 1733 the same. The town also voted to build a new meeting house near the old one. The value of money, in comparison with other articles, however, had then depreciated so much, in consequence of the emission of large quantities of paper money by the Colony, that perhaps his compensation at this time was worth little more than his original salary. (2.) This, though it may seem to us a small sum, [£80, or $270.00] was no mean salary in those days, when the Colony gave the Governor but £100 a year, and when Portsmouth, the Capital, and which had been settled a century, gave its minister a salary of only £130. (1.)

NOTES:

(1.) Mass. *Ecclesiastical Records*, 1705.

(2.) *Mass. Ecclesiastical Records*, 1707, page 239. Mr. Hunt graduated at Harvard College, 1700.

(1.) *Mass. Ecclesiastical Records*, 1707, *page* 239.

(2.) *Mass. Ecclesiastical Records*, 1709, 1710, 1711.

(3.) *Upham's Lectures on the Salem Witcheraft.* Mr. Parris died in Sudbury, Mass.

(1.) 1 *Belknap*, 186.

(2.) *Penhallow.* 1 *N. H. Hist. Coll.*, 89.

(1.) **1** *N. H. Hist. Coll.*, 150, 5. 109 *Rev. Mr. Sperry's Sketch.*

(1.) 1 *N. H. Hist. Coll.*, 180.

(2.) 1 *Belknap*, 223: *note.*

(1.) Others say in 1735.

(2.) See table of values of money in Appendix.

(1.) Adams' Annals of Portsmouth.

CHAPTER VII.
INDIAN ATTACK OF 1724

THE mournful story of Indian massacre must now be resumed. After the close of Queen Anne's war, by the ratification of the treaty of peace between France and England, at Utrecht, a treaty was made with the Indians at Portsmouth, N. H., in July, 1713, and quiet reigned throughout the frontiers for many years. The emigrants pushed their settlements farther and farther into the wilderness, and the smoke curling up from many a cabin along the green hill sides, and in the rich valleys, gave signs of advancing civilization. The distant Indians, however, were still hostile and treacherous, although, being deserted by France, they were compelled to make peace.

In 1717 they began to be more and more insolent, killing the cattle and threatening the lives of the settlers, and occasioned so much alarm that a Fast was ordered. These outrages were imputed to the instigations of the French missionaries, (the Jesuits) who were jealous of the growth of the English plantations. In August, 1717, however, a congress was held with them at Arrowsick on the Kennebec River, and the treaty of 1713 was renewed. (1.) This apparent friendship lasted but a short time, owing, as was said, to the advice of Father Rasle and the Jesuits, for in 1720 they began to threaten again, and in June,

1722, attacked the settlement at Merry Meeting Bay, on the southern shore of Lake Winnepisiogee, and "carried off nine families." (*1.*)

During all the previous Indian wars, Dunstable was the *frontier town*, and therefore exposed to greater dangers than its more interior neighbors. Now other settlements had commenced beyond us, although yet in their infancy, and incapable of affording much protection. As early as 1710 settlements were made in Hudson. Londonderry (then called Nulfield) was settled in 1719, and Litchfield (then called Brenton's Farm, or by its ancient Indian name, Naticook) in 1720. Chester was also settled in 1720, and Merrimac and Pelham in 1722. During the years 17223-4, frequent ravages were committed and much alarm excited. As we look around on our beautiful villages and thickly peopled towns, we can scarcely realize that a little more than a century ago the yell of the Indian was heard even here, and the shriek of the murdered settler went up to heaven with the flames of his desolated home.

In the summer of 1723 the Indians attacked Dover and Lamprey River, and fearing an attack upon the settlements in this vicinity, a garrison of thirty men was posted in Dunstable. It was still considered a *frontier* town, and was the rendezvous of all the scouting parties which traversed the valleys of the Merrimack and the Nashua. The scouts were drafted from the different regiments, and were constantly out upon excursions against the Indians. In Nov. 1723, Capt. Dan'l Peeker arrived at Dunstable with such a company from Haverhill, and having received recruits here, marched to Penichook brook, Souhegan, Anconoonook hills, Piscataquog, Amoskeag, Annahooksit, Contookook, Cohasset, [Goffe's Falls] and Beaver brook, but "discovered no enemy." A small party was sent out by him "under the command of Jona. Robbins of Dunstable," and were gone several days but without success. (1.)

At the same time a company under the command of Lt. Jabez Fairbanks of Groton, was also scouting up and down the Nashua. In this company were six men from Dunstable; viz: Joseph Blanchard, Thomas Lund, Isaac Farwell, Eben'r Cummings, John Usher, and Jonathan Combs. Upon a petition from the selectmen of the town, stating its exposed situation, and the necessity that they should be allowed to stay at home to guard it, they were all discharged, upon the condition, however, that they should perform duty at Dunstable. (2.)

January 19, 1724, died Hon. Jonathan Tyng, aged 81. He was the oldest son of Hon. Edward Tyng, and was born Dec. 15, 1642. He was one of the original proprietors of the town, and the *earliest permanent settler*, having remained here, alone, during Philip's war, when every other person had deserted the settlement for fear of the Indians. That he was a man of much energy and decision of character we may judge from this fact. That he was a man of probity and of considerable distinction at an early period, we may infer from his appointment as Guardian over the Wamesit Indians in 1676, and from the numerous other important trusts confided to him from time to time by the Colony.

In 1687, he was appointed (as well as his brother, Edward Tyng) (1.) in the royal commission of James II. as one of Sir Edmund Andros's Council. In 1692 he was chosen representative of Dunstable, and for many years as selectman, and otherwise was much engaged in the public business of the town. For many years during the wars of 1703, he was Colonel of the upper Middlesex regiment, and was entrusted with the care of all the garrisons within its bounds.

Col. Tyng married Sarah, daughter of Hezekiah Usher, who died in 1714. After her death, he married Judith Fox of Woburn, who died June 5th. 1736, aged 99. His children were, 1. *John*, grad. of Harvard College, 1691, who was killed by the Indians in 1710; 2. *William*, born 22d. April, 1679, the first child horn in town; 3. *Eleazar*, grad. of Harvard College, 1712; 4. *Mary*. who married Rev. Nathaniel Prentice, minister of the town; and others who died at an early age.

In the winter and spring of 1724, Lieut. Fairbanks and his company were scouting about "Nashuway River," "Nisitisit Hills," "The Mines," or Mine Falls, "Penichnck Pond,' "Naticook," "Souheganock," "Nesenkeag," "Dunstable meeting house," and other places in this vicinity. In May, 1724, men were at work planting both north and west of Nashua river, and a part of this company were posted here as a garrison. (2.)

In August, 1724, the English sent a body of troops to attack the Indian town at Norridgewock, Me. The town was surprised, and a large number of Indians slain, together with Father Rasle, the Jesuit, their priest, who was considered by the English as the instigator of all these outrages. By this attack the Eastern Indians were much alarmed and weakened. But about this time a party of French Mohawks, to the number of 70, made an incursion into this neighborhood. "Sept. 4th they fell on Dunstable, and took *two* in the evening. Next morning Lt. French with *Fourteen men* went in pursuit of them, but being way-laid, both he and one half of his men were destroyed. After this as many more of a fresh company engaged them, but the enemy being much superior in number, overpowered them, with the loss of one man killed and four wounded." (1.) A more particular account of this mournful event has been preserved and collected from various sources with much care and labor. It must prove interesting, at least to the descendants of the actors in these scenes, many of whom still reside among us, and may serve to make us all realize more fully the nature, extent, and worth of the sufferings of those into whose labors we have entered.

"The two captives mentioned above were Nathan Cross and Thos. Blanchard. (2.) They had been engaged in the manufacture of turpentine on the north side of the Nashua, in Nashville, near the spot where the upper part of the village now stands, and were seized while at work and carried off by the Indians. As there were at that time no houses or settlements on that side of Nashua River at that place, these men had been in habit of returning every night to lodge in a saw mill on the south side of the river. – This mill was probably John Lovewell's, which stood on Salmon Brook at the bridge, by the house of Miss Allds, the mud sills of which are now visible. The night following their capture they came not as usual, and an alarm was given, as it was feared they had fallen into the hands of the Indians.

"A party consisting of *ten* of the principal inhabitants of the place, beside their leader, started in pursuit of them, under the direction of Lieut. Ebenezer French. In this company was Josiah Farwell, who was next year Lieutenant at Pequawkett under Lovewell. When this party arrived at the spot where these men had been laboring, they found the hoops of the barrels cut and the turpentine spread upon the ground. – From certain marks made upon the trees with wax mixed with grease, they understood that the men were taken and carried off alive.

"In the course of the examination, Farwell perceived that the turpentine had not ceased spreading, and called the attention of his comrades to this circumstance. They concluded that the Indians had been gone but a short time, and must be near, and decided on instant pursuit. – Farwell advised them to take a circuitous route to avoid an ambush; but unfortunately he and French a short time before had a misunderstanding, and were then at variance. French imputed this advice to cowardice, and cried out, "I am going to take the direct path: if any of you are not afraid let him follow me." French led the way and the whole of the party followed, Farwell following in the rear.

"Their route was up the Merrimac, towards which they bent their course to look for their horses upon the intervals. At the brook (1.) near Satwych's [now Thornton's] Ferry they were way-laid. The Indians fired upon them and killed the larger part instantly. A few fled, but were overtaken and destroyed. French was killed about a mile from the place of action under an oak tree lately standing in a field belonging to Mr. John Lund, of Merrimac. Farwell in the rear, seeing those before him fall, sprung behind a tree, discharged his piece, and ran. Two Indians pursued him. The chase was vigorously maintained for some time, without either gaining much advantage, till Farwell passing through a thicket, the Indians lost sight of him, and probably fearing he might have loaded again, they deserted from farther pursuit. He was the only one of the company that escaped.

"A company from the neighborhood immediately mustered, and proceeded to the fatal spot to find the bodies of their friends and townsmen. Eight of them were found and conveyed to the burying place. 'Coffins were prepared for them, and they were decently interred in one capacious grave.' The names of these persons given in the Boston News Letter, were Lt. Ebenezer French, Thomas Lund, Oliver Farwell and Ebenezer Cummings, who belonged to Dunstable, and all of whom, excepting the last, left widows and children, Daniel Baldwin and John Burbank, of Woburn, and Mr. Johnson, of Plainfield."

Cross and Blanchard, the first named, were carried to Canada; after remaining there some time they succeeded, by their own exertions, in effecting their redemption, and returned home." (1.)

The place of their interment was the ancient Burial Ground near the State line, in which there is a monument still standing, with the following inscription, copied *verbatim et literatim.*

"Memento Mori.
Here lies the body of Mr Thomas Lund
who departed this life Sept. 5th 1724 in the
42d year of his age.
This man with seven more that lies in
this grave was slew all in a day by
The Indians."

Three other grave stones stand close beside the above, very ancient, moss covered and almost illegible. One was erected to "Lt. Oliver Farwell, aged 33 years"; one to "Mr Ebenezer Cummings, aged 29 years", and one to "Mr Benjamin Carter, aged 23 years".

It is related by Penhallow, that after the first attack "a fresh company engaged them" but were overpowered "with the loss of one killed and four wounded." The Indians, elated with their success, moved forward to Nashua River, and this second fight is said to have taken place at the ancient fordway, where the highway crossed the Nashua, and very near its mouth. – It was probably at this time that the circumstance occurred which has given to that portion of the village its name. Tradition reports that the Indians were on the north side of the river and the English on the south, and that after the fight had lasted a long time across the stream without decisive result, both parties drew off, and that after the Indians had departed, upon a large tree which stood by the river side, near the Concord Railroad Bridge, the figure of an *Indian's Head* was found carved by them, as if in defiance. Such was the origin of "Indian Head."

There is another version of the account, indeed, which relates, that a fight once took place there between the whites and the Indians; that the latter were defeated, and all of them supposed to be slain; but that one escaped, and carved upon a tree The *Indian Head* as a taunt and a threat of vengeance.

Sometime during this year, William Lund, "being in the service of his country, was taken prisoner by the Indian enemy and carried into captivity, where he suffered great hardships and was obliged to pay a great price for his ransom." The time, place and circumstances of his capture and return are not known, and this brief record is all that remains. (1.)

NOTES:

(1.) *Penhallow.* 1 N. H. *Hist. Coll.,* 89. 1 *Belknap* 189.

(1.) 1 *Belknap,* 201.

(*1.*) *Mass. Records. Journals of Scouts, page 47.* Robbins was a volunteer, and a Lieutenant under Capt. Lovewell in 1725

(2.) *Mass. Military Records,* 1723, *page* 111 – 145.

(1.) Edward Tyng was appointed Governor of Annapolis, but sailing for it, was taken prisoner and carried into France where he died. His children were; – 1. *Edward,* a brave naval commander, born *1683* and died at Boston 8*th.* Sept. 1755 2. *Jonathan,* who died young. 3. *Mary,* who married Rev. John Fox of Woburn. 4. *Elizabeth,* who married a brother of Dr. Franklin. Edward Tyng was a Lieutenant in the great Narraganset swamp fight, Dec. 19, 1675, and commanded the company after Capt. Davenport was killed.

(2.) *Mass. Records. Journal of Scouts, page* 51.

(1.) *Penhallow. 1 N. H. Hist. Coll..* 109.

(2.) A Grand-daughter of Thomas Blanchard, Mrs. Isaac Foot – is still living.

(1.) Naticook Brook, the stream which crosses the road just above Thornton's. The scene of the ambush must have been near the present highway.

(1.) 1 *Belknap, 207: note.* Manuscript corrections thereof by John Farmer, Esq., in the possession of Isaac Spalding, Esq.

(1.) *Mass. Military Records,* 1734.

CHAPTER VIII.
LOVEWELL'S WAR AND LOVEWELL'S FIGHT

In consequence of this attack, and of the devastation everywhere committed by the Indians, John Lovewell, Josiah Farwell and Jonathan Robbins petitioned the General Assembly of Massachusetts for leave to raise a company, and to scout against the Indians. The original petition, signed by them, is still on file in the office of the Secretary of State in Boston, and is as follows:

"The Humble memorial of John Lovel, Josiah Farwell, Jonathan Robbins, all of Dunstable, sheweth:

"That your petitioners, with near forty or fifty others, are inclinable to range and to keep out in the woods for several months together, in order to kill and destroy their enemy Indians, provided they can meet with Incouragement suitable. And your Petitioners are Imployed and desired by many others, Humbly to propose and submit to your Honors' consideration, that if such soldiers may be allowed five shillings per day, in case they kill any enemy Indian and possess their scalp, they will Imploy themselves in Indian hunting one whole year; and if within that time they do not kill any, they are content to be allowed nothing for their wages, time, and trouble.

JOHN LOVEWELL.

JOSIAH FARWELL.

Dunstable Nov. 1724.   *Jonathan Robbins."*

Lovewell was a man of great courage and fond of engaging in adventurous enterprises. He was particularly successful in hunting wild animals, and in time of war was engaged in exploring the wilderness to find the lurking places of the In- dians who ravaged the settlements in New England. His father, it is said, had been an ensign in the army of Cromwell, and a soldier under the famous Capt. Church in the great Narraganset Swamp fight, and his sons inherited his military taste and ardor. This petition was granted, changing the conditions into a bounty of £100 per scalp. The company was raised and a commission of Captain given to Lovewell. They became greatly distinguished, first by their success, and afterwards by their misfortunes.

Lovewell was then in the prime of life, and burning with zeal to distinguish himself. With his company of picked men he started upon an excursion into the Indian country. The *head quarters* of the Peqnawketts, a fierce and dangerous tribe, were in the region between Lake Winnepiseogee and the pond in Fryeburg, Me., since known as *"Lovewell's Pond."* It was called Pequawkett, is filled with lakes, ponds and streams affording excellent fishing and hunting, and embraces the present towns of Conway, Wakefield, Ossipee, Fryeburg, &c. Dec. 10th. 1724, while northward of Lake Winnepiseogee, the party came "on a wigwam wherein were two Indians, one of which they killed and the other took, for which they received the promised bounty of *one hundred pounds* a scalp, and two shillings and six pence a day besides." (1.)

Other similar expeditions had been attempted, but without much success. Some had fallen into ambuscades, and some after long and dangerous journeys through the pathless wilderness had returned without meeting an enemy. But the success of Capt. Lovewell roused their spirits, and he determined upon another excursion. This company was soon augmented to eighty-eight (1.) He marched again, February, 1725, and visiting the place where they had killed the Indian, found his body as they had left it two months before. Their provisions falling short, thirty of them were dismissed by lot and returned home.

The remaining fifty-eight continued their march till they discovered a track, which they followed until they saw a smoke just before sunset, by which they judged that the enemy were encamped for the night. This was February 20th. 1725. "They kept themselves concealed till after midnight, when they silently advanced and discovered *ten* Indians asleep around a fire by the side of a frozen pond. Lovewell was determined to make sure work, and placing his men conveniently, ordered a part of them to fire, five at once, as quick after each other as possible, and another part to reserve their fire. He gave the signal by firing his own gun, which killed two of them. His men firing according to order killed five more on the spot. The other three starting up from their sleep, two of them were immediately shot dead by the reserve. The other though wounded attempted to escape by crossing the pond, but was seized by a dog and held fast till they killed him.

"Thus in a few minutes the whole company was destroyed, and some attempt against the frontiers of New Hampshire prevented; for these Indians were making from Canada well furnished with new guns, and plenty of ammunition. – They had also a number of spare blankets, mockaseens and snow-shoes, for the accommodation of the prisoners which they expected to take, and were within two days' march of the frontiers.

"The pond where this exploit was performed is at the head of a branch of Salmon Falls River, in the township of Wakefield, and has ever since borne the name of *Lovewell's Pond.*" "The action is spoken of by elderly people at this distance of time," says Belknap in 1790, from whom the above is chiefly taken, "with an air of exultation, and considering the extreme difficulty of finding and attacking Indians in the woods, and the judicious manner in which they were so completely surprised, it was a capital exploit."

"The brave company, with the ten scalps stretched on hoops and elevated on poles, entered Dover in triumph, and proceeded thence to Boston, where they received the promised bounty of *one hundred pounds* for each scalp out of the public treasury." (1.)

Penhallow adds that "the guns were so good and new that most of them were sold for seven pounds ($23.33) a piece. The plunder was but a few skins, but during the march our men were well entertained with moose, bear and deer, together with salmon trout, some of which were three feet long, and weighed twelve pounds a piece." (2.) Scarcely had Lovewell returned from this successful excursion, when Capt. Eleazar Tyng of this town, collecting a large company of volunteers, many of them also from this town, marched into the wilderness. They scouted around Pemigewasset river and Winnepiseogee lake for a month but returned without accomplishing any thing. (1.)

"Encouraged by his former success, and animated still," as Penhallow says, "with an uncommon zeal of doing what service he could," Lovewell marched a third time into the wilderness, intending to attack the Pequawketts in their head-quarters on Saco River. Just before he left, it is said, that being at a house in what is now Nashua, he was warned to be upon his guard against the ambuscades of the enemy. He replied, "That he did not care for them," and bending down a small elm beside which he was standing into a bow, declared "that he would treat the Indians in the same way." This elm is still standing, a venerable and magnificent tree.

He set out from Dunstable with 46 men, include a chaplain and surgeon. Two of them proving lame returned. Another falling sick, they halted and built a fort fortified by pointed stakes, on the west side of Ossipee Pond. Here the surgeon was left with the sick man, and eight of the number for a guard. The number of the company was now reduced to thirty-four. (2.)

"The names of this brave company are worthy of preservation, and their numerous descendants may trace back their descent to such ancestry with pride. They were Capt. John Lovewell, Lt. Josiah Farwell, Lt. Jonathan Robbins, Ensign John Harwood, Ensign Noah Johnson, Robert Usher and Saml. Whiting, all of Dunstable; Ensign Seth Wyman, Corporal Thos. Richardson, Timothy Richardson, Ichabod Johnson and Josiah Johnson of Woburn: Eleazer Davis, Joseph Farrar, Josiah Davis, Josiah Jones, David Melvin, Eleazer Melvin and Jacob Farrar of Concord; Chaplain Jonathan Frye of Andover; Sarg't Jacob Fullam of Weston; Corporal Edward Lingfield of Nutfield, (now Londonderry;) Jonathan Kittredge and Solomon Keyes of Billerica; John Teffts, Daniel Woods, Thomas Woods, John Chamberlain, Elias Barson, Isaac Lakin and Joseph Gilson of Groton; Abiel Asten and Ebenezer Alger of Haverhill, and one who deserted them in battle, and whose name has been considered unworthy of being transmitted to posterity."

"Pursuing their march northward they came to a pond about twenty-two miles distant from the fort, and encamped by the side of it. Early the next morning May 8th. 1725, (May 19th. New Style,) while at their devotions they heard the report of a gun, and discovered a single Indian standing on a point of land which runs into the pond more than a mile distant. They had been alarmed the preceding night by noises round their camp, which they imagined were made by Indians, and this opinion was now strengthened. They suspected that the Indian was there to decoy them, and that a body of the enemy was in their front.

A consultation being held they determined to inarch forward, and by encompassing the pond, to gain the place where the Indian stood. That they might be ready for action they disencumbered themselves of their packs, and left them without guard at the northeast end of the pond, in a pitch pine plain, where the trees were thin, and the brakes at that time of the year small." Penhallow adds that fearing a snare, "the Captain calling his men together, proposed, whether it was best to engage them or not?" They boldly replied, *"That as they had come out on purpose to meet the enemy, they would rather trust Providence with their lives and die for their country, than return without seeing them."* Upon this they proceeded." (1.)

"It happened that Lovewell's march had crossed a carrying place, by which two parties of Indians, consisting of forty-one each, commanded by Paugus and Wawha, who had been scouting down Saco river, were returning to the lower village of Pequawkett, distant about a mile and a half from this pond. Having fallen on this track they followed it till they came to the packs which they removed, and counting them found the number of his men to be less than their own. They therefore placed themselves in ambush to attack them on their return. The Indian who stood on the point, and who was returning to the village by another path, met them and received their fire, which he returned and wounded Farwell and another with small shot. Lieut. Wyman firing again killed him and they took his scalp.

"Seeing no other enemy they returned to the place where they had left their packs, and while they were looking for them the Indians rose and ran towards them with a horrid yelling. A smart firing commenced on both sides, it being about ten of the clock. Capt. Lovewell and *eight* more were killed on the spot. Lieut. Farwell and *two* others were wounded. Several of the Indians fell, but being superior in numbers they endeavored to surround the party, who perceiving their intention, retreated hoping to reach a shelter behind a point of rocks which ran into the pond, and a few large pine trees standing on a sandy beach. In this forlorn place they took their station. On their right was the mouth of a brook at that time unfordable; on their left was the rocky point. Their front was partly covered with a deep hog, and partly uncovered, and the pond was in the rear. The enemy galled them in front and in flank, and had them so completely in their power, that had they made a prudent use of their advantage, the whole company must either have been killed or obliged to surrender at discretion, being destitute of a mouthful of sustenance, and escape being impracticable.

"Under the conduct of Lieut. Wyman, they kept up their fire, and shewed a resolute countenance all the remainder of the day, during which their Chaplain, Jonathan Frye, Ensign Robbins, and one more were mortally wounded. The Indians invited them to surrender by holding up ropes to them, and endeavored to intimidate them by their hideous yells, but they determined to die rather than to yield. By their well directed fire the number of the savages was thinned, and their cries became fainter, till just before night they quitted their advantageous ground, carrying off their killed and wounded, and leaving the dead bodies of Lovewell and his men unscalped. The shattered remnant of this brave company collected themselves together, and found *three* of their number unable to move from the spot; *eleven* wounded, hut able to march; and n*ine* only who had received no hurt. All the rest, *eleven* in number, were slain.

"It was melancholy to leave their dying companions behind, but there was no possibility of removing them. One of them, Ensign Robbins, (1.) desired them to lay his gun by him charged, that if the Indians should return before his death, he might be able to kill one more. After the rising of the moon they quitted the fatal spot, and directed their march towards the Fort, where the surgeon and guard had been left. To their great surprise they found it deserted. In the beginning of the action one man (whose name has not been thought worthy to he transmitted,) quitted the field, and fled to the Fort. Here, in the style of Job's messengers, he informed them of Lovewell's death, and the defeat of the whole company, upon which they made the best of their way home, leaving a quantity of bread and pork, which was a seasonable relief to the retreating survivors."

The fate of the survivors was scarcely less pitiable than that of the dead. "Lieutenant Farwell, (of Dunstable) and the Chaplain, who had the journal of the march in his pocket, perished in the woods for want of dressing their wounds. Mr. Frye languished three days and died." "He was a very worthy and promising young man," says Penhallow, "and graduated at Harvard College in 1733." "Mr. Farwell held out until the *eleventh* day, during which time he had nothing to eat but water and a few roots which he chewed." Josiah Jones "after long fatigue and hardships got safe into Saco." Solomon Keyes "being wounded in three places, lost so much blood as disabled him to stand any longer; but by a strange Providence, as he was creeping away, he saw a canoe in the pond which he rolled himself into, and by a favorable wind, without any assistance of his own, was driven so many miles on, that he got safe into the Fort. Eleazer Davis was the last that got *in*, who after wandering about many days, and being nearly famished, came at last to Berwick, and thence to Portsmouth. The others, after enduring the most severe hardships, and meeting many providential escapes, came in one after another. They were received not only with joy, but were recompensed for their valor and sufferings, and a generous provision was made for the widows and children of the slain.

"Mr. Wyman, who distinguished himself in such a signal manner, was at his return, presented with a Captain's commission. Edward Ling-field was also made an Ensign, and the General Assembly gave the sum of *fifteen hundred pounds* to the widows and orphans." (1.)

"In 1 Samuel, xxxi. Chap., 11, 12, 13 verses," says Penhallow, "it is recorded in the immortal honor of the men of Jabesh-gilead, that when some of their renowned heroes fell by the hands of the Philistines, they prepared a decent burial for their bodies. Now so soon as the report came of Capt. Lovewell's defeat, about *fifty* men from New Hampshire, well equipped, marched into Pequawkett for the like end, but were not so happy as to find them. (2.) But in the Spring another company from Dunstable, under the command of Col. (Eleazer) Tyng, went to the scene of the action, and having found the bodies of *twelve,* buried them, and carved their names upon the trees where the battle was fought. – At a little distance they found the Indian graves which he opened, in one of which he found the celebrated warrior, Paugus, "a vile and bloody wretch," as Penhallow mildly adds.

The news of Lovewell's defeat and death reached Dunstable before the twentieth day of May. All was consternation and grief. What reports were brought by the survivors we know not, but immediate attack upon the town was feared by the inhabitants. The alarm extended through the settlements, and even reached Boston. The Governor odered Col. Eleazer Tyng into the wilderness to protect the frontiers against the anticipated invasion of the victorious foe. The state of excitement and alarm which pervaded the town may be conjectured from the following Petition addressed to the Governor and Council of Massachusetts. (1.)

"The Petition of the Selectmen of Dunstable,

Humbly Sheweth:

"That whereas your Honors hath found it necessary to order Col. Tyng and his men into the woods, on the sad occasion of Capt. Lovewell's defeat, we are extremely exposed and weak, by reason of so many of our fighting men being cut off last summer, and so many killed now in the Province's service. We would beg leave to represent to your Honors our case as very sad and distressing, having so many soldiers drawn out, and our inhabitants reduced to so small a number by the war. Several families have removed, and more are under such discouragement, not daring to carry on their planting or any other business, that they fully design it. We hope your Honors will take our deplorable circumstances into your compassionate consideration, and order such measures to be taken for our defence and support, until our men return, as you in your wisdom shall think fit. And your Petitioners, as in duty bound, will ever pray.

SAMUEL FRENCH,		JOHN CUMMINGS,
JOSEPH SNOW,		Selectmen. JOHN CUMMINGS, Jr.,
JOSEPH FRENCH,		NATH'L CUMMINGS.
JOHN LOVEWELL,		JONATHAN CUMMINGS,
JOHN FRENCH,		JONATHAN COMBS.

John Lovewell, the aged father of Capt. Lovewell also petitioned the General Assembly at the same time, for "some assistance from the country to defend his garrison, or that he must leave it to the enemy." (1.)

The petitions were granted. A guard of twenty-five soldiers was posted in town. Companies of scouts under Capt. Seth Wyman, Capt. Joseph Blanchard and Capt. Willard, were scouring the valleys of the Merrimac and the Nashua, during the whole summer and autumn, but no enemy appeared. With Joseph, a Mohawk, as a guide, and Nessa Gawney for an interpreter, they ranged as far as Penacook, "Win- ipisocket," and "Cocheco Path," but excepting killing a moose and a bear between. Dunstable and Penacook, they found nothing. (2.)

This incursion into the head-quarters of the Pequawketts, and the destruction of Norridgewock, alarmed the Indians so much that they resided no more at either place until after the peace. Nor after this did they commit any serious depredations. Their power was broken. – "Our encountering them at such a distance was so terrible and surprising," says Penhallow, "that they never formed any body after." – These conflicts were the themes of eulogy throughout the New England settlements. The names of their actors were upon all men's tongues "familiar as household words." The story of *"worthy Captain Lovewell"* was the subject of many a ballad, and was sung by every fireside. The mother taught it to her child to excite in him a hatred of the "Indian enemy," and to set before him an example of valor and patriotism, which he was to imitate when he should become a man.

Public gratitude kept pace with private enthusiasm. In addition to the gifts above cited, other donations were made, and the Township of Pembroke, first called *"Love-*

welVs Town," was granted by the General Assembly of Massachusetts, "in May, 1727, to Capt. Lovewell and his brave associates in consideration of their services against the Indians. The whole number of grantees was 60, 46 of whom accompanied Lovewell in his last march to Pequawkett, and the remainder were among the 62 who attended him in his first enterprise." (1.)

Of this company, as has been said, *seven* or more belonged to Dunstable, including nearly all the officers. Of these every man was killed or wounded. Capt. Lovewell, Ensign Harwood, and Robert Usher were killed on the spot. Lt. Robbins was left on the field mortally wounded. Lt. Farwell died on the march home. Samuel Whitney was wounded, and probably died not long after, as no mention of him is found in the Records of the town after May, 1725. Noah Johnson was so severely "wounded in the fight as to be disabled" for many years, but was the last survivor of the company. In 1727 a pension of £10 per annum for seven years was granted him by the Colony of Massachusetts, and after its expiration in 1734, the sum was increased to £15 per annum, and continued for many years. (2.) He died at Pembroke, N. H., 13 August, 1798, in his hundredth year. The grand children of some of these still survive in this town and vicinity.

Several of the ballads which were written to commemorate this event, one of the most important in our early history, have been preserved. If they do not possess high poetic merit, they answered well the purpose for which they were designed. "Let me make the *ballads* of a people," said (he great Chatham, "and I care not who makes the laws." There was deep wisdom in the remark, and such ballads, rude though they were, nurtured the free, bold, self-sacrificing spirit, which wrested Canada from the French in 1755, and finally achieved our Independence. One of the oldest of these ballads, composed, as is said, the year of the fight, "the most beloved song in all New England." is here inserted. (1.)

SONG OF LOVEWELL'S FIGHT.

I.

Of worthy Captain Lovewell I purpose now to sing,
How valiantly he served his country and his king;
He and his valiant soldiers did range the woods full wide,
And hardships they endured to quell the Indians' pride,

II.

'Twas nigh unto Pigwacket, on the eighth day of May,
They spied a rebel Indian soon after break of day;
He on a bank was walking, upon a neck of land,
Which leads into a pond as we're made to understand.

III.

Our men resolved to have him and traveiled two miles
                    round,
Until they met the Indian who boldly stood his ground;
Then speaks up Captain Lovewell,
                    "Take you good heed," says he,
"This rogue is to decoy us I very plainly see.

IV.

"The Indians lie in ambush in some place nigh at hand,
"In order to surround us upon this neck of land;
"Therefore we'll march in order, and each man leave
his pack,
"That we may briskly fight them when they shall us attack."

V.

They come unto the Indian who did them thus defy;
As soon as they come nigh him two guns he did let fly,
Which wounded Captain Lovewell and likewise
one man more, (1.)
But when this rogue was running they laid him in his gore.

VI.

Then having scalped the Indian they went back to the spot
Where they had laid their packs down, but there
they found them not;
For the Indians having spied them when they them
down did lay,
Did seize them for their plunder and carry them away.

VII.

These rebels lay in ambush this very place near by,
So that an English soldier did one of them espy:
And cried out, "here's an Indian"; with that they started out
As fiercely as old lions, and hideously did shout.

VIII.

With that our valiant English all gave a loud huzza,
To show the rebel Indians they feared them not a straw;
So now the fight began as fiercely as could be;
The Indians ran up to them but soon were forced to flee.

IX.

Then spake up Captain Lovewell when first the fight began, –
"Fight on my valiant heroes! you see they fall like rain:"
For as we are informed, the Indians were so thick,
A man could scarcely fire a gun and not some of them hit.

X.

Then did the rebels try their best our soldiers to surround,
But they could not accomplish it, because there was a pond,
To which our men retreated, and covered all the rear;
The rogues were forced to flee them although
                  they skulked for fear.

XI.

Two logs that were behind them so close together lay,
Without being discovered they could not get away;
Therefore our valiant English they travelled in a row,
And at a handsome distance as they were wont to go.

XII.

'Twas ten o'clock in the morning when first the fight begun,
And fiercely did continue till the setting of the sun,
Excepting that the Indians some hours before 'twas night.
Drew off into the bushes, and ceased a while to fight.

XIII.

But soon again returned in fierce and furious mood.
Shouting as in the morning, but yet not half so loud;
For as we are informed, so thick and fast they fell,
Scarce twenty of their number at night did get home well.

XIV.

And that our valiant English till midnight there did stay,
To see whether the rebels would have another fray;

But they no more returning they made off toward
their home,
And brought away their wounded as far as
they could come.

XV.

Of all our valiant English there were but thirty-four,
And of the rebel Indians there were about fourscore;
And sixteen of our English did safely home return:
The rest were killed and wounded for which
we all must mourn.

XVI.

Our worthy Captain Lovewell among them there did die; (1.)
They killed Lieutenant Robbins, and wounded
good young Frye, (2.)
Who was our English chaplain; he many Indians slew,
And some of them he scalped when bullets round him flew.

XVII.

Young Fullam, too, I'll mention, because he fought so well,
Endeavoring to save a man, a sacrifice be fell;
And yet our valiant Englishmen in fight
were ne'er dismayed,
But still they kept their motion, and Wyman Captain made

XVIII.

Who shot the old chief *Paugus* which did the foe defeat;
Then set his men in order and brought off the retreat;
And braving many dangers and hardships by the way,
They safe arrived at Dunstable the thirtieth day of May.

The statement in the last verse that Paugus was killed by Wyman is not correct. He was slain by John Chamberlain, who afterwards settled in Merrimac. After the heat of the conflict was over, weary and faint, Paugus and Chamberlain both went down to the pond to quench their thirst, and to wash out their guns which had become foul by continued firing. There they met and at once recognized each other, for Paugus was known personally to many of the company. Seeing the useless condition of each others' guns, they tacitly agreed to a truce while they were cleaning them.

During this process some words were exchanged, and Paugus said to Chamberlain, "It is you or I." Cautiously but with haste they proceeded in their work, for it was a case of life or death. Paugus had nearly finished loading, and was priming his piece, when Chamberlain struck the breech of his gun violently upon the ground, thus causing it to prime itself, and shot Paugus through the heart, the bullet of Paugus at the same instant grazing the head of Chamberlain. (1.)

There is another ballad of more poetic merit, written in imitation of the ancient Chevy Chase. As it is somewhat rare and curious, it is thought best to insert it. (1.)

LOVEWELL'S FIGHT.

A BALLAD.

What time the noble Lovewell came,
With fifty men from Dunstable,

The cruel Pequ'at tribe to tame,
With arms and bloodshed terrible, –

Then did the crimson streams that flowed
Seem like the waters of the brook,
That brightly shine, that loudly dash,
Far down the cliffs of Agiochook. (2.)

With Lovewell brave, John Harwood came:
From wife and twin babes hard to part;
Young Harwood took her by the hand,
And bound the weeper to his heart.

"Repress that tear, my Mary dear,"
Said Harwood to his loving wife;
"It tries me hard to leave thee here,
"And seek in distant woods the strife.

"When gone, my Mary, think of me,
"And pray to God that I may be
"Such as one ought that lives for thee,
"And come at last in victory."

Thus left young Harwood wife and babes;
With accent wild she bade adieu;
It grieved those lovers much to part,
So fond and fair, so kind and true.

Seth Wyman who in Woburn lived,
(A marksman he of courage true,)

Shot the first Indian whom they saw;
Sheer through his heart the bullet flew.

The savage had been seeking game.
Two guns and eke a knife he bore,
And two black ducks were in his hand, –
He shrieked and fell to rise no more.

Anon there eighty Indians rose,
Who'd hid themselves in ambush dread;
Their knives they shook, their guns they aimed,
The famous Paugus at their head.

Good Heavens! They dance the Powow dance!
What horrid yells the forests fill!
The grim bear crouches to his den,
The eagle seeks the distant hill.

"What means this dance, this Powow dance!"
Stern Wyman said, with wondrous art;
He crept full near, his rifle armed,
And shot the leader through the heart. (1.)

John Lovewell, Captain of the band,
His sword he waved that glittered bright;
For the last time he cheered his men,
And led them onward to the fight.

"Fight on! Fight on"! brave Lovewell said:
"Fight on while Heaven shall give you breath!"
An Indian ball then peirced him through,
And Lovewell closed his eyes in death,

John Farwell died, all bathed in blood,
When he had fought till set of day;
And many more, we may not name,
Fell in that bloody battle fray.

When news did come to Harwood's wife
That he with Lovewell fought and died, –
Far in the wilds had given his life
Nor more would in their home abide, –

Such grief did seize upon her mind,
Such sorrow filled her faithful breast,
On earth she ne'er found peace again,
But followed Harwood to his rest.

T'was *Paugus* led the Pequa't tribe;
As runs the fox would Paugus run;
As howls the wild wolf would he howl, –
A huge bear skin had Paugus on.

But Chamberlain of Dunstable,
(One whom a savage ne'er shall slay, –)
Met Paugus by the water side,
And shot him dead upon that day.

Good Heavens ! is this a time for prayer ?
Is this a time to worship God ?
When Lovewell's men are dying fast,
And Paugus' tribe hath felt the rod.

The Chaplain's name was Jonathan Frye;
In Andover his father dwelt;

And oft with Lovewell's men he'd prayed
Before the mortal wound he felt.
A man he was of comely form,
Polished and brave, well learned and kind:
Old Harvard's learned walls he left
Far in the wilds a grave to find.

Ah ! now his blood red arm he lifts;
His closing lids he tries to raise;
And speak once more before he dies,
In supplication and in praise.

He prays kind heaven to grant success,
Brave Lovewell's men to guide and bless.
And when they've shed their heart blood true
To raise them all to happiness.

"Come hither, Farwell," said young Frye;
"You see that I'm about to die;
"Now for the love I bear to you,
"When cold in death my bones shall lie;

"Go thou and see my parents dear,
"And tell them you stood by me here;
"Console them when they cry, alas !
"And wipe away the falling tear."

Lieutenant Farwell took his hand,
His arm around his neck he threw,
And said, "brave Chaplain I could wish
That heaven had made me die for you."

The Chaplain on kind Farwell's breast,
Bloody and languishing he fell;
Nor after this said more, but *this*,
"I love thee soldier; fare thee well!"

Ah! many a wife shall rend her hair,
And many a child cry out "wo is me !"
When messengers the news shall bear
Of Lovewell's dear bought victory.

With footsteps slow shall travellers go
Where Lovewell's Pond shines clear and bright,
And mark the place where those are laid
Who fell in Lovewell's bloody fight.

Old men shall shake their head and say,
"Sad was the hour and terrible,
When Lovewell brave 'gainst Paugus went,
With fifty men from Dunstable."

Thus ended "Lovewell's War." Deep and universal was the gratitude at the restoration of peace. Well might the people rejoice. For fifty years had the war been raging with little cessation, and with a series of surprises, devastations and massacres which seemed to threaten annihilation. "The scene of this desperate and bloody action is often visited with interest to this day; and the names of those who survived are yet repeated with emotions of grateful exultation." (1.) And a century after upon that spot strangers came together, from a broad and populous region won from the savages in that conflict, to pay their tribute of gratitude, with festive celebration, song, and eulogy to the waning memory of "Lovewell's Fight." (2.)

After this fight no other attack was made by the Indians upon this town, although many years subsequently, during the French Wars, the inhabitants were alarmed at the ravages committed in the neighborhood at Bedford, Pembroke, Dunbarton, Concord, and upon Connecticut River. Garrisons were built, and armed scouts kept out constantly, but the *frontiers* were now beyond us. Sometimes, indeed, individual Indians appeared mysteriously, seeking the life of some offending settler who had slain a relative, to appease his restless spirit by the sacrifice of "blood for blood." Such tales they tell of Chamberlain, the slayer of Paugus, of Ford, and others noted in fight, and how, mysteriously disappearing, the layer in wait became the victim.

Perilous conflicts, providential escapes and strange adventures were thickly woven in the romance of our early history, but the remembrance of most of them has passed away utterly, and of others but dim and doubtful traditionary shadows remain. These traditions, handed down from the survivors long since departed, too direct and circumstantial to be entirely fictitious, and fixing neither time, nor place, nor actors of the scene, meet the enquirer at every step in his investigations, and excite longings and questions which cannot be gratified. If there were indeed "tongues in trees, books in the running brooks," and "sermons in stones," what thrilling tales might not some of our old denizens of field and forest unfold!

Many anecdotes which have been handed down, if not entirely authentic, are at least characteristic of the times in which they are said to have occurred, and probably possess some foundations. The following are specimens:

A party of Indians, it is said, once came suddenly upon Ford, "the Indian Fighter," so that he had no chance to escape. He was splitting logs for vails, and had just driven in his wedge and partly opened a log. Pretending to be very anxious to complete the work, he requested them to put their hands in the cleft, and pull it open, while he drove in the wedge. Suspecting nothing they did so, but watching his opportunity he dexterously knocked the wedge *out* instead of *in*. The log closed tight upon their fingers, and held them fast, and the whole party became his prisoners.

"At a later period an Indian appeared in Dunstable enquiring for 'Joe Snow,' who at some former time had slain his kinsman. The duty of revenge had long been transmitted, and the desire nourished; and the descendants of the aggrieved and restless warrior had now come thus far through the wilderness, even from Canada, guided by tradition alone, to avenge and pacify his spirit. This errand, however, was vain, for 'Joe Snow' had long ago departed."

At some period during "Lovewell's War," William Cummings of this town, was wounded by the Indians, but bow, when, or where, no record tells. For bis wounds he received the sum of £10 from the Colonial Treasury. (1.)

"An Indian once called upon Chamberlain at his saw mill, intending to way-lay him on his return homeward at nightfall, through the forest. It was a time of peace, but Chamberlain suspected the character of his pretended friend, and the motive of his visit. While engaged in his work, he invited the Indian to examine the wheelpit, and seizing the opportunity, knocked him on the head with a handspike without compunction."

"Among those indefinite traditions which have been assigned to a period subsequent to Lovewell's War, is the following: – A party once went from this town to the East-ward upon a hunting expedition in early winter. While absent they were attacked by a party of predatory Indi-ans, and nearly all of them were killed. A few escaped and returned home bringing the sad tidings of the death of their companions and neighbors.

"One man, however, who was left in the field for dead, survived. His name was Whitney, and he lived in what is now the southerly part of Nashua, near Long Hill. He was too weak to think of returning home alone through the trackless and unpeopled forest, so he built him a hut of logs, and bark, and branches of trees, and there passed the winter, subsisting chiefly on roots and cranberries. In the Spring another party went out to find and bury the dead, and came to this hut which they sup-posed to he that of an Indian. As they approached they saw something stir within it. One of the party fired, – a

groan followed, but the victim, to their great astonish-
ment and grief, proved to be the unfortunate Whitney.
He was just preparing to return home, having survived
his wounds and all the perils and hardships of a winter
in the wilderness, only to perish by the hands of his own
friends and townsmen."

NOTES:

(1.) *Penhallow.* 1 N. H. Hist. Coll. 100. 1 *Belknap*, 208.

(1.) So says Report of Committees on the subject in *Mass. Records
   – Towns.* 1728.

(1.) Belknap, 208. The original journal *of* this expedition, in Lovewell's hand writing, is still preserved among the papers in
   the office of the Secretary of State, at Boston. Many of the
   company were from this town, but the names of few have
   been preserved. – Beside the officers already named, and
   those who accompanied them to Pequawkelt, were Zaccheus Lovewell, Thos. Colburn, Peter Powers, Josiah Cummings, Henry Farwell, Win. Avers.

(2.) 1 N. H. Hist. Coll. 113.

(1.) Mass. Records. Tyng's Journal, J725.

(2.) The report of the committee upon Lovewell's tour says that
) he started with 47 men, 3 of whom returned home sick and
   lame. – *Military Records and tour,* 1728. They had his muster
   roll before them.

(1.) 1 N. H. Hist. Coll., 114.

(1.) Robbins lived on Long Hill, in the south part of Nashua.

(1.) *Penhallow.* 1 N. H. Hist. **Coll.,** 118.

(2.) Under Capt. Joseph Blanchard, of this town, in July, 1725.
   Mass. Military Records, 1725.

(1.) *Military Records,* 1725, *page* 233.

(1.) *Mass. Military Records,* 1725: Original Petition, *page* 263.

(2.) *Mass. Military Records*, 1725: *page* 263.

(1.) *Farmer's N. H. Gazetteer. Pembroke.* – There seems, however, to be an error in this – the Report of the Committee upon the subject of the grant says, that the whole number was 88, of whom 62 were in the second expedition, and 26 in the last as well as the second expedition.

(2.) Johnson, it is said, occupied the farm on the south side of the Nashua at its mouth, extending probably as far as the house of Judge Parker. Lovewell is said to have occupied the farm near Luther Taylor's house.

(1.) *Drake's Book of the Indians*, 132.

(1.) Lt. Farwell, of this town.

(1.) The powder horn worn by Lovewell in this fight is preserved in the family, and the cellar of the house where he lived is still visible a little distance from Salmon Brook in Nashua.

(2.) Robbins was from Dunstable. Frye was a son of Rev. Mr. Frye of Andover, as before mentioned. Their notions were all Jewish, and in slaying the "Heathen Indians" they thought themselves obeying the voice of God.

(1.) *Rev. Mr. Symme's Narrative of the fight. Allen's Chelmsford*, 37.

(1.) *Farmer's and Moore's Hist. Coll.*, 95. *Book of the Indians*, 179.

(2.) The Indian name of the White Mountains. *Book of the Indians*, 191.

(1.) The *chief* Powow or Priest who led the ceremonies.

(1.) *North American Review.*

(2.) Its centennial anniversary was celebrated on the spot of the Fight, in Fryeburg, Me., May 19. 1825, when an address was delivered by Charles S. Davis, Esq., of Portland.

(1.) *Mass. Military Records*, 1734.

CHAPTER IX.
CIVIL HISTORY OF THE TOWN UNTIL ITS DIVISION BY THE NEW STATE LINE IN 1741

THE settlement of the town which had been so much and so long retarded, – which for *forty* years had scarcely advanced at all, now increased rapidly. But the inhabitants were extremely poor. In addition to the heavy public taxes occasioned by the long and expensive Indian Wars, they had suffered much from the incursions of the enemy – from the loss of the ransoms paid for the release of their captive friends, and from the obstruction of all regular employment.

In consideration of the universal scarcity of money, the General Assembly of Massachusetts issued bills of credit in 1721 to the amount of £50,000, to be distributed among the several towns in proportion to the public taxes. They answered the purpose of money for the time. – Nov. 7, 1721, Lt. Henry Farwell and Joseph Blanchard were appointed Trustees to receive and loan out "the share" of this town, in such sums that "no man shall have more than five pounds, and no man less than three pounds," and shall pay *five per cent.* interest for the use of the same to the Town.

In 1727 the General Assembly, finding this mode of making money popular, issued £60,000 more. The share belonging to this town was received and loaned to Rev. Mr. Prentice, to be applied in payment of his *future* salary as it should become due. Thus early and easily did men discover and adopt the practice of throwing their debts upon posterity. The consequence of these issues was a ruinous depreciation in their value – a nominal rise in the value of every species of property, speculation, and at last universal distress. In 1750 the bills were worth but *12* per cent.

The general poverty of the inhabitants may also be inferred from the fact, that *no representative* was sent to the General Assembly, although directed so to do, the Town voting regularly from 1693 to 1733 "not to send." Whenever the interests of the Town were in danger, however, a special agent was sent to see that they were protected. As an illustration of the feelings and peculiarities of those times it may be added, that, February 1, 1631, it was "voted not to choose any person as Representative, *deeming ourselves not obliged by Law."* But in order to be certain as to their rights and duties, the next year they took legal advice upon this subject, and again voted "not to send, *finding the Town not obliged by Law."* At that time the representative received no compensation for attendance. but bis expenses were paid by the town. In 1718 the compensation was fixed by statute at *three shillings* per day. At one period the General Assembly hired an inn-keeper to board all of the members at a stipulated price per day, including wine, "but not to exceed one cup of sack each." This was done not only for economy, but for the greater despatch of business.

For many years little occurred here which would be of general interest. The records are chiefly valuable as serving to shew the contrast between the past and the present, and the slow and painful steps by which towns arrive at maturity. Some memoranda of this period, therefore, may serve to amuse and perhaps instruct the curious reader.

In 1716 a committee was appointed by the town to lay out a road to Dracut, and "to state the Country road from Capt. Tyng's to Nashaway River." Its width was declared to be "four rods."

"Sept. 2, 1718, voted, that John Lovewell Senior, and his son John, [the Hero of Pequawkett,] should hav liberty to bild a dam in the highway over Salmon Brook, not to incommodate the highway." This was at the little bridge near the house of Miss Allds, where the mud sills are still visible, and the *"highway"* was the "Country road" just mentioned.

"March 31, 1819, Joseph French was *chosen to make coffins* where there be need for the year ensuing." Friendly Indians still lived here, and this singular vote may have referred to them, as we find a charge made by him not long after, "for Jacob Indian's coffin 7s."

The Selectmen and other persons in the employment of the town at this period charged 5s. per day for their services.

The humble Meeting House which had served for the worship of all the inhabitants, since no division into sects existed, was a rude, one story, unsteepled edifice, and would shew but poorly beside the erections of the present day. It was divided by an aisle in the centre, with rows of benches on either side, one of which was appropriated for the use of the women, and the other for the use of the men. Such a separation was not unfrequent in those primitive days. (1.)

But even among our grave and simple fore-fathers, luxury and ambition crept in. March 2, 1720, it was "Voted that Lt. Henry Farwell and Joseph Blanchard should hav the libety to erect for themselves two Pewes on there own charge at the west end of the Meeting House." The example was contagious, so dangerous is a precedent. If Lt. Farwell and Capt. Blanchard could afford "Pewes," why might not others? May 18, 1720, it was "Voted that there be four Pewes erected in our Meeting House; one on the hack side of the lowermost seats, and one seat to be taken up; Sargt. Colburn, one pew; Sargt. Perham, one pew; Nathaniel Cummings, one pew; Oliver Farwell, one pew."

The *first pauper* in town appears to have been Joseph Hassell, a son probably of him who was slain by the Indians in 1691. He was supported by the town, who appointed a person *"to take care of"* him in 1722 or 1723.

In 1723 *Grand Jurymen* were chosen by the town at the annual meeting by ballot. This was probably done as a precaution against the encroachments of the officers of the crown, and as a safeguard of popular rights. One tribunal was secure from royal influence, and no individual could be unjustly condemned. This mode of choice continued till after the revolution, and was a source of great annoyance to the enemies of America, who complained that the Towns chose the most active opponents of England for their Grand Jurors, so that those guilty of political offences could not be indicted. (1.)

In 1723 the choice of a *Tything man,* Thomas Blanchard, is first recorded. The Town raised *£20* [about $70] to defray all town expenses, and the collector had "3 pence in the pound *[1* 1-4 per cent] for gathering all Town rates for ye year."

In 1724 the Town was again called upon to assist in keeping "the great bridge in Billerica in good repare," and chose Henry Farwell "to jine with the committy appinted" for that purpose. 1729 they united with Dracut, Chelmsford, and Billerica in further repairs, and 1731 expended £3 10s. for the same purpose. This bridge was over the Concord river on the main road to Boston, and of great importance.

The method of voting for all the more important officers was *"by ballot,"* while others of less importance were chosen "by holding up of ye hands." So early did our forefathers recognize that truly republican principle and safeguard of popular rights, the secret ballot.

In those days *offices* were not only places of honor and profit, but also of good cheer. Those were glorious times for dignitaries. Among the accounts presented for acceptance, and which were allowed and paid by the Town without scruple, we find the following:

"Town of Dunstable to Samuel French, Dr 1726. To dining the Selectmen 6 meals, £0 6s 0d for *rhum* and *cyder* bad at Mr William Lund's *for the Selectmen*, 0 12 6."

We are accustomed to look back upon that early period as an age of primitive simplicity and virtue. Yet what would be said of such an account in these Temperance days? But their faults were only those of rude and hardy pioneers, and of the age, and we would institute no comparison. They laid a noble foundation for our Republic. "Every man who was *forty* years old," says Belknap, "had seen twenty years of war." Such continual dangers and hardships, although affording no good school for cultivation and refinement, furnished a race of hardy soldiers and sterling patriots for the "times that tried men's souls."

In March, 1727, the town raised "eight pounds for building a boat," and it was directed "that Capt. Blanchard should return the boat within the year to the Town." This was probably for a Ferry-boat over the Merrimac at the Blanchard farm, [now Little's] as Hudson was then included in Dunstable, and a few settlers had located themselves on that side of the river. – The bridge existed for a century after.

October 29 and 30, 1727, at night a shock of an earthquake was felt here. It effected chiefly "the towns upon the Merrimac." "The shock was very loud and was attended with a terrible noise like thunder. The houses trembled as if they were falling. Divers chimnies were cracked, and some had their tops broken off. Flashes of light broke out of the earth, and the earth broke open." The shocks lasted until February, 1728. (1.)

At this time taverners were licensed by the County-Court. In the fall of 1727, Capt. Joseph Blanchard, who had been the inn-keeper of the town for many years, died, and as the Court was not in session in December, 1727, Henry Farwell Jr., petitioned the General Assembly for a license which was granted. (2.)

In 1728 a *boom* was built across Merrimac River by the town.

Among the early settlers of New England the principles of jurisprudence were but little known, and there were few lawyers. The jurisdiction of courts of law was limited, and as many of the judges had received no preparatory legal education to fit them for the bench, but were taken directly from the counting room or camp, all settled rules of law were of course unknown and disregarded. The people, therefore, in all cases of difficulty applied at once to the General Assembly, who assumed and exercised jurisdiction in imitation of the English Parliament, as a court of Errors and of Chancery in all cases whatsoever, where their assistance was needed for the purposes of Justice.

A committee having been appointed by the town to purchase the ministerial farm of Rev. Mr. Coffin as a parsonage for Mr. Prentice, and refusing to convey it as directed, the Town applied to the General Court of Massachusetts by a "petition for some redress, if it may be obtained, touching the premises." This was not done, however, without a division, and several persons entered their *desent* [dissent] or protest against the proceeding.

The amount of taxes raised from 1726 to 1733 for the general expenses of the Town, including the support of the ministry, varied from $250 to $400 per year.

The subject of *education* was one of deep interest to the early settlers of New England. – To them must be awarded the enviable distinction of their being the first to lay down the noble principle, that "every child should be taught to read and write," and the first to establish common schools to carry it into effect. It was ever the custom, and became the law in Puritan New England as early as 1642, that "none of the brethren should suffer so much barbarism in their families, as not to teach their children and apprentices so much learning, as may enable them perfectly to read the English Language." A fine of *20* shillings was imposed for every neglect, and, if after reproof by the Selectmen, they still neglected this duty, the children were to be taken from them, and bound out, males until *21*, and females until 18 years of age.

In 1646 it was enacted that "if any child above 16 years old, and of sufficient understanding, shall curse or smite his natural father or mother, he shall be put to death, unless *it can* be sufficiently *testified, that the parents have* been VERY UNCHRISTIANLY NEGLIGENT IN THE EDUCATION OF SUCH CHILDREN." This was the Mosaic Law, but with an important and characteristic qualification.

"To the end that learning may not be buried in the graves of our forefathers," it was ordered in 1647, "that every township, after the Lord hath increased them to the number of *fifty householders,* shall appoint one *to teach all the children* to read and *write:* And when any town shall increase to the number of *one hundred, families* they shall set up a grammar school, the master whereof being able to instruct youth so far as they may be fitted for the university." These provisions, furnishing the best academic education to every child gratuitously, go far beyond our present School Laws, and we might do well to retrace our steps. For non-compliance the Towns were liable to indictment, and a fine was imposed for the benefit of the school in the next Town.

One reason which determined the Puritans upon a removal from Leyden was, "That the place being of great licentiousness and liberty to children, they could not educate them; nor could they give them due correction without reproof or reproach from their neighbors." Their ideas of government, family and national, were all derived from the Mosaic code, and, as was said of the Connecticut settlers, they "agreed to take the laws of God for their guide until they had time to make better."

But, deeply as the settlers felt the importance of Education, it was no easy matter in a frontier town, where a fierce Indian War was raging, when the inhabitants dwelt in garrisons and the settlement was every day liable to an attack, to establish common schools. The dense forest, where the quiet of the school room might be broken at any time by the yell of the savage, was no fitting time or place for helpless children; still at home education was not neglected, as the state of our ancient records everywhere attests. So much were the inhabitants scattered that no school was kept in Town until 1730. In that year, it seems, the Town having increased to the requisite number of *"fifty house-holders,"* and having neglected to provide *a teacher* according to Law, had been indicted by the Grand Jury. Nov. 3, 1730, it was accordingly voted, that "it be left with the selectmen to provide and agree with a person to keep a writing school in the town *directly";* and, that "the sum of Ten pounds be granted and raised for defraying the charges in the last mentioned concern and *other Town charges."* How liberal this provision was we may judge from the fact that the same sum, and even more, had been annually raised for Town charges alone, and that Dunstable then included the greater part of Hollis and Hudson within its limits !

How many inhabitants the Town then contained we are unable to ascertain. If there were fifty house-holders or families, the number was probably about *two hundred and fifty.* How slow was the increase and how disastrous must have been the effect of the long Indian Wars, we may conjecture when we remember that as far back as 1680, there were thirty families, or nearly one hundred and fifty inhabitants, most of whom were settled within the present limits of Nashua.

After this indictment, however, had been arranged, it appears that the Town relapsed into its ancient neglect and no further notice was taken of it. No record of any vote to raise money for the support of Schools, or to choose any school committee, or to build any school-house, or any allusion to the subject of schools is found for many years. The Town was too much distracted, at this period, perhaps, by exciting religious and sectional questions, to attend to or agree upon any general plan of education. The inhabitants of Hollis and Hudson were desirous of being erected into separate townships. Then came the question of erecting "a decent meeting house," and similar divisions ensued.

The controversies about the boundary line between New Hampshire and Massachusetts, which finally divided Dunstable nearly in the middle, leaving one half of the territory within the jurisdiction of Massachusetts, and transferring the northern portion, with a large majority of the inhabitants, to New Hampshire, gave rise to an excitement still more intense and protracted. Then followed a succession of sectarian disputes about the *Orthodox* and *New Lights*, Congregationalists and Presbyterians, all of which were discussed and decided in Town meetings. – These, and similar controversies, with their consequent victories and defeats, protests and reconsiderations must have occupied their time sufficiently to prevent their union upon any subject, where there might be conflicting interests or prejudices.

After Love well's War, so great was the security felt by the settlers, that they plunged boldly into the wilderness in every direction. In July, 1729, the lands lying three miles north and south on Merrimac River, extending three miles east and four miles west of it, and bounded southerly by the Souhegan, [now the northerly part of Merrimac] were granted to Joseph Blanchard and others. Even as early as May, 1726, a settlement was commenced at Concord. In Dunstable the outlands were taken up, and soon the wilderness was alive with population. So numerous had they become that "for greater convenience of public worship", they desired on every hand to be erected into townships.

In 1731 the inhabitants on the east side of the Merrimac petitioned the town to be set off, which was granted to take effect "whenever the General Court should think it advisable." Leave was obtained accordingly from the Assembly of Massachusetts, and the new township was called Nottingham. On the establishment of the boundary line it fell within the State of New Hampshire, obtained a new charter in 1746, and changed its name to Nottingham-West, there being already a Nottingham in the eastern section of the State.

In 1732 the inhabitants on the northerly side of Nashua River petitioned to be set off also with Brenton's Farm, but the petition was not granted by the town. In 1733, however, part of the town lying west of Merrimac River was incorporated by the General Assembly into a township by the name of Rumford, but soon after was called Merrimac.

July 3, 1734, Litchfield was incorporated. – In the petition for incorporation, dated May, 1734, and signed by "Aquila Underwood for the Town", it is stated, as a reason for the grant, that they have "supported a minister for some time."

While the jealousies and divisions, to which reference has been made, were existing in such strength, "the old meeting house," it seems, had grown so old and out of repair, as not to be "*decent*." Upon a vote taken in 1732 whether the town "would build a decent meeting house or rectify and mend the old one", it was decided not to "*rectify*", but to build. After quarrel- ling a year and holding various meetings, it was voted to build it "about 4 rods westward of where the meeting house now stands", upon which 19 persons, chiefly from that part of the town now lying in Massachusetts, *entered their dissent* of record against the location.

In 1736 Hollis was set off from Dunstable by the name of "*the west parish of Dunstable*"; but after the establishment of the boundary line, it received a new act of incorporation from the State of New Hampshire, by the name of Hollis. Its Indian name was Nissitisset. In the mean time settlements were extending rapidly all around, and the forest was bowing before the onward tread of civilization. In 1734, Amherst was settled, and in 1736 a bridge was built across Souhegan River, then the northerly boundary of Dunstable, and a road laid out and built "from the bridge to Dunstable meeting house."

In 1732 Townsend was incorporated, taking in the southerly part of the town, including Pepperell. Thus township after township had become parcelled out from the original body of "old Dunstable", until in 1740 the broad and goodly plantation was reduced to that portion only which is now embraced within the limits of Nashua and Nashville, Tyngsborough and Dunstable. At length, after a long and violent controversy, and against the wishes of the inhabitants, the boundary line between New Hampshire and Massachusetts was established in 1741, severing Dunstable very nearly in the middle, and leaving the present towns of Nashua and Nashville within the limits of New Hampshire. With the exception of a small section set off to Hollis, this portion retains the territory which it had in 1741, and contains by computation, about 18,878 acres.

After the death of Rev. Mr. Prentice, Rev. Josiah Swan received a call to settle over the church and town. He accepted the call, and was ordained Dec. 27, 1738. Mr. Swan is said to have been a native of Dunstable, and graduated at Harvard in 1733. In 1739 he married Jane [Mr. Sperry says erroneously *Rachael,*] Blanchard, daughter of Joseph Blanchard, Esq., of this town. In 1741, however, on the division of the town by the new boundary, it became more difficult to support a minister. Not long afterwards the sect then called *"New Lights"*, but since known as Methodists, appeared, and a division in his society ensued. The churches were "infected with lay exhorters, and some ministers who have left their parishes and charges and undertaken to play the bishop in another man's diocese", as the regular clergy complained, and "distracted by such persons exhorting and preaching in private houses without the consent of the stated pastor." (1.)

We have seen that the question of building a new meeting house was discussed as far back as 1732, and a vote taken fixing its location. In November, 1734, John Kendall and others remonstrated to the General Assembly against its location, and asked for a committee. (2.) The records of the town from 1733 to 1746 are lost, but it is known that the vole was inoperative and the house not built until 1738, when Mr. Swan was settled. It stood near the old burying ground not far from the State line, having been built for the accommodation of the original township. Immediately after the division of the town, it became necessary to erect a new meeting house in a more central situation. But so diverse were the interests and the feelings of our then widely scattered population, that no location was satisfactory. June 20, 1746, the town voted "that the *place of preaching the gospel this summer be at Ephraim Lund's barn.*" After sundry votes, protests and reconsiderations, committees, reports and compromises, the town voted to accept the proposal of Jona. Lovewell and others to build the meeting house on their own account, and to have the liberty of selling all the wall pews for their own benefit.

The House was built accordingly in the autumn of 1747, *"on a spot of rising ground about six rods west of the main road"*, which is a few rods northerly of the present South meeting house. it was about twenty-eight feet by forty; had a small gallery, and was divided like the old one, into the "men's side" and the "women's side."

NOTES:

(1.) The following is a description of the early Meeting Houses as drawn up by Rev. Leonard Bacon of New Haven: – "Immediately before the pulpit, and facing the Congregation was an elevated seat for the *ruling elder,* and before that, somewhat lower, was a seat for the Deacons behind the Communion Table. On the floor of the house there were neither pews nor slips, but plain seats. – On each side of what we may call the centre aisle were *nine* seats of sufficient length to accommodate five or six persons. On each side of the pulpit at the end were five cross seats, and another shorter than the five. Along each wall of the house, between the cross seats and the side door, six seats.

The men and women were seated separately, on opposite sides of the house, and every one according to his office, or his age, or his rank in society, and his place was assigned by a committee appointed for that purpose. The children and young people at the first seating seem to have been left to find their own places, away from their parents, in that part of the house which was not occupied with seats prepared at the town's expense."

(1.) *Gov. Hutchinson's Letters.*

(1.) 4 N. H. *Hist. Coll.,* 93.

(2.) *Mass. Assembly Records,* 1727.

(1.) *Allen's Chelmsford,* 116.

(2.) *Ecclesiastical Records, 1734, page 70.*

CHAPTER X.
HISTORY OF DUNSTABLE, N. H., TO THE OLD FRENCH WAR

APRIL 4, 1746. the town was first incorporated by the State of New Hampshire, having previously acted under their charter, obtained from the General Court of Massachusetts, in 1673. – It retained the ancient name of Dunstable.

In 1746 the great road to Tyngsborough was stated anew and recorded. There would seem to have been but few houses upon this road at that time. The following are all that are mentioned: – Capt. Joseph French's house was *8* rods north of the State line; Col. Joseph Blanchard's house, 300 rods north of the State line, and 29 rods south of "Cummings's Brook"; Cyrus Baldwin's near Col. Blanchard's; John Searles' house *66* rods north of Cummings's Brook; Henry Adams's 80 rods north of Searles' house; the old ditch which led to the Fort was 90 rods north of Adams's house; Thomas Harwood's house was 90 rods north of the old ditch; no other house mentioned between Harwood's and Nashua River, excepting Jonathan Lovewell's, which was 283 rods south of the River, or at the Harbor, south of Salmon Brook.

About this time the difficulties with Mr. Swan having increased, he was dismissed. He did not leave town, however, immediately, for we find his name recorded the next year as having voted against a successor. He settled in full with the town. March 2, 1747. He did not remain here long, but returned to Lancaster, Mass., his former place of residence. Here he was engaged in the tuition of a school, which had been his occupation previous to his entrance upon the ministry, and became "a famous teacher." He remained at Lancaster until about 1760, when he removed to Walpole, N. H., where he died. (1.)

Of his character little is known, and a single anecdote has reached us. From this, however, from his dealings with the town in regard to his salary, and from the amount of his taxes, for he owned a farm, we may infer that he amassed some property, and was a prudent, stirring, thrifty, but not over spiritual man. One Sabbath morning, it is said, during the latter part of his ministry, while old Mr. Lovewell was alive, he forgot the day and ordered his hired men to their work. They objected, telling him it was Sunday. He would not believe it, but finally, says he, "if it is Sunday, we shall soon see old father Lovewell coming up the hill"; and sure enough, punctual as the clock to the hour, the old man, then more than a hundred years of age, hut who never missed a Sunday, was seen making his way to church, and Mr. Swan was convinced of his mistake.

At this time there was neither school nor schoolhouse in town. Sept. 29, 1746, it was voted that "Jona. Lovewell be desired to hire a school master until the next March for this town, upon the cost and charge of the town." – Two dwelling houses, one in the northern and one in the southern portions of the town, were designated, in which the school should be kept, "if they could be obtained." But one teacher was employed, and he was to keep school half of the time at each place. The number of inhabitants was probably about 400.

During this year the Indians committed much havoc in the frontier towns, around and above us. Many settlements above us were nearly or quite deserted. "The defenceless state they were in obliged them all, namely, Peterborough, Salem Canada, [Lyndeborough,] New Boston and Hillsborough, [so called,] entirely to draw off, as well as the forts on the Connecticut river. (1.) In the winter of 1745 and 1746 scouts were furnished by this State and Massachusetts for the protection of those towns.

In May, 1747, the inhabitants of Souhegan West, [Amherst,] and Monson, [a town formerly lying between Amherst and Hollis, afterwards divided and annexed to those towns,] petitioned Gov. Wentworth for a guard, being "in imminent danger." The petition was granted, and his "Excellency was desired to give orders for enlisting or *impressing* fifteen good and efficient men, to scout and guard, under proper officers, said Souhegan West and Monson, till the twentieth day of October next, if need be, and that said men be shifted once a month."

It was about this time, probably, that Jonathan Farwell and Taylor were taken captive by the Indians, while hunting in the south part of this town. They were carried to Canada, and sold to the French, where they remained in captivity three years; but finally succeded in obtaining their release, and returned to their friends. A daughter of Farwell, Mrs. Rachael Harris, a grand daughter also of Noah Johnson, one of Lovewell's men, is still living [1840] in this town.

After the dismission of Mr. Swan, in May, 1747, Rev. Samuel Bird preached here. Aug. 31, 1747, he received a call to settle, and was soon after ordained. By the terms of his contract he was to have *"100 ounces of coined silver, Troy weight, sterling alloy, or the full value thereof in bills of public credit,"* or about $100,00 yearly, for his salary, *provided "that he preach a lecture once in three months at least in this town,"* and "visit and catechise the people." At this choice there was much dissatisfaction, and the town was nearly equally divided.

Mr. Bird was a "New Light," and his ordination was a triumph. His friends, however, at the head of whom was Jonathan Lovewell, stood by him, and by them the new meeting house, before mentioned, was erected. His opponents, at the head of whom was Col. Blanchard, complained of the injustice of being compelled to pay Mr. Bird, and all who were dissatisfied were freely excused. But the quarrel was sectarian, and could not be appeased. A division in the church ensued, and a new church was organized, which worshipped in the old meeting house, in conjunction with members from Tyngsborough and Dunstable. Lovewell and Blanchard were both distinguished men, and had been much in public life. The question soon assumed a *party* shape and laid the foundation of political differences, which after the lapse of a century are not entirely forgotten or obliterated.

It was soon discovered by Blanchard that neither by the new charter of the town, nor by any existing law of the State was there any provision for calling the first meeting of the town, after its recent incorporation by New Hampshire. Massachusetts having no legal jurisdiction over the town, any organization under its old charter was illegal and void. He, therefore, petitioned the legislature of New Hampshire that an investigation might be had into the authority and proceedings of the town meeting, which gave Mr. Bird *a call*, and that all its transactions should be set aside as contrary to law.

An investigation was held accordingly. Much evidence was introduced, and long and learned arguments made on both sides. The petitioners contended that they paid *two thirds* of the taxes, and Mr. Bird's friends rejoined that they had a majority of the voters. Finally, it was decided that the meeting was illegal – all its proceedings were set aside, and a special act was passed providing for the call of a new meeting, and the legal organization of the township under its new charter. This was in 1748. (1.)

After this decision, and the triumph of Blanchard, Mr. Bird left town, and settled in New Haven, Conn., but afterwards became Chaplain in the Army, in the French War of 1755. At what period he left Dunstable is uncertain. Mr. Farmer says it was in 1751, (2.) but it was probably earlier. His name is not mentioned in the town records after 1748, nor was any money raised for the support of preaching by the town. In January, 1751, Jonathan Lovewell was at length chosen a committee to hire preaching, and in March, 1751, it was voted that the preaching should then again be held at the new meeting house, *formerly* occupied by Mr. Bird.

How strong was the feeling about the settlement of Mr. Bird, and how bitter the hostility between his friends and his opponents, we may judge from sundry remarks contained in a petition of the inhabitants of Pine Hill to be set off to Hollis. The petition was dated June, 1763. "Soon after Dunstable was incorporated," says the petition, "they got into parties about the settlement of Mr. Bird. Each courted Pine Hill's assistance, promising to vote them off to Hollis as soon as the matter was settled. And so Pine Hill was fed with Sugar Plums for a number of years, till at length Dunstable cast off the mask and now appears in their true colours." After alluding to the objections raised by Dunstable, they add: – "Their apprehension must arise from some other quarter. They wish to keep us as a whip for one party or the other *to drive out every minister that comes there, for they are always divided with respect to these things.*" (1.)

In 1749, the town *"voted to hire a school for eight months."* One teacher only was to be employed, and the school was to be kept in *four places* in different parts of the town, alternately. Soon after this the French War commenced, which was very burdensome to the Province, and exposed the frontiers to Indian attacks, and no other record of any school is found until 1761, when the town raised a small sum, "to hire schooling and houses for that end." This was at the commencement of the difficulties with the mother country, and the importance of education began to be more sensibly felt. After this time money was raised for this purpose almost every year, but it was not until the Revolution that the people were fully awakened. In 1772, Joseph Dix was *"the Schoolmaster,"* and he continued to teach in town for many years. In 1775 the town was divided into *five School Districts,* and school houses were first erected. In 1777 each district received its proportion of money from the town, and hired its own teachers, which had been formerly done by the town. – Females now began occasionally to be employed. From this period until 1790, about £30, or $100 was raised *annually* for the support of schools, or twenty dollars to each district. From this fact we may imagine the advantages of education enjoyed by our fathers at that period, and compare them with the privileges of children at the present day.

The bridges over the Nashua have always been a source of much trouble and expense to the town. At what period, and where the first bridge was erected, cannot be ascertained with certainty, but there was a bridge over the Nashua not far from the present one at Main street, previous to 1746, when the road was surveyed and recorded anew by the Selectmen in very near its present location. In the spring of 1753 it was carried away by a freshet, and rebuilt the same summer at an expense of £150. Before 1759 it was in a ruinous condition, and the town petitioned to the General Court far "liberty to raise a *Lottery* for repairing the Bridge, or building a new one." The lottery was not granted, but a new bridge was built, partly by subscription, and partly by the town in 1746. It stood "a little above" the old bridge, but below the present. In the spring of 1775 it was again carried away by a freshet, but was rebuilt the same season in the same place.

Between 1752 and 1756, (1.) died JOHN LOVEWELL, at the great age of *one hundred and twenty years,* the oldest person who ever deceased in New Hampshire. He was one of the earliest settlers of Dunstable, after Philip's War, but of his history little is known. He came, it is said, originally from England, about 1660, and settled some years before 1690. It is not improbable that he came to this town from Weymouth, as a person of the same name, from that town, was in the great Narragansett Swamp Eight, Dec. 19, 1675, and throughout Philip's War, under the famous Capt. Church; and the hand-writing of this person corresponds very closely with that of John Lovewell of Dunstable. (2.) He is said, according to the tradition in the family, to have been an Ensign in the army of Cromwell, and to have left England on account of the Restoration of Charles II. in 1660. This army of 30,000 men was raised in 1653, and Cromwell died in 1658. During the Indian difficulties, about 1700, it is said that he was often spared by the Indians in their incursions, because he had been kind to them in time of peace. (3.) He is represented as being even then old and white haired, and for such scalps the French Governor paid no bounty. The cellar of his house may still be seen on the north side of Salmon Brook, just above the bridge, by the road side, and there for a long time, when very much advanced in years, he kept a small store. There, too, he had a mill, and his farm reached far to the south of Salmon Brook. He must have been extremely vigorous, for as late as 1745, when more than one hundred years old, he was very constant in his attendance upon church, and after 1752 used to chase the hoys out of his orchard with his cane. The children were, 1. John, the hero of Pequawkett; 2. Zaceheus, a Colonel in the army; 3. Jonathan. (1.)

In 1753 the town contained 109 polls, and *one female slave*. There were *four* mills in town, and the valuation was £3795.

In the fall of 1753, Rev. Benjamin Adams, (a graduate of Harvard College in 1738,) preached here for *three months*, and the greater portion of the time during the next two years.

December 21, 1753, the town voted to build a new meeting house, "at the crotch of the roads as near as can be with convenience near the house where Jonathan Lovewell now dwells." – This was the tavern stand now owned by Jesse Gibson, about two miles below Nashua Village, and the meeting house was built upon the little triangular green in front of it. It was finished in 1754, and a part of the materials of the old meeting house in the south part of the town, were used in its construction.

NOTES:

(1.) *Willard's History of Lancaster, citing 2 Mass. Hist. Coll. ,55.*

(1.) *Province Records, 1747. 5 N. H. Hist. Coll., 253.*

(1.) *Original papers in the office of Secretary of State, at Concord. Province Papers, Dunstable.*

(2.) *1 N. H. Hist. Coll., 150.*

(1.) *Dunstable **Papers,** in office of Secretary of State, Concord.*

(1.) *Farmer's Manuscripts.*

(2.) *Original papers in Mass. Records, 1676, 1725.*

(3.) *N. H. Hist. Coll., 136. Farmer's Historical Catechism, 88.*

(1.) From a note in Mr. Fox's manuscript, afterwards crossed out by him, he appears to have entertained doubts as to the extreme age of John Lovewell, but to have subsequently dismissed them. – The following is the note referred to:

"I am inclined to think that his age is somewhat overstated, and that the father and grandfather of Capt. John are confounded. In 1691 we find in the records of the town the names of John Lovewell and John Lovewell, Jr. The former probably came from England – the latter was in Philip's War, and the person above described.

This note was crossed out, and the following written, in connection with the reference to Farmer's manuscripts.

"He was certainly alive in 1732, as appears by a deed in which he styles himself "the original proprietor." He must have been aged, however, since he did not write his name as usual, and his mark is faint."

It has been thought best to insert both the above notes.

CHAPTER XI.
HISTORY OF DUNSTABLE FROM THE FRENCH WAR TO THE REVOLUTION

However distracted and divided our predecessors may have been in relation to religious affairs, we may justly be proud of them for their unanimity in patriotism. Exposed for so many years to the dangers of a border warfare, every citizen was a soldier. The story of Indian atrocities, and French instigation had been handed down from father to son, and not a few had shared personally in the conflicts. To hold a commission was then a high honor, and an object worthy of any man's ambition, for it was only bestowed upon those who had given proofs of courage and capacity. Every officer might bo called at any moment into actual service. The military spirit was fostered as a duty, and New England freedom, which placed in the hand of every child a *gun* as well as a *spelling-book*, made necessarily of every child not less a marksman than a scholar.

When the French War broke out in 1755, an expedition under General Sir William Johnson, was planned against Crown Point, then in possession of the French. A regiment of *five hundred men* was raised in New Hampshire for this purpose, and the command of it was given to Col. Joseph Blanchard of this town. One of the companies which composed the regiment was the famous *Rangers, of* which Robert Rogers was Captain, and John Stark, (afterwards General,) was Lieutenant. The regiment was stationed at Fort Edward, and "was employed in scouting, a species of service which none could perform so successfully as the Rangers of New Hampshire. Parties of them were frequently under the very walls of the French garrisons, and at one time killed and scalped a soldier near the gate of the fort at Crown Point. Late in the autumn the forces were disbanded, and the regiment returned to their homes." One of the companies composing the regiment went from Dunstable and the vicinity, and was commanded by Capt. Peter Powers of Hollis. Among the officers of the regiment we find the names of Jonathan Lovewell of this town, Commissary, Rev. Daniel Emerson of Hollis, Chaplain, and John Hale of Hollis, Surgeon. (1.)

The war still continued, and New Hampshire still furnished her quota of troops for the service. In 1759 another regiment, consisting of one thousand men, were ordered out from this State. Col. Blanchard having died the year previous, the command of it was given to Col. Zaccheus Lovewell of this town, a brother of Capt. John Lovewell. This regiment, of which one or more companies were from this vicinity, joined the main army under Lord Amherst, and was present at the taking of Ticonderoga and

Crown Point, where it did good service. The next year a regiment of eight hundred men was raised, chiefly from this vicinity, commanded by Col. John Goffe of Bedford. They were present at the capture of St. John's, Chamblee, Montreal, and Quebec, which wrested all Canada from France and put an end to the war. (1.)

There is scarcely in the annals of America a company of troops more famous than "Rogers's Rangers." Their life was one scene of constant exposure, and their story reminds one of the days of romance. The forest was their home, and they excelled even the Indian in cunning and hardihood. Everywhere they wandered in search of adventures, fearless and cautious, until their very name became a terror to the enemy. Even in the post of danger, when the army was advancing, they scouted the woods to detect the hidden ambush, and when retreating they skirmished in the rear to keep the foe at bay. If any act of desperate daring was to be done, the *Rangers* were *"the forlorn hope."* At midnight they traversed the camp of the enemy, or carried off a sentinel from his post as if in mockery. Their blow fell like lightning, and before the echo had died away or the alarm subsided, another blow was struck at some far distant point. They seemed to be omnipresent, and the enemy deemed that they were in league with evil spirits. The plain, unvarnished tale of their daily hardships and perilous wanderings, their strange adventures, and "hair breadth 'scapes" would be as wild and thrilling as a German legend.

Of this company, and of others similar in character, a large number belonged to this town. The records are lost and their names are princicipally forgotten. Besides the two Colonels, Blanchard and Lovewell, and the Commissary, Jonathan Lovewell, it is known that the sons of Noah Johnson, the last survivor of Lovewell's Fight, were in the war, both of whom were killed. One of them, Noah was an officer, and was killed at the storming of Quebec, fighting under Wolfe. Nehemiah Lovewell was a Lieutenant in 1756, and a Captain in 1758 and 1760. Jonathan Farwell, William Harris, Thomas Killicut, Thomas Blanchard, Jonathan Blanchard, Eleazer Farwell, Benjamin Hassell. James Mann, Ebenezer Fosdick, Bunker Farwell, John Lamson, Simeon Blood, Thomas Lancey, Ephraim Butterfield, John Carkin, James French, Henry Farwell, Nathaniel Blood, Joseph Combs, John Gilson, James Harwood, John Huston, Joshua Wright, William Walker, John Harwood and William Lancey, were also out during the war. as was also Lt. David Alld, and the gun which he then carried is still in the possession of his daughters.

In the expedition of 1760, Col. Goffe commanded the regiment winch mustered at Litchfield. His destination was Crown Point and Canada. A select company of Rangers was formed from the regiment, and the command given to Capt. Nehemiah Lovewell of this town. As a specimen of the military dress and discipline of the time, the following order is inserted. It is copied from Adjutant Hobart's record, and is dated Litchfield, May

25, 1760: – "Col. Goffe requires the officers to be answerable that the men's shirts are changed twice every week at least; that such as have hair that will admit of it must have it constantly tyed; they must be obliged to comb their heads, and wash their hands every morning, and as it is observed that numbers of the men accustom themselves to wear woollen nightcaps in the day time, he allows them hats; they are ordered for the future not to be seen in the day time with any thing besides their hats on their heads, as the above mentioned custom of wearing nightcaps must be detrimental to their health and cleanliness; the men's hats to be all cocked, or cut uniformly as Col. Goffe pleases to direct." (1.)

September 26, 1757, the town voted, "that some measures be taken *to settle the Gospel* in this town"; and four persons were selected to preach one month each, on probation. Nov. 7, they gave a call to Rev. Elias Smith, (a graduate of Harvard in 1753,) but difficulty ensued, and Dec. 16, the call was retracted. (2.) It was a custom for those dissatisfied to enter their protest and as a curiosity and a specimen, the following is inserted:

"We the subscribers, being freeholders in Dunstable, do for ourselves protest against the choice of Mr. Elias Smith for our minister, which they have essayed to choose, and for these reasons; *first*, because we are not of the persuasion he preaches and indevors to maintain; we are Presbyterians, and do adhere to the Westminster Confession of faith; and do declare it to be the confession of our faith; and that we are members of the Presbyterian Church in Londonderry – some 18 years – some 15 years, and have partaken of Baptism, and of the Lord's supper as frequently as we could, they being the sealing ordinances, and that we cannot in conscience join in calling or paying Mr. Smith. Therefore we plead the liberty of conscience that we may hear and pay where we can have benefit." *John Alld, Jeremiah Colburn.*

There was also a protest of David Hobart and others against his settlement, because, as they say, "Mr. Smith's preaching is contrary to our persuasion, and as we judge favors the Arminian scheme, which we judge tends to pervert the truths of the Gospel, and darken the counsels of God."

April 7, 1758, died Col. Joseph Blanchard, aged 53. He was born Feb. 11, 1704, and his grandfather, Deacon John Blanchard, was one of the first settlers of the town. His father, Capt. Joseph Blanchard, was town clerk, selectman and proprietor's clerk for many years, a very active and useful citizen, and died in 1727. On the death of his father, although young, Joseph Blanchard was chosen proprietor's clerk, which office he held, with a slight interval, during his life, and was constantly engaged in town business until his death. In early life he became distinguished as a surveyor of land, and was almost constantly employed in that capacity. – In conjunction with Rev. Dr. Langdon, of Portsmouth, he projected a map of New Hampshire, which was published after his death, in 1761, and inscribed to "Hon. Charles Townsend, his Majesty's Secretary of War."

At this period no accurate maps of the State existed, and to prepare one from the then scanty materials must have been a work of great magnitude. Surveys were to be made, and information collected from every quarter. Most of the labor, of course, fell on Col. Blanchard. The greater part of our territory was then a wilderness, for our whole population scarcely exceeded 50,000, and the means of intercommunication were limited and difficult. But settlements were springing up rapidly, and the lands were becoming every day more and more valuable, and accurate information of the localities was important. Under these circumstances the map was considered of great value, and as a token of their estimate of it, Mr. Townsend procured from the University of Glasgow, for Mr. Langdon, (Col. Blanchard having deceased,) the honorary degree of Doctor of Divinity. (1.)

Upon the dissolution of the connexion between New Hampshire and Massachusetts in 1741, and the accession of Benning Wentworth as Governor, Mr. Blanchard received the appointment of Counsellor of State by mandamus from the Crown. This was an office of great dignity and authority, and next to that of Governor, was the most honorable and responsible in the colonies, in the gift of the king. This office he held for a number of years, and probably until his death. In 1749, on the death of Chief Justice Jaffrey, he was appointed a Judge of the Superior Court of Judicature of the State, which office he held during life.

When the old French War broke out in 1755, an expedition was planned against Crown Point. New Hampshire raised a regiment of 500 men, and Mr. Blanchard was appointed Colonel. Of this regiment, the famous *Rangers*, under the command of Rogers and Stark, formed a part. The regiment was stationed at Fort Edward, and returned home in the autumn of the same year.

Col. Blanchard married Rebecca Hubbard, [Hobart?] by whom he had twelve children. – He died in this town and is buried in the Old South Burying Ground; his tombstone bears the following inscription: – "The Hon. Joseph Blanchard, Esqr., deceased April the 7th, 1758, aged 53."

November 27, 1758, the town voted to give Rev. Josiah Cotton a call, and offered 178 milled dollars salary. Jan. 29, 1758, they added £5 sterling, making his salary about $200. The call was accepted, – the day of ordination appointed, and the churches invited to attend to assist in the services. But a quarrel ensued as usual, – the opposition prevailed, and Mr. Cotton was not ordained. Protests were entered at every meeting by the minority, as each party in turn prevailed.

In 1759, in consequence of the divisions and the bitterness of feeling which existed, an Ecclesiastical Council was called to settle the difficulties. For many years there had been two churches and two meeting-houses, but no minister. – After much trouble and effort, a compromise was made, and an union effected. Mr. Bird's meeting house was purchased by Jona. Lovewell, removed, and converted into a dwelling house, which is

now occupied by Jesse Bowers, Esq., and the two societies again became one.

As the town at its public meetings settled and paid
the minister, so it determined his creed, and we find accordingly, the following to us curious record. In 1761,
a town meeting was called expressly "to see what doctrines the town would support"; and it was voted, "that
the Doctrines contained in the New England Confession
of Faith are the standing doctrines to be defended by this
Town."

July 19, 1762, an invitation was given to Mr. Jonathan Livermore to settle here. He was to receive £100,
for a settlement, and £40 sterling per annum salary, "if
he will fulfil the duties of a Gospel minister agreeably to
the Congregational persuasion, according to Cambridge
Platform, and New England Confession of Faith." This
proviso was adopted by a party vote, and was a renewal
of the old sectarian difficulties of past years. Mr. Livermore would not accept and afterward settled in Wilton.

During the next two years various preachers were
heard, but not to general satisfaction. Although nominally
united there was still a variance at heart, and no attempt
was made to settle a minister until August 1764. A call
was then given to Mr. Thomas Fessenden, (a graduate of
Harvard college in 1750,) and an offer of £100 settlement,
and £50 sterling salary. Against this call *three* separate protests were entered by persons styling themselves "*Presper-
terions,*" or Presbyterians, because this mode of settlement
was "contrary to the fundamental doctrines of Christian-

ity,"and "of our persuasion." Mr. Fessenden accepted the call, but such was the spirit of discord that he was never ordained. He left town very soon after, for he commenced a suit at law against the town, for the recovery of his salary before May, 1765, and recovered judgment.

For nearly *twenty* years the town had been without a settled minister. Sept. 12, 1766, they gave a call to Mr. Joseph Kidder, (a graduate of Yale College in 1764,) and offered him £132 6s. *8d.* [about $450,] for a settlement, and a salary of £53 6s. *8d.* lawful money, [or about $180.] Mr. Kidder accepted the invitation, and more fortunate than his predecessors, succeeded in being ordained March 18, 1767. After many years, old difficulties revived, and new ones arose. – Parties were again formed, and in 1796, by a reference of all disputes to a committee mutually chosen, the civil connection between Mr. Kidder and the town, ceased. He was the last minister over the town. He continued his relation to the church, however, as before, and preached to bis society until his death, Sept. 6, 1818. Nov. 3, 1818, Rev. Ebenezer P. Sperry was ordained as his colleague, but was dismissed in April, 1819. (1.)

A picture of Dunstable as it was before the Revolution, and of the manners and customs, opinions and feelings, doings and sayings of the inhabitants, would be highly interesting. To sketch such a picture would require the hand of a master, as well as materials, which can now hardly be obtained. A few facts and anecdotes must serve instead.

Slavery was then considered neither illegal nor immoral. Several slaves were owned in this town; one by

Paul Clogstone. She was married to a free black named Castor Dickinson, and had several children born here, but before the Revolution he purchased the freedom of his wife and children. Slavery in New Hampshire was abolished by the Revolution.

In those days it was customary to drink at all meetings, whether of joy or of sorrow. The idea which was long after in vogue – "to keep the spirits up, by pouring spirits down" – seems to have been then universally prevalent. Even at funerals it was observed, and in the eyes of many it was quite as important as the prayer. – The mourners and friends formed themselves in a line, and an attendant with a jug and glass passed around, and dealt out to each his or her portion of the spirit; and the due observance of this ceremony was very rarely omitted. It is said that sometimes "one more thirsty than the rest," after having received one "portion," would slily fall back from the line, under some pretext or other, and re-appear in a lower place, in season to receive a *second portion.* (1.)

NOTES:

(1.) 5 *N. H. Hist. Coll.,* 217, 218. 1 *Belknap,* 319.

(1.) 1 *Belknap,* 319, 320.

(1.) *Regimental Records, in Secretary's office, Concord.*

(2.) Perhaps the founder of the sect of *Christians.*

(1.) 1 *Belknap,* 312.

(1.) Mr. Sperry is now or was recently Chaplain of the House of Correction, at South Boston.

(1.) This is stated on the authority of Mrs. Kidder, wife of Rev. Mr. Kidder, an eye witness.

CHAPTER XII.
REVOLUTIONARY HISTORY OF DUNSTABLE

From the commencement of our Revolutionary difficulties, a deep and universal feeling of indignation pervaded the community. The men who had settled in the wilderness, and defended their homes from the attack of the "Indian enemy," and had built them up a great and goodly heritage, unaided by stepdame England, were not the men quietly to yield up their dear bought rights without a struggle. Their love for the mother country was never very strong, for there was little cause for gratitude, and the first approach of oppression and wrong was the signal for resistance. This feeling was stronger in New England than in the other colonies, and manifested itself, at an earlier period, because the Puritans, having been forced to leave their Father land by oppression and insult, and having made for themselves a new home in the wilderness, unassisted and unprotected, felt it a more grievous and insufferable wrong, that England should seize upon the first moment of prosperity, to heap upon them new oppression and new insults here.

The division of New England into townships, – those "little democracies" as they were aptly called, – each self-governed, where every citizen feels that he is a part of the commonwealth, has municipal rights and duties, and learns to think and act for himself, was an excellent school for training up the Fathers of our Republic, and teaching them the principles of self-government upon a more extended scale.

During the long succession of encroachments, which preceded and caused the Revolution, the inhabitants of this town were not indifferent. – They had watched the storm as it gathered, and knew its consequences must be momentous. – After the establishment of the boundary line in 1741, which severed us from Massachusetts, no right to send a representative was conceded for many years. At that period this right was a *favor* granted by his majesty, through his "beloved, and trust-worthy Benning Wentworth, Governor of his. Majesty's Province of New Hampshire," and bestowed only upon the loyal and obedient. In 1774, however, when a collision with England began to be very generally expected, the General Assembly of New Hampshire claimed for itself the exercise of this right, and allowed certain representatives from towns not heretofore represented a seat and a voice in their councils. Immediately a petition was presented from this town, asking the privilege of representation, which was granted. (1.)

September, 1774, Jonathan Lovewell was sent as a delegate to the Convention, which met at Exeter soon after, for the purpose of choosing delegates to the First Continental Congress. – At the same town meeting the town voted to raise a sum of money *"to purchase a supply of ammunition"*; and also voted to pay their proportion of the "expenses of the Delegate to the Grand Continental Congress," which met at Philadelphia the same month, and which published a Declaration of Rights, and formed an *"association not to import or use British Goods."* From this time every movement for liberty met with a hearty response.

January 9, 1775, Joseph Ayers and Noah Lovewell were chosen to represent the town in the Convention which met at Exeter, April 25, 1775, for the purpose of appointing delegates, to act for this State m the Grand Continental Congress, to be held at Philadelphia. May 10, 1775. At this meeting, with a spirit characteristic of the times, and evidently anticipating a Declaration of Independence, they chose "Saml. Roby, Jona. Lovewell, Joseph Eayers, Benjamin Smith, John Wright, Benjamin French, James Blanchard and John Searle, a *Committee of Inspection* to see that the Result of the late Continental Congress be carried into practice, and that *all persons in this town conform themselves thereto."*

Another meeting of this Convention was holden at Exeter, May 17, 1775; at which the same delegates attended, and which after several adjournments, formed a Constitution for the Government of the State. This Constitution, which is dated January 5, 1776, was the earliest one formed in the United States. (1.) It was adopted at the suggestion of the Continental Congress of May, 1775; but it was a bold step, for it was a denial of the right of

England to rule over us, and a virtual Declaration of Independence. It provided for a House of Representatives, and a Council of twelve men to be chosen by the House, and to form a separate body like our Senate. – There was to be no Governor, but the powers of the executive were vested in the Council and House jointly. If the dispute with England continued longer than one year, the members of the Council were to be chosen by the people. Of this Council, Jona. Blanchard of this town, was a member in 1776.

From the first the people of New Hampshire, who as the royalists complained, "had never set any good example of obedience," were desirous and prepared for a collision: and no sooner did the news of the fight at Lexington on the nineteenth of April, 1775, reach the State, than the whole population rushed to arms. In these movements the citizens of Dunstable were among the most zealous; and the military spirit derived from their fathers, and the military *experience* of many in the French Wars, was roused at once into activity by the noise of the Conflict. Instantly they hurried to Concord to avenge the blood of their fellow-citizens. Who and how many were these "minute men" we do not know; but the town paid over $110.00 for their expenses. Within less than a week a company of sixty-six men was organized at Cambridge, under Capt. Wm. Walker of this town, forty of whom, including the officers, were also from Dunstable. The following is the Company Roll: (1.)

William Walker, Captain.

*James Brown, 1st Lieut.,

* Daniel Warner, Sergeant,

*John Lund, do.,

†William A. Hawkins, do.,

†Francis Putnam, do.,

*Medad Combs, Corporal,

*Abijah Reed, do.,

*John Lovewell, do.,

*Phineas Whitney, do.,

*William Harris, Drummer,

*Paul Woods, Fifer,

*Simeon Butterfield,

*Peter Honey,

*Paul Clogstone,

*Joel Stewart,

* David Adams, jr.,

*Nehemiah Lovewell,

*Henry Lovewell,

*William Roby, 2nd Lieut.,

*Eleazer Blanchard,

*Richard Adams,

*Ebenezer Fosdick,

* William Butterfield,

*James Gibson,

David March,

*John Snow,

* Philip Roby,

*Jonathan Harris,

*William Harris, jr.,

*Archibald Gibson,

*Benjamin Whitney,

*Jonathan Danforth,

*David Adams,
Jason Russell,

*Benjamin Bagley,

Moses Chandler,

*Eliphalct Bagley,

‡Stephen Chase,

‡Joshua Severance,

‡Nehemiah Winn,

‡Joseph Greeley,

†Henry Stevens,

†Jonathan Gray,

†Isaac Brown,

†Asa Cram,

†Hart Balch,
†Stephen Blanchard,

* Abel Danforth,

*Simeon Hills,

*James Harwood,

*Ichabod Lovewell,

*Jacob Blodgett,

Moses Chamberlain,	Silas Chamberlain,
†Nathan Abbott,	Mansfield Tapley,
†Timothy Darling,	*Oliver Woods,
†Daniel Brown,	*Nehemiah Wright,
†Theodore Stevens,	†Israel Howe,
†Henry Lovejoy,	*Jonathan Emerson.
†Eliphalet Blanchard, jr.,	

The whole male population of the town at this time between the ages of sixteen and fifty, was only 128; so that nearly one half the able-bodied inhabitants must have been in the army, at the first call of liberty, a month before the battle of Bunker Hill. From no other town in New Hampshire was there so large a number in the army, as appears by the returns; and we record a fact, so honorable to their patriotism and courage, with a feeling of no little pride.

The Convention which met at Exeter, April 25, 1775, a few days after the fight at Lexington, organized two regiments, for the assistance of their brethren in Massachusetts. But the men were not to be recruited; they were already in the field. Within two weeks, more than two thousand men from New Hampshire had joined the army around Boston; or more than one seventh of the whole population of the State, between the ages of sixteen and fifty. From these the two regiments were formed and placed under the command of Col. Stark and Col. Reed, of which this company formed a part.

It may be a matter of curiosity worthy of record, to give the abstract of returns of population, number of soldiers in the army, in May, 1775, number of males between the ages of sixteen and fifty not in the army, and ratio of soldiers to the male population. This had been required at an early period by the Convention, in evident anticipation of a rupture with the mother country, in order to ascertain our actual condition and resources. The original returns also included the number of arms, deficiencies, quantity of powder, &c., all of which are now in the office of the Secretary of State, and furnish an admiral specimen of the forethought of the patriots of that day. (1.)

Counties.	Population.	Number of males in army.	Num. negr's and slaves forlife	No. males from 16 to 50 net in the army.	Ratio of soldiers to male population from 16 to 50.
Rockingham,	37,850	927	437	6,383	12⅔ in 100
Strafford,	12,713	275	103	2,282	10¾ "100
Hillsborough,	15,948	650	87	2,723	19¼ "100
Cheshire,	10,659	376	7	2,009	15¾ "100
Grafton,	3,880	156	24	834	15¾ "100
Total,	81,050	2,384	656	14,231	14⅓ "100

From this table we may gather some facts which will enable us to appreciate more truly the spirit and the sacrifices of that period. More than fourteen hundred of the whole male population of the State, between the ages of sixteen and fifty years, were in the army in May, 1775, or nearly one out of every five who was able to bear arms. Our own county, old Hillsborough, excelled them all, however, having at that time in the army more than nineteen in every hundred males, between sixteen and fifty, or at least one quarter part of all the able-bodied inhabitants. – A few days after the battle of Bunker Hill, another regiment from New Hampshire, under the command of Col. Poor, joined the army at Cambridge.

Previous to the battle the New Hampshire troops were stationed at Medford, and formed the left wing of the American Army. "These troops," says Major Swett, (1.) "were hardy, brave, active, athletic and indefatigable. Almost every soldier equalled William Tell as a marksman, and could aim his weapon at an oppressor with as keen a relish. Those from the frontiers had gained this address against the savages and beasts of the forests. The country yet abounded with game, and hunting was familiar to all; and the amusement most fashionable and universal throughout New England was trial of skill with the musket."

At eleven o'clock on the morning of the battle, the New Hampshire troops received orders to reinforce Col. Prescott, at Charlestown. "About *fifteen charges* of loose powder and balls were distributed to each man, and they were directed to form them into cartridges immediately. Few of the men, however, possessed cartridge boxes, but employed powder horns, and scarcely two of their guns agreeing in calibre, they were obliged to alter the balls accordingly." (2.)

As soon as the British troops landed at Charlestown, the New Hampshire regiments were ordered to join the other forces on Breed's Hill. – A part were detached to throw up a work on Bunker Hill, and the residue, under Stark and Reed, joined the Connecticut forces, under Gen. Putnam, and the regiment of Col. Prescott, at the Rail fence. This was the very point of the British attack, the key of the American position. Here Captain Walker's company was formed, awaiting the attack. To be stationed there, in the post of danger, was a high honor, and well did the New Hampshire troops merit it, although not a few paid for the distinction with their lives.

As soon as the British moved forward to the attack, our troops under Stark, engaged in fortifying Bunker Hill under the direction of Putnam, joined their brethren. The battle commenced. – The Americans, forbidden to fire upon the enemy until "they could see the whites of their eyes," swept them down by companies. Again and again were the British driven back, and not until their scanty supply of ammunition was exhausted, and the British assaulted the works at the point of the bayonet, did the Americans retire from their position. Even then they retreated like the lion, disputing every step with stones and clubbed muskets, and lay upon their arms during the night at Winter Hill, directly in the face of the enemy.

The number of Americans engaged in the battle was fluctuating, but may be fairly estimated at little more than two thousand men. Their loss was 115 killed, 305 wounded, and 30 captured; in all 450. The New Hampshire regiments lost 19 men killed, and 74 wounded, a large proportion of those engaged. The British loss was 1054, including 89 officers. One regiment, the Welsh Fusiliers, lost every officer except one. (1.)

None of Capt. Walker's company were killed; two only were wounded – Joseph Greeley and Paul Clogstone. The latter died soon after. – William Lund, of this town, however, who was in another company, was killed in the battle. – The original return of Capt. Walker, including articles lost by the company, in the battle and in the retreat, is now on file in the office of the Secretary of State. It is as follows: "6 great coats, 31 shirts, 24 pair of hose, 18 haversacks. 1 pistol, 1 fife, 2 guns, 1 cartridge box, 5 strait body coats, 2 jackets, 10 pair of trowsers, 6 pair of leather breeches, 2 pair of shoes, 12 blankets." The unusual heat of the day compelled them to lay aside their knapsacks, which were lost in the excitement and hurry of the retreat.

The bond of allegiance to Great Britian was severed by this battle, never to be again united. The people of New England expected a Declaration of Independence, and awaited it impatiently, long before the 4th of July, 1776. In February, 1776, we find the officers of this town warning the annual meeting, not as heretofore, "in his Majesty's name," but, "in the name *of* the peo*ple of the State of New Hampshire.*"

At this meeting the "spirit of '76" was strongly manifested. "Sam'l Roby, Noah Lovewell, William Walker,

Joseph Eayrs, Joseph French, Jr., Capt. Benjamin French and Thomas Butterfield, were chosen delegates to the County Congress."

"Jona. Lovewell, Robert Fletcher. Joseph Eayrs, Capt. Benjamin French, Noah Lovewell, Samuel Roby, Joseph Whiting and Thomas Butterfield, were chosen a committee of safty."

"Samuel Roby, Benjamin Smith, Thomas Butterfield, John Searls, David Alld, James Blanchard, William Walker, John Wright and Henry Adams, were chosen a committee of inspection to see that no British Goods were sold in town."

In November, 1776, in consequence of the great depreciation of paper money, the exorbitant prices asked by the speculators who had forestalled the markets, and the consequent discouragement to the exertions of those who were laboring to sustain the heavy public burdens, a meeting was holden at Dracut, to petition Congress, and the State Legislature, upon the subject; and to devise such other measures as might be necessary for the protection of the people. A large number of delegates were present, and Dunstable was represented by Capt. Benjamin French, Capt. Noah Lovewell and Joseph Eayrs. The Convention met November 26, 1776, at the house of Major Joseph Varnum, and prepared a Petition to the Legislature, praying that the resolves of the Continental Congress of 1775, respecting prices, &c., might be enforced more strictly. (1.)

Early in 1776, New Hampshire raised *three* regiments of 2,000 men, which were placed under the command of

Colonels Stark, Reed and Hale. They were sent to New York to join the army under Gen. Sullivan for the invasion of Canada. They proceeded up the Hudson, and down the lakes to Canada, but were obliged to retreat to Ticonderoga. A part of Capt. Walker's company enlisted in these regiments. They suffered severely, and lost one third of their number by sickness and exposure. (2.) Of those who were in the army at this time, in the company commanded by Capt. William Reed, and said to belong to Dunstable, we find the following names: Joel Lund, ensign, Silas Adams, James Blanchard, Peter Honey, John Wright, jr., Jonathan Butterfield, John Lovewell, Oliver Wright, Nehemiah Wright, Daniel Wood, Timothy Blood, Asa Lovejoy, Daniel Blood, Jonathan Wright,

The following persons were in the company of Capt. Daniel Wilkins, in Col. Timothy Bedell's regiment, which was stationed on our northern frontier; Philip Abbot Roby, Ebenezer Fosgett [or Fosdick,] Joseph Farrar, James Harwood, and Reuben Killicut.

In July, 1776, Capt. William Barron raised a company for Canada, in which there were the following Dunstable men: – John Lund, 1st Lieut., Richard Whiting, 2d Sergt., Abijah Reed, 3d Sergt., John Fletcher, 2d Corporal, Ephraim French, Benjamin Bailey, Charles Butterfield, William Butterfield, Abraham Hale, John Comb, Thomas Blanchard, Thomas Killicut, Israel Ingalls, Medad Combs, Levi Lund, Thomas Harris, Peter Henry, James Jewell, William Stewart.

In consequence of the loss sustained by the New Hampshire regiments, Jonathan Blanchard, Esq., of this town, was sent by the Legislature to Ticonderoga in October, 1776, to recruit the army. In December, 1776, Capt. Walker, of this town, raised a company from Dunstable and vicinity. It was attached to a regiment commanded by Col. Gilman, of which Noah Lovewell, of this town, was Quarter-Master, and ordered to New York. Among those who enlisted we find Phineas Whitney, Silas Swallow, Joseph Dix and Jacob Adams.

In 1777, also, three regiments, consisting of 2,000 men, were raised in this State, for three years, and placed under the command of Colonels Cilley, Hall and Scammel; Stark and Poor having been promoted to the rank of Brigadier-Gen- eral. The same quota of troops was furnished by New Hampshire during the war, besides voluntary enlistments in other regiments, which were very numerous. In every levy of 2,000 men, the proportion to he furnished by this town, was about sixteen. More than twice this number, however, must have been constantly in the army. (1.)

In March. 1777, the town offered a *bounty of one hundred* dollars to every soldier who would enlist, and a large number joined the army. Besides those already mentioned, we find the following: – Jonathan Emerson, Lieutenant in Cilley's regiment: James Blanchard, Quarter-Master in Scammel's regiment; John Butler and James Harwood killed at Hubberton, Vt. July 7, 1777, on the retreat from Ticonderoga, John Manning taken prisoner there, and afterwards re-taken; Simeon Butterfield, David Alld, Israel Ingalls, John Lund, William Gibbs, Paul Woods, Eliphalet Manning, John Manning, James Seal,

Isaac Adams. Noah Downs, Jeremiah Keith who served in a Massachusetts regiment; Ephraim Blood, William Mann and John Crocker, in the Artillery corps. Just before the battle of Saratoga, Lt. Alld returned for volunteers, and a large number from this town and vicinity hastened to join the army, and arrived in season to compel and witness the surrender of Burgoyne. In November, 1777, the town voted to raise "£735 lawful money to defray the extraordinary *expenses* of the present war."

By the Constitution of 1776, no provision was made for a Governor, or any chief Executive Officer of the State. The Legislature was itself *the Executive,* and upon every adjournment, therefore, it became necessary to give to some body the power of acting in case of emergency during the recess. This power was voted in a Committee of Safety, varying in number from six to sixteen, composed of the wisest, best, and most active men in the different sections of the State, and those who had shown themselves the truest friends of their country. Their duty was like that of the Roman Dictators – "ne quid Republica detrimenti caperet" – to take care that the Republic received no injury; and a corresponding power to effect this object was given them. Of this most responsible committee, two members belonged to this town. Jonathan Lovewell was a member from June 20, 1777, to January 5, 1779, and Jonathan Blanchard from January 6, 1778. (1.)

The complaints of the people respecting the high prices of all the necessaries of life still continuing, and the recommendations of Congress having no effect upon many of the extortioners, it was then recommended that a Convention should he holden at New Haven, Conn., January 15, 1778, to be composed of Delegates also appointed by the Legislatures of the several States. Its object was "to regulate and ascertain the price of labour, manufactures, internal produce, and commodities imported from foreign ports, military stores excepted, and also to regulate the charges of inn-holders, and to make Report to the Legislatures of their respective States." – Jonathan Blanchard, of this town, and Col. Nathaniel Peabody, were appointed delegates from New Hampshire, and acted accordingly.

After the Declaration of Independence, which was the abolition of all existing government, it became necessary to form some plan of Government, both for the State and the Union. The people in their primary assemblies had commenced and carried on the Revolution, and they entered with the same zeal into the discussion of their political rights and duties, and the best mode of preserving and perpetuating them. – February 9, 1778, *in town meeting*, "the articles of Confederation formed by the Honorable Continental Congress having been taken into consideration were *consented to unanimously.*"

April 17, 1778, Capt. Benjamin French, and Dea. William Hunt were chosen delegates to the Convention, which was to be holden June 10, 1778, for the purpose of forming a Constitution for the State. We may see with what jealousy the people watched their servants, and regarded the powers of Government, from the fact that they appointed a committee of *eleven*, viz.: Cyrus Baldwin, Joseph Whiling, Robert Fletcher, Esq., Jonathan

Lovewell, Esq., Capt. Daniel Warner, Joseph Eayrs, Capt. Benjamin Smith, Lieut. David Alld, Col. Noah Lovewell, Lieut. Joseph French, and Lieut. Jacob Taylor "*to assist* said members during the Convention's session." So early was the right of *instruction* claimed, practised, and acknowledged. A Bill of Rights and a Constitution was drafted accordingly, and an able Address to the People issued, signed by John Langdon, President of the Convention. But the people would not sanction either. Their experience of royal usurpation, and the fear of giving too much power to their rulers prevailed, and both were negatived by a great majority. This town voted *unanimously to* reject them."

In August, *fourteen* men went from this town to Rhode Island, as volunteers, with Col. Noah Lovewell. The town voted to pay them a bounty of about thirty-five dollars each. Of this number were James Jewell, Eleazer Fisk, Isaac Foot, and others. During this year a very large number of soldiers from this town were in the army in New York and at the South.

In December, 1778, Col. Noah Lovewell was chosen "Representative for one year," being the *first* representative elected by the town under the Constitution.

How many soldiers were furnished to the army from this town during that long and bloody struggle, it is impossible now to ascertain with correctness, but the number continued to be very large during the war. It is estimated that New Hampshire sent to the army at various times, 14,000 men, a number nearly equal to the whole able-bodied population of the State at the commencement of the wars, and of whom 4,000 died in the service.

The whole male population of this town in May, 1775, between the ages of sixteen and fifty years, was only 128, and nearly every inhabitant, either as a volunteer upon an alarm, or as a drafted man, was at some period in the service. They were in almost every fight from Bunker Hill to Yorktown, and their bones are mouldering upon many a battle field from Massachusetts to Virginia. When the news of *"the Concord Fight"* flew hither on the wings of the wind, our *"minute men"* saddled their horses and hastened to the scene of conflict, and, although they did not reach there in season to share in its dangers, they formed a portion of that fiery mass of undisciplined valor which "hung upon the steps of the retreating foe like lightning on the edge of the cloud." They were at Bunker Hill in the post of danger and honor, and shared largely in the glory of that day. They were at Ticonderoga, where, borne down by sickness, by pestilence, and by want, they were compelled to retreat, fighting step by step, in the face of a victorious enemy. They were at Bennington, under Stark, where the first gleam of light broke in upon the darkness which was lowering over our prospects, cheering every heart to new efforts, and at Stillwater and Saratoga, where this first omen of victory was converted into a triumph most glorious and enduring.

They wintered at Valley Forge with Washington, where, "without shoes or stockings, their pathway might be tracked by their blood." – They were at Trenton and Princeton, where, under the very eye of Washington, they surprised and captured the Hessians, and gave new hope and courage to the disheartened nation. They fought at Germantown and Monmouth, and at the memorable conflicts on Long Island. At Monmouth, the New Hampshire regiment, under Cilley and Dearborn, was "the most distinguished, and to their heroic courage the salvation of the army was owing." General Washington acknowledged the service, and sent to enquire what regiment it was. "*Full blooded Yankees*, by G-d, sir," was the blunt reply of Dearborn. – And at Yorktown, when the whole British army capitulated, they were there with Scammel, a glorious and fitting finale to the great Revolutionary drama, whose opening scene was at Lexington.

Of those who, during this long period, when the fears of even the stout-hearted prevailed over their hopes, and darkness seemed resting upon their freedom, rallied around the standard of their country, and perilled "their lives, their fortunes, and their sacred honour" in its defence, few – very few – now survive, the shadows only of their manhood. It is no easy task even to collect their names, and they ought not to be forgotten. They were in humble station, and familiarity may have reduced them in the eyes of the present age; yet their service was no holiday sport, and to them, their exertions, and their sufferings, do we all owe the birth-right of our liberty. From the records of the town, and musty papers on file; from Legislative Journals; from company and regimental returns in the office of the Secretary of Stale; from vouchers and loose memoranda accidentally preserved, – and from personal enquiry of the survivors and descendants of the actors, we have gathered with no little care and labor, a portion of their names. Some of them sound strangely in our ears, but most of them are known positively to have been in the service, and are called of this town. (1.)

NOTES:

(1.) 2 *Province Papers. Towns,* 253. *In Secretary's office.*

(1.) 4 *N. H. Hist. Coll.*

(1.) In the office of the Secretary of State.

*From Dunstable. †From Wilton. ‡From Hudson.

*From Dunstable. †From Wilton.

(1.) 1 *N. H. Hist. Coll.,* 231. *Original returns in Secretary's affice.*

(1.) *Bunker Hill Battle,* 20.

(2.) *Major Swett's Bunker Hill Battle,* 40.

(1.) 2 *N. H. Hist. Coll.,* 145. *Mrs. Adams's Letters. Original papers in office of Secretary of State.*

(1.) 2 *N. H. Hist. Coll.,* 50.

(2.) 1 *Belknap,* 370.

(1.) The regiment of militia to which Dunstable was attached, was then commanded by Col. Moses Nichols, of Amherst. It embraced the following towns, containing the number of males between the ages of sixteen and fifty, in each respectively: – Amherst 321; Nottingham West [Hudson] 122; Litchfield 57; Dunstable 128; Merrimac 129; Hollis 234; Wilton 128; Rindge 20; Mason 113. – This was the basis for all drafts of soldiers for the army. In May, 1777, one hundred and fifty-five men were drafted from the regiment, or one in every eight.

(1.) 2 *N. H. Hist., Coll,* 39.

(1) For the list *of* soldiers in the army from Dunstable [Nashua] Appendix

CHAPTER XIII.
HISTORY TO THE ORIGIN
OF NASHUA VILLAGE

WE can form but a faint idea of the sacrifices which were made for Independence. Beside perilling life in battle and submitting to privations of every description, so large a proportion of the able-bodied population were in the army, that the fields were often left untilled. Yet they gave both time and treasure to their country, without measure and without a murmur. "Our efforts are great," Mr. Adams said in 1780, "and we give this campaign more than half our property to defend the other. He who stays at home cannot earn enough to pay him who takes the field." (1.) The amount annually expended by the town, during the war, was several thousand dollars:- – a heavy burden upon a population, numbering in 1775, only 705. Yet this small number had diminished, in 1783, to 578, shewing a decrease of 127, or 18 per cent.; a fact which proves better than pages of description, the amount of the exertions which were put forth, and the sacrifices which were made, and the consequent paralysis of the energies and prosperity of the community.

In 1781, another Convention was holden at Concord, for the purpose of forming a State Constitution; and Jonathan Lovewell, Esq., was chosen a delegate. But the same jealousy continued to exist as heretofore, and the new Constitution, which was our present one with slight modifications, was rejected by the town "unanimously." In December, 1782, Jonathan Blanchard, Esq., was chosen Representative, and it was again voted "not to receive the Bill of Rights and Plan of Government" as adopted, and the town chose Capt. Benjamin French, Joseph Whiting, Jonathan Lovewell, Esq., and Col. Noah Lovewell, a committee to state the reasons of rejection.

March, 1784, Capt. Benjamin French was chosen Representative.

March 6, 1786, Col. Noah Lovewell was chosen Representative, and the town voted, that "the Selectmen with Jona. Blanchard, Esqr., Jonathan Lovewell, Esqr., Mr. Joseph Whiting and Deacon William Hunt be a committee *to give instructions to the Representatives."* In 1787, the same proceedings were renewed.

January 10, 1788, Dea. William Hunt was chosen a delegate to the Convention, which met at. Exeter in February of the same year, to consider of. and adopt, the Constitution of the United States, which had recently been formed and sent out for the approval of the people. Throughout the country, as well as in the Convention, which formed it, there was a great diversity of opinion respecting it, and much opposition. It contained no hill of rights as it now does; as its opposers thought no limitation of powers. The States had long been sovereign and independent democracies, and hesitated to give up any of their rights. The confederation had been inefficient from the want of central authority.

Thus, while some believed that the Constitution vested too much power in the General Government, which would eventually swallow up the several States, others feared that it possessed too little power to protect itself from the encroachments of the States; and would soon share the fate of the old confederacy. There was danger on both sides: on the one side *anarchy* – on the other *usurpation*. It was an untried experiment, and every little community was divided. It was discussed in town meeting, and the town voted "not to accept said Constitution," and chose a committee of *nine* to give their delegates instruction to oppose its adoption by the Convention. This committee reported a list of objections, which were adopted by the town, and forwarded to the Convention. The Constitution, however, was adopted. It was a medium and a compromise, between the doubts of conflicting parties, and the fears of both have happily proved vain.

July 16, 1788, died Hon. Jonathan Blanchard, aged 50 years. He was the son of Col. Joseph Blanchard, and was born September 18, 1738. – He had not the advantage of a collegiate education, but was early initiated, by his father, into the active business of life. After the death of his father, which occurred in his 20th year, he was called upon to fill his place as proprietors' clerk and surveyor, and was soon deeply engaged in the management of town affairs, and other public business.

When the events which preceded the revolution occurred, the people of New Hampshire were among the
first to resist the usurpations of the crown. When in 1685,
Cranfield forbade the ministers to preach, unless they
would administer the communion to all who requested
it, in the Episcopal form, they refused obedience, de-
nounced him from the pulpit, and went to prison rather
than yield. When the Governor at a later day, levied a tax
upon the lands of the people, for his private advantage,
the women resisted the collection, and drove his officers
from their houses with water scalding hot. The "broad
R," cut by some "prowling official," upon their choicest
trees, thus devoting them to the Royal Navy, without redress or compensation, was a continued eye-sore.

Early in 1775, the legislature of New Hampshire, first
of all the States, and evidently anticipating Independence,
sent a request to the Continental Congress, which met at
Philadelphia, May 10, 1775, to advise them as to the organization of an Independent Government. Agreeably to
their recommendation, given with much hesitation, (1.)
a Convention met at Exeter, and adopted a Constitution,
bearing date January 5, 1776. It was the earliest adopted
by any colony, and was violently opposed by the more
timid, as a virtual Declaration of Independence. (2.) It
provided, as has before been mentioned, for a House of
Delegates, and a Council of twelve, to be elected annually by the people, and which were similar to our Senate
and House of Representatives. No provision was made
for a Governor, and the whole Executive, as well as Leg-

islative, authority was placed in these two bodies. Of this Council, Jonathan Blanchard was chosen a member in 1776, and continued such for three years. No better testimony to his worth could be given than the bestowal of such an office at such a period.

In October, 1776, Gen. Blanchard was sent by the Legislature to recruit our regiments, which had been wasted by sickness, suffering, and defeat at Ticonderoga. In 1777, he was appointed Attorney General of the State, in conjunction with Col. Nathaniel Peabody, and is said "to have discharged his duties in a manner satisfactory to the Government, and advantageous to the people." (1.) January 6, 1778, he was appointed a member of the "Committee of Safety" for the State, an office of unlimited responsibility and power, and which he held for a long period. (2.)

He was a delegate from this State, in conjunction with Col. Peabody, to the Convention, which met at New Haven, January 1778, "to regulate prices." enforce the recommendations of Congress, and relieve the distress of the people; and he prepared a report to our Legislature accordingly. (3.) In 1784, soon after the adoption of our State Constitution, Gen. Blanchard was appointed Judge of Probate for the County of Hillsborough, an office which he held nearly or quite up to the time of his death.

In 1787, during the confederation of the States, he was elected a delegate from this State to the Continental Congress. They were chosen annually, and whether he was again elected and died in office is uncertain. (4.) Soon after the death of his father he was appointed agent, by the Masonian Proprietors, to manage and dispose of all the unsettled lands within the State of New Hampshire. The territory of this State had been granted originally, to Robert Mason, hut after many years, finding that it yielded very little income and caused him much trouble, he disposed of the land, as far as it remained in his possession, to a company of individuals who were called the Masonian Proprietors. As their agent, Gen. Blanchard conveyed most of the lands within the State, and this circumstance caused that many of the original proprietors of a very large number of towns resided here, and from this town were drawn many of their first settlers.

Gen. Blanchard died in this town and is buried in the Old South burying ground. He married Rebecca Farwell, who died August 20, 1811, and left five children, one only of whom is now living.

In 1790, the population of the town was 632.

In 1792, died Jonathan Lovewell, Esq., aged 79. He was a brother of Capt. Lovewell, "The Indian Fighter," and of Col. Zaccheus Lovewell, and was born in this town, May 14, 1713. Early in life he took an active part in town affairs, and became one of the proprietors of "common lands" in the township of Dunstable. For many years he was proprietor's clerk, and a magistrate under the crown. About the year 1746, under the preaching of Rev. Mr. Kirk, he became a convert to the doctrine of the "New Lights," as the followers of Whitefield were then called, and soon after became a preacher. This probably, however, was of short duration, as he never left town, and in 1755, he was commissary of the New Hampshire regiment, sent out against Crown Point, under the command of Col. Joseph Blanchard. A gun taken from the French during that campaign, and brought home by him, is still in the possession of the family.

In the earliest stages of the Revolution, Mr. Lovewell was an ardent and efficient friend of liberty. In April, 1774, he was chosen agent of the town to petition the General Court for leave to send a Representative, a privilege which they had not hitherto enjoyed. In September, 1776, he was chosen a delegate to represent the town in the Convention holden at Exeter, for the purpose of sending a delegate to the First Continental Congress, to be holden soon after at Philadelphia. These were the first steps towards Independence.

January 9, 1775, Mr. Lovewell was chosen a member of the "Committee of Inspection" for the town, to see that none of the inhabitants purchased or used British Goods. February, 1776, he was chosen a member of the "*Commit*tee of Safety" for the town, a situation of no little trust, and continued a member of almost every such Revolutionary committee during the war. These committees were of the highest utility in diffusing information, and in exciting and concentrating the efforts of the patriotic, and demanded men of great energy and decision. – June 20, 1777, he was chosen a member of the "COMMITTEE OF SAFETY" for the State, and served in that capacity until January 5. 1779, about which period the necessity for the exercise of their functions in a great measure ceased.

NASHUA CORPORATION

April, 1778, he was chosen a member of the Committee to "assist" the delegates from this town in the Convention for framing a Constitution for the State. In 1781, he was chosen a member of the committee which formed our present State Constitution. After its adoption he was appointed a Judge of the Court of Common Pleas for this County, which office he held for several years. He lived and died unmarried.

CHAPTER XIV.
HISTORY OF NASHUA VILLAGE

For a number of years little occurred in the history of the town which would be of general interest. It was slowly recovering from the effects of the war, and its exhausting sacrifices. About 1795 the first stage coach was put upon this road, and was an occasion of great public interest. It was a two horse covered vehicle, owned and driven by Mr. Joseph Wheat, and ran from Amherst to Boston and back again once a week. It stopped at Billerica over night, making the trip both ways in about four days. They had not then learned the advantages of changing horses, and the same team performed all the journey. People came from a distance of several miles to look at "the stage," and gaze upon it with the same feeling of wonder that they now do upon a locomotive engine.

About this time the locks and canal around Pawtucket Falls were built, and boating upon the Merrimac began. At this time there were no dwellings where our village now stands, and but one or two at the Harbor.

In 1800 the population of Dunstable had increased to 862. In the spring of 1803 a Canal Boat was built in the village, by Robert Fletcher, Esq. It was a singular structure, having sides five or six feet in height all around it, and doors, and was looked upon as "a wonder." It was the first canal boat ever built in this vicinity for the regular transportation of goods, and the fact was considered of as much importance to the infant village as the opening of a railroad at the present day. It was launched on the Fourth of July, which was celebrated by a public meeting, and an oration by Daniel Abbot, Esq. (1.) – There was a great gathering of the people, and great rejoicing. Already was it a place of some trade, and the more sanguine saw in imagination its trade and population doubled or even trebled. The landing was on the Merrimac near the mouth of the Nashua, and a store was there erected. – The boat was christened "the Nashua," with much parade, and the village which had until then been called "Indian Head," received the name of Nashua Tillage. (2.) That may be considered the birth-day of Nashua, and forms an important epoch in its history.

Let us endeavor to picture to ourselves Nashua Village as it appeared July 4th, 1803. A large, one story dwelling house stood on the site of the Indian Head Coffee House, (of which it now forms a part) and was kept as a tavern by Timothy Taylor, Esq. A large, one story store, owned and conducted by Robert Fletcher, who resided in Amherst, stood where Kendrick & Tuttle's store now stands. Abbot and Fox's office was a dwelling house occupied by "uncle" John Lund, his brother and sisters. A dwelling house, three stories in front and two in rear, had just been erected by Mr. Fletcher, but was then unfinished. It stood on the north-east corner of Main and Franklin streets, opposite the Baptist meeting house, and here upon a temporary platform the oration was delivered. The Amherst and Concord roads with Main street, and a road down the northern bank of the Nashua to the Boating house and Ferries were all the highways then existing.

At the Harbor the dwelling house of Gen. Noah Lovewell, now occupied by Hon. Jesse Bowers, with two other small houses on the south side of Salmon Brook, were the only buildings. As the greater part of the inhabitants lived west and south of this, the meeting house was built on the little triangle in front of Silas Gibson's house. Here was the largest village in town, a tavern, store, shops, and dwellings, and here resided the physician and the lawyer, (Mr. Abbot.) But in September, 1803, the "Old Tontine," the long, low, building at the head of Main street, in Nashville, was built, and soon after occupied by Mr. Abbot, (who removed here Dec. 1, 1803;) Dr. Elias Maynard, physician; Dea. James Patterson, bookbinder, and a Mr. Clements, saddler. There was no dam across the Nashua, and its waters flowed far down its natural channel over its rocky bed. The *"pilgrims"* who then settled here must have seen some light from the future breaking through the surrounding darkness, for there was not a building between Salmon Brook and Nashua river, and a broad, unfenced, desolate, white-pine forest spread in every direction beyond.

In 1803 a Post Office was first established in town, and Gen. Noah Lovewell appointed Post Master. Previously letters for this town were received from the Post Office at Tyngsborough. (1.)

In 1804 a farther impulse was given to the growth and business of the village by the completion and opening of the Middlesex canal. – This opened a direct channel of communication with Boston, and rendered the place, as the head of navigation, one of considerable trade. Hitherto the principal markets of this region had been Haverhill and Newburyport.

From this period the growth of the settlement was gradual, but constant. The whole plain, upon which the village stands, was covered with its native growth of pines, and was considered generally of but very little value. "Dunstable Plains" were often the subject of much merriment, and seemed to some the embodiment of the idea of poverty of soil. It is said that some wicked wag, in our Legislature, once undertook to disparage our soil, declaring that "it would not support one chipping squirrel to the acre but this, as well as the story that "a grasshopper was once seen perched upon the top of a dry mullen stalk, with the tears rolling down his cheeks, looking in vain to discover one stalk of green grass," is a grievous slander, and a device of the enemy.

The soil of our plains was, indeed, naturally sandy and barren, and of little value for cultivation when other and more desirable locations for tillage were scattered all around. From this circumstance, we may believe the statement to he quite credible, that the *rise* of Main street from the Bridge over Nashua river, to the present place of Messrs. Kendrick & Tuttle's store in Nashville, was "the *worst hill* between Amherst and Boston." We must remember, however, hat a great change has taken place in its appearance and situation. The present bridge is raised some twenty or twenty-five feet above the old one, the water under the present bridge being not the natural stream, but a pond occasioned by the dam at Indian Head, and many feet in depth. – While the bridge has been raised many feet and the road filled in accordingly, the slope of the hill on either side of the river has been cut down, and graded, so that the ascent now, in either direction, is comparatively slight.

In 1812, the old meeting house, which stood in the little square in front of the Gibson tavern, and which had been standing there more than sixty years, had become too old and dilapidated to answer the purposes of its erection. A new and more costly house was built accordingly, nearly half a mile northerly of the old one. – This is the one now called the Old South," and was dedicated November 4, 1812, upon which occasion the sermon was preached by Rev. Humphrey Moore, of Milford. (1.)

November 3, 1813, Rev. Ebenezer P. Sperry was ordained, as the colleague of Rev. Mr. Kidder. He remained in Dunstable until April, 1819, when he was dismissed, and has been Chaplain of the House of Correction, at South Boston. During his ministry, September 6, 1818, Rev. Mr. Kidder died, aged 77, on which occasion a discourse was delivered by Rev. H. Moore. (1.)

About 1817, a dam was thrown across Nashua river, a few rods above Main street; a Grist-mill erected at one end of it by Dea. James Patterson, and a saw-mill at the other by Willard Marshall. Some time after, another dam was built near the spot, where the present dam of the Jackson Company stands, and a mill erected. – At this time the village had increased so much that it contained about a dozen or twenty houses, and being a central thoroughfare had become a place of considerable business. The population of the town was 1,142.

In 1820, when the census was taken, there were returned from Dunstable: 1 meeting house; 9 school districts and school houses; 6 taverns; 5 stores; 3 saw mills; 3 grist mills; 1 clothing mill; 1 carding machine; 2 bark mills; 3 tanneries.

Soon after 1820, public attention began to be turned towards manufactures. Many years previously Judge Tyng, of Tyngsborough, in a conversation with George Sullivan, predicted that the valley of the Merrimac would be a great manufacturing region, and he pointed out the locations at Lowell, at Nashua, and at Amoskeag. (2.)

It was considered a visionary idea, but what was then prophecy is now history. The erection of mills at Lowell awakened the minds of enterprising men and of capitalists, to the manufacturing advantages of other places. The leading citizens of the town seem to have been peculiarly far-sighted, public spirited, and energetic, and the manufacturing capacities of Nashua river did not escape their notice.

The idea, which first suggested itself, was that of building mills at Mine Falls; the water power was great,

and a saw mill had been erected there at a very early period, probably before 1700. It was not, however, for some
time that the idea occurred to them of erecting the mills
upon their present location, and building up a village
here, by bringing the water from Mine Falls by means of a
canal. It was a great undertaking, and of doubtful result,
but a survey was made, and its practicability ascertained.

The few individuals, who had conceived the idea,
formed an association, and in 1822 and 1823, purchased
the greater portion of the lands in and around the village, and up to the Falls. – In June, 1823, a charter was
granted to Daniel Abbot, Moses Tyler, Joseph Greeley,
and others, by the name of the "Nashua Manufacturing
Company," with a right to increase their capital to one
million dollars. The capital stock was at first fixed by
them at $300,000; and was divided into three hundred
shares, of $1,000 each. Of these Daniel Webster took 60
shares; Daniel Abbot 30 shares; J., E. & A. Greeley 30
shares; Augustus Peabody 75 shares; Benj. F. French 30
shares; Foster & Kendrick 30 shares; John Kendrick 15
shares; Moses Tyler 30 shares.

In 1824, a considerable portion of the stock was disposed of to capitalists, and the works were commenced.
The dam at Mine Falls was. built, and the excavation of
the canal began under the superintendence of Col. James
F. Baldwin. This canal, which supplies the water for the
factories of the Nashua Manufacturing Company, is
about three miles in length, 60 feet wide, and 6 feet deep,
and affords a head and fall of about 33 feet. Ira Gay, Esq.,

was also engaged as machinist, and Col. William Boardman as wheel-wright and engineer; and the first Factory
was commenced. December 25, 1824, the Machine Shop
was completed and went into operation. The works advanced. Mill No. 1, of the Nashua Corporation was erected and went into partial operation in December, 1825,
and into full operation in 1826.

In December, 1824, a charter was obtained by the
Nashua Manufacturing Company for the purpose of
building "a canal with the necessary dams and locks" to
connect the Nashua with the Merrimac. They were built
in 1825, and opened for the transportation of goods in the
spring of 1826. The lower dam across the Nashua was
built at this time. The Locks are of solid stone, 24 feet
high; each lift being ten feet wide and eighty-two long.
They were built under the superintendence of Col. Baldwin, and cost $20,000. The canal dam cost a further sum
of $10,000. – This canal was of very great advantage to
the rising village, which was now becoming the centre
of business for the neighboring towns, by affording such
increased facilities for the transportation of goods and
produce, and its beneficial effects were soon sensibly felt
in the increase of trade and enterprise.

In May 1825, a portion of the lower water privilege,
now occupied by the Jackson Company, was sold by the
Nashua Manufacturing Company to Charles C. Haven
and others, who were incorporated by the name of the
"Indian Head Company." for the purpose of erecting
Woollen Factories. Their works were commenced imme-

diately, and went into operation in 1826, under the agency of Mr. Haven.

In 1825, the meeting house, now occupied by Rev. Mr. Richards's Society, was erected by the Nashua Company; and November 8th. 1826, Rev. Handel G. Nott was settled over the church and society, which had been destitute since the dismission of Mr. Sperry, a period of eighteen years. In 1834 the society was divided, in consequence of a change in the sentiments of their pastor, and the church, in its organized capacity, under the name of the "First Congregational Church in Nashua," left the meeting house in possession of Rev. Mr. Nott's society, and worshipped for a time in Greeley's Hall. They invited Rev. Jonathan McGee to become their pastor, and his installation took place January 1, 1835. During the same year a spacious meeting house was erected at an expense of more than $10,000. – June 8th. 1842, Mr. McGee was dismissed and Rev. Matthew Hale Smith was installed October 19th. of the same year. Mr. Smith was dismissed August 20th. 1845, and Rev. Samuel Lamson, the present pastor, was installed April 8th. 1846. This church consists of 450 members, and has connected with it a Sabbath school, which usually numbers more than 300 scholars. There is a library for the use of the school. There are two benevolent societies sustained by the ladies, a Maternal Society and a Young Men's Missionary Association. Contributions are annually taken up in aid of the following objects: the Foreign and Home Missionary, the Education, Bible, Tract and Seaman's Friend Societies, with other occasional objects of benevolence.

A portion of the church, embracing 142 members, remained with Mr. Nott's society, and formed a new church, which was organized Oct. 26, 1835, under the name of the "First Congregational Church in Nashua Village." Feb.9, 1846, thename of this church was changed to "Olive Street Congregational Church." Shortly after the change in Mr. Nott's views, he withdrew from his connection with the church and society, and Rev. Austin Richards, the present pastor, was installed April 6th. 1836. The number of church members at the present time, (1846,) is 506. The Sabbath school contains 500 scholars, and has a library of 409 volumes. With the exception of the Ladies' Charity Circle and the Seaman's Friend Society, there are no regularly organized benevolent societies distinct from the church, but contributions are taken up during each year for the benefit of the Foreign and Home Missionary, the Tract, Bible, Education, Sabbath School, Seaman's Friend, and Foreign Evangelical Societies.

In the Fall of 1824 and spring of 1825, fifty new tenements or more had been erected, and all was bustle and prosperity. In 1825 a new bridge was built over the Nashua river in Alain street, in consequence of the raising of the water by the dam at Indian Head. Lots of land were selling at the rate of "about $1,000 per acre," according to the report of the Directors for that year.

In 1826 a charter was granted to several individuals, by the name of the "Proprietors of Taylor's Falls Bridge," for the purpose of building a bridge across the Merrimac. At this time the people crossed by a ferry, there being no bridge across the river between Lowell and Amoskea\g.

This bridge was completed and opened for public travel the same year. It is thirty-three rods in length, and its total cost was about $12,000. It was no small undertaking in the then feeble state of the village, and was deemed by many persons a hazardous investment, but the prosperity of the place required it. and success has rewarded the effort.

In the winter and spring of 1827, the Unitarian church was erected. The society enjoyed preaching in 1824; and from 1825 to 1826, hired and occupied the meeting house built by the Nashua Company. June 27, 1827, the church was dedicated, and Rev. Nathaniel Gage ordained. In 1834 Mr. Gage asked a dismission; and in 1835, Rev. Henry Emmons was ordained as pastor. In 1837 Mr. Emmons also asked a dismission, and May 16, 1838, Rev. Samuel Osgood was ordained; In December 1841, Mr. Osgood requested a dismission, having received an invitation to settle at Providence, R. I. From this time the society was without a settled minister until October 25, 1843, when Rev. A. C. L. Arnold was ordained. He was dismissed August 25, 1844. Rev. S. G. Bulfinch, the present pastor, was installed September 17, 1845. The Sabbath School consists of 112 pupils. There is a S. S. Library containing about 400 volumes, and a Church Library of 180 volumes. A Benevolent Circle is sustained by the ladies of the society.

March 19, 1835, the proprietors appropriated the grounds around the meeting house to the purpose of a burial place, under the name of the Nashua Cemetery. Of this an account will be given in the Appendix.

In 1827, Mill No. 2, of the Nashua Corporation was built and went into partial operation, and into full operation in 1828. Mill No. 3, was built in 1836. Mill No. 1, is 155 feet long, 45 feet wide, and 5 stories high. It contains 6,784 spindles, and 220 looms, manufacturing No. 14 shirtings and drills. Mill No. 2, is 155 feet long, 45 feet wide, and 6 stories high. It contains 12,170 spindles, and 315 looms, which manufacture No. 24 printing cloths and jeans. Mill No. 3, is 160 feet long, 50 feet wide, and 5 stories high, it contains 6,400 spindles, and 205 looms, and manufactures No. 14 sheetings. Mill No. 4, was built in 1844, and was put into operation in December of the same year. It is 198 feet long, 50 feet wide, and 5 stories high, and contains 6,720 spindles, and 200 looms, manufacturing No. 12 sheetings. The whole number of spindles in the four mills is 32,074, looms 940. Number of female operatives 835. Number of males 225. – These mills manufacture 11,500,000 yds. of cloth per annum; and use 8,000 bales of cotton, weighing 3,250,000 lbs., 150,000 lbs. starch, 8,000 gallons sperm oil, $1250 worth leather, 700 cords of hard and pine wood, annually. There are 48 tenements for overseers and boarding houses, and two brick houses for the agent and clerk. Thomas W. Gillis, Esq., is the agent; J. A. Baldwin, clerk. The capital is $800,000; the number of shares 1600, at $500 each.

The Savings Bank deposites in 1845 were $44,000, by 364 depositers, three fourths of whom are females. No interest is allowed on any sum exceeding $500, and the privileges of the Bank are limited to individuals in the employ of the company. The rate of interest is 5 per cent.

– On the first of June of every year interest is credited on all amounts and added to the principal, and interest computed on the total sum from that date, – thus giving to those who permit their savings to remain in the hands of the company for any length of time, the advantage of compound interest. The following table, arranged October 13, 1845, shows the number of females employed in the N. M. Co.'s Mills and the proportion thereof who attend meeting, are members of the Sabbath School, and are professors of religion:

	Whole no. girls empl'd.	No.who attend meeting	Attend Sab. School.	Memb's of church's
No. 1 Mill,	214	194	116	67
No. 2 Mill,	216	206	131	82
No. 3 Mill,	192	167	88	52
No. 4 Mill,	170	151	73	43
Cloth Room,	8	8	3	6
Total,	800	726	411	250

About 1828, the Indian Head Company became embarrassed, and soon after the works stopped. The whole property was then disposed of to a new company, which was incorporated in 1830 by the name of the Jackson Company. They took out the old machinery, and converted the establishment into a cotton manufactory. The capital stock of this company is $480,000. They have two Mills, 150 and 155 feet in length, by 48 feet in width, and 4 stories high. These contain 11,588 spindles and

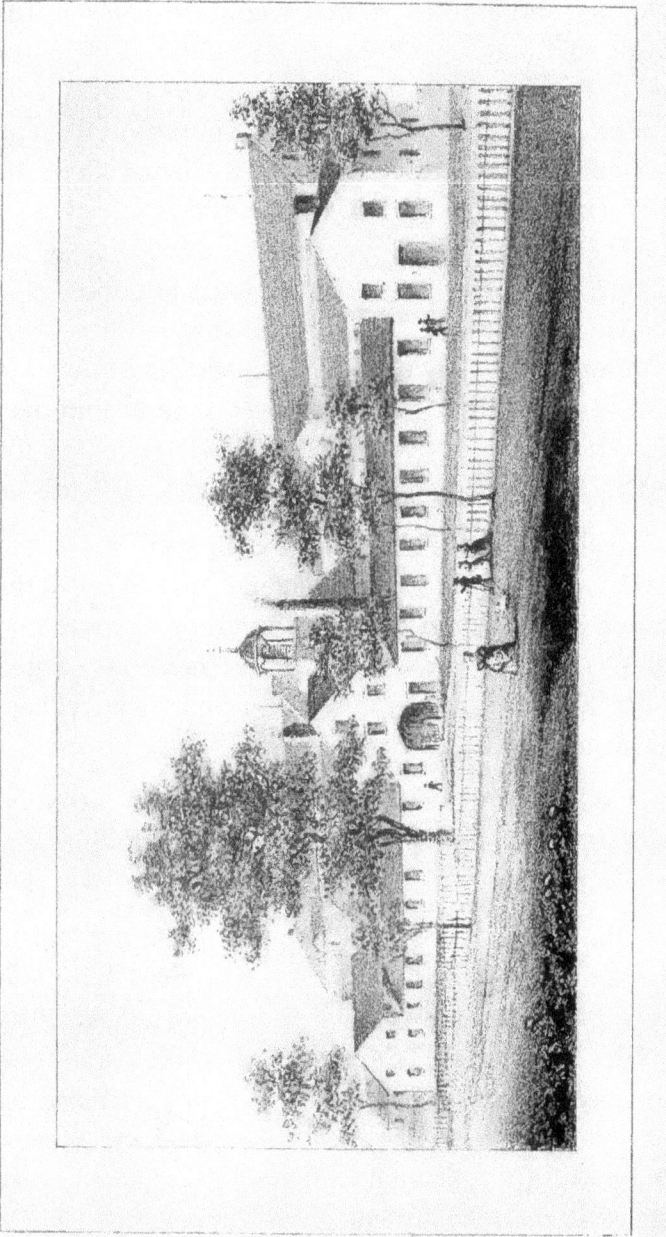

JACKSON CORPORATION

378 looms, and employ 90 males and 350 females. The amount paid males per annum, is $30,000, – to females, $60,000. They use 5,000 bales of cotton a year, averaging 400 pounds each, from which they manufacture five and a half million yards of cloth of the following kinds: 46 and 37 inch sheetings, and 30 inch shirtings, all of No. 14 yarn. The value of wood per annum is $2,500; oil $3,700; starch $2,500; leather $1,000. The amount of deposites in the Savings Bank is $18,000, on which 5 per cent. compound interest is allowed. The depositing is confined to operatives, and no interest is allowed on any sum over $500. The number of depositers is 150. The agent of the company is Edmund Parker, Esq.; George F. Beck, clerk.

In February. 1827, the first newspaper was established in town by Andrew E. Thayer, Esq., and called the "Nashua Constellation." After a short lime it passed into the hands of Israel Hunt, Jr., Esq., and its name changed to "The Nashua Gazette." Its present editor is William Butterfield.

In 1830, the population of Dunstable had increased to 2,417 of which number about 1,500 resided within the village.

In the winter of 1831, a new paper called the "Nashua Herald" was started by Dr. Simeon J. Bard, but it did not prosper, and was soon given up. In September, 1832, the "New Hampshire Telegraph," a weekly paper, was established by Alfred Beard, and is now conducted by Albin Beard. "The Oasis" was established in January, 1843, by Murray & Sawtell, and is now published every Wednesday morning, by Murray & Kimball.

In the fall of 1832, the First Baptist Society was organized, and obtained its present pastor, Rev. Dura D. Pratt.
It was formed as early as 1818, and a church organized in
1822; but they were few and feeble, and preaching was
maintained but a small portion of the time. A large and
commodious meeting house was now erected, at a cost of
nearly $8,000; and January 23. 1833, it was dedicated, and
Rev. Mr. Pratt ordained. The church now comprises over
500 members. The Sabbath School consists of 350 members, and has a library of 300 volumes.

The First Methodist Episcopal Society was organized
November 3,1832. A meeting house was erected in 1833,
and enlarged, and a parsonage attached in 1837. Their
ministers have been as follows: – Rev. A. P. Brigham,
1834; Rev. Wm. D. Cass. 1835; Rev. Wm. H. Hatch, 1836;
Rev. Jared Perkins, 1838; Rev. Samuel Kelley, 1840; Rev.
J. W. Mowry, Rev. L. D. Barrows, Rev. J. Smith. Rev. Mr.
Pike is the present pastor.

April 1, 1844, after the separation of Nashville, a new
church was organized, under the name of the First Methodist Episcopal Church in Nashua, and during the same
year the society purchased the meeting house formerly
occupied by the Second Baptist Society, for $15,000, about
half the original cost. Rev. E. A. Rice, of Lowell, Mass.,
supplied the pulpit for the first three months. From July
1, 1844, to July 1, 1845, the church was under the pastoral
care of Rev. C. C. Burr. Rev. J. Boyce is the present pastor.
This church contains 160 members. There are 268 scholars in the Sabbath School, and 360 volumes in the library.

From 1830 to 1837 the growth of the village was rapid and constant. The population of the village had nearly trebled in number. Trade and travel had increased proportionally. In the spring of 1835, the project was conceived of extending the Lowell Railroad to Nashua. June 23, 1835, a charter for this purpose was granted, by the Legislature of New Hampshire; and by that of Massachusetts, April 16, 1836. In 1831, the preparatory surveys were made and the location filed. Uriah A. Boyden, Esq., was engaged as engineer. In May, 1837, the work upon the road was commenced, and October 8, 1838, the NASHUA AND LOWELL RAILROAD was first opened for the transportation of passengers as far as the *great elms* near Judge Parker's house, where a temporary depot was erected. December 23, 1838, the bridge over the Nashua, and the depot near Main street, were completed, and the cars for the first time came up to the present terminus. The length of the road is about fourteen and a half miles, exclusive of double tracks, and its total cost about $380,000, or about $25,000 per mile, including fixtures and apparatus.

June 27, 1835, the Concord Railroad Company was incorporated. This Railroad was commenced in the spring of 1841, under the direction of William S. Whitwell, Esq., as engineer, and finished to Concord, September 1, 1842. Its length is 34 miles, 3048 feet. The net profits have been 10 per cent. per annum from its commencement. The amount of capital is $800,000. The officers of the Road are:

ADDISON GILMORE, of Boston, President.

ISAAC SPALDING, of Nashua, Treasurer.

CHARLES H. PEASLEE, of Concord, Clerk.

June 19, 1835, the NASHUA BANK was incorporated, with a capital of $100,000; and went into operation soon after.

In 1835, the steamboat Herald was also built, and placed upon the Merrimac in the summer of 1836. It was intended to ply between Nashua and Lowell, but the shortness of the distance, – the inconvenience of the landing places, and the necessity for the shifting of passengers and baggage, rendered the enterprise a failure.

In 1835, the First Universalist Society was organized, under the pastoral charge of Rev. Woodbury M. Fernald. He preached until 1837, when Rev. A. P. Cleverly became their preacher. In 1839, a large meeting house was erected, and in October of that year, Rev. Lewis C. Browne was ordained as their pastor. In consequence of ill health, Mr. Browne requested a dismission in September, 1848, and Rev Wm. H. Ryder, the present pastor, was installed December 25th. of the same year. The church was organized in 1841, and contains 104 members. There are two benevolent societies sustained by the ladies of the society. The Sabbath School embraces 20 teachers, and 175 scholars. The Sabbath School Library numbers 600 volumes.

In April, 1836, the population had increased to 5065, of which number 2105 were males, and 2960 females.

During this year, a Second Baptist Society was formed under Rev. N. W. Smith, and a meeting house erected. In 1838, Rev. Samuel C. Pratt was ordained as its pastor. In 1839, the society was again united to the First Baptist Society.

January 1, 1837, the township laid aside its ancient name of DUNSTABLE, which it had worn from its infancy, through good and evil fortune a hundred and sixty years, under which it had witnessed two revolutions and formed a portion of a Colony, a Province, and a sovereign State, – under which it had passed through many wars, and grown up from obscurity and poverty; and adopted in order to distinguish it from its neighbor "t'other Dunstable," its present name, that of the river from which its prosperity is chiefly derived – NASHUA.

The First Free-Will Baptist Church was organized November, 1838, and was under the pastoral care of Elder Silas Curtis, to September, 1839. He was succeeded by Elder Thomas M. Preble, who was dismissed September, 1841. in December of the same year, Elder Benjamin Phelon was chosen pastor. He was dismissed December, 1842, since which time the church has been without a settled pastor. Religious services have been regularly observed every sabbath. The number of church members is 40. The Sabbath School numbers 56 members, and has a Library of 150 volumes. The present house of worship was erected in 1844, at an expense of $600. Rev. S. Stearns is the present minister.

In 1840, the First Christian Society was organized under the pastoral care of Rev. Mr. Robinson. They have no meeting house.

In November, 1845, the services of the Protestant Episcopal Church were, for the first time, regularly observed in Nashua. The court-room of the town house has been occupied for this purpose. Rev. Milton Ward is the officiating minister.

In 1845, a large machine shop, built of brick and slated, was erected by the Nashua Company on the site of the old one. The main building is 150 feet long, with an addition of 158 feet, used for a blacksmith's shop, furnace, &c. The main building is occupied by shuttle and bobbin makers, locksmiths, gunsmiths, manufacturers of axes, hoes, ploughs, and by artisans in other branches. The whole number of workmen employed in the building is two hundred and eighteen. A portion of this building is occupied by the extensive establishment of Messrs. J. & E. Baldwin, for the manufacture of shuttles and bobbins, which gives employment to a number of workmen.

The manufacturing business of the Nashua Lock Company is also done here. This establishment, of which L. W. Noyes and David Baldwin are the proprietors, is employed in the manufacture of mortise locks and latches for dwelling house doors, and rose wood and brass knobs for the handles of the same. They usually have in their employment about 40 men, and manufactured, during the last year, $35,000 worth of goods. These manufactures embraced 56,617 locks and latches, and 35.000 pairs of rose wood knobs.

Another portion of this shop is occupied by Mr. John H. Gage for building turning engines, machines for planing iron, engines for cutting gears, scroll chucks, and all other tools requisite to fill a large machine shop for building cotton and other machinery, and for doing railroad work. Mr. Gage now employs sixty-four workmen, and does business to the amount of about $40,000 per annum.

The "Nashua Manufacturing and Mechanics Association" was chartered January 2, 1829, with liberty to have a capital to the extent of $30,000. This company was organized under the charter August, 1845. The present capital is $10,000, with 200 shares at $50 each. The contemplation is to erect a brick building 100 feet long, two stories high, with two wings, each 150 feet long and 40 feet wide, one story, with an attic. The work in this shop is to be conducted by means of a steam engine of fifty horse power, and is intended to embrace all kinds of mechanical work similar to the Nashua Company's shop. – One wing of the building is now completed, and is occupied by Mr. Edwin Chase, for the manufacture of doors, window blinds and sashes.

The officers of this association are:

THOMAS CHASE President
THOMAS CHASE
L. W. NOYES
BARTLETT HOYT
ISRAEL HUNT jr.   } Directors
JOHN H. GAGE
JOHN A. BALDWIN Treasurer.
FRANCIS WINCH Clerk.

In the summer of 1845, the Iron Foundry of S. & C. Williams was erected. They manufacture, from pig iron, 4000 pounds of castings per day, and consume in the same time, 1300 pounds Lehigh coal and six feet of wood. Their arrangements are such that they can melt nine or ten tons of iron at a melting, or eighteen tons in twelve hours. They now employ thirty men, and have room for twenty more. The amount of their business is not far from $40,000 a year.

In 1845, Mr. Alanson Crane commenced a cotton manufacturing establishment on Salmon Brook at the Harbor. His mill is 30 by 40 feet on the ground, two stories high, with an attic. When in full operation this mill will contain 500 spindles, for making cotton yarn of various numbers and qualities. The yarn, when manufactured, is worked up into braids and cords of various descriptions; also twine for weavers' harnesses, knitting cotton, &c. The number of operatives employed is 20, 4 males and 16 females. About $30,000 worth of goods are manufactured annually. A dye house is connected with this establishment for dyeing braids, cords, yarn, &c. From a survey recently made it is estimated that there is sufficient water running in Salmon Brook to operate 1500 spindles, and Mr. Crane contemplates erecting another mill with about 1000 spindles and looms for the manufacture of cotton shirtings, sheetings, and drillings.

At the annual meeting of the town of Nashua, March, 1842, it was voted to erect a Town House. Of this structure, now completed, an account will be given in the Appendix.

In 1842, the town of Nashua was divided, and a part of the territory, chiefly lying north of the Nashua river, received the name of Nashville. – The following act of incorporation, passed by the Legislature, June 23, 1842, defines the limits of the new town:

"Be it enacted by the Senate and House of Representatives in General Court convened, – That all that part of the town of Nashua, in the County of Hillsborough, lying westerly and northerly of a line commencing upon the Nashua river at the east side of Hollis, and running thence down said river, to the bridge erected over said river by the Nashua and Lowell Railroad Company; thence from the southwest corner of said bridge, eastwardly by said railroad to the Old Ferry road so called, thence by said last mentioned road to the Merrimack river, be and the same is severed from the town of Nashua, and made a body politic and corporate, by the name of Nashville."

The town was organized July 11, 1842.

What a contrast our villages now present to their condition but twenty-*six* years ago ! Then there was one small religious society, without a minister: now there are ten. most of them in a flourishing condition, and enjoying the services of settled clergymen. Then there was one meeting house: now there are seven others, built at an expense of more than $45,000. It is a singular fact that for more than 100 years not a settled minister died in town. Then the receipts of the Post office were about $250 yearly and now they exceed $2,500. Then a single stage coach passed three times a week through the village. Now there are six daily lines, five tri-weekly lines, and two weeklies, besides extras and the railroad. – Then two stores supplied the town and neighborhood. Now there are near a hundred, several of which are wholesale stores, with an aggregate trade of more than half a million dollars. Then a canal boat dragging its "slow length along," and occupying days in its passage, laid our goods at the mouth of the Nashua: now by the magical power of steam they are brought to our doors almost in as many hours. The little village of less than fifty souls has increased one hundred and fifty fold. By the wondrous alchemy of skill and enterprise, out of the waters of the Nashua and the sands of this pine barren, from some half dozen dwellings, have been raised up within these twenty-six years these thronged, and beautiful villages of near seven thousand people.

We have now traced this History through a period of nearly two centuries. From its wilderness state, by toil and privations, by bloodshed and sufferings, by enterprise and capital combined, has this place been brought to its present condition. Its prosperity must now depend upon its trade and manufactures, and for the increase of them every effort should be made. Its central position and its facilities of transportation are advantages, which cannot be too highly appreciated.

The multiplication of shops and stores, and the amount of their trade, are evidences of what has been accomplished by enterprise, and offer strong encouragements for the future. Other manufactures besides cotton are creeping in, thus far with great success, and should be encouraged. The manufactures of shuttles and bobbins, locks, guns, ploughs, edge tools, machinery, iron, brass, and tin ware, carriages, saddlery, sashes, blinds, doors, hats, caps, boots and shoes, reeds, cigars, furniture, time-pieces, boxes, stoves, and of patent leather, and book-binding, employ a large amount of capital and furnish employment to a large number of persons.

When we consider the ease and cheapness of communication with Boston and the comparative lowness of the price of land, of materials, and of board among us, it is manifest that all kinds of manufactures may be greatly extended and multiplied, and to much advantage. If all will but labor permanently for this end, thus, and thus only, will the means of support be afforded to additional thousands, a market for all the neighborhood furnished, and the foundation be laid, broad and deep, and immovable, for the permanent prosperity of Nashua and Nashville.

NOTES:

(1.) Mrs. *Adams's Letters*, 152.

(1.) Mrs. *Adams's Letters*, 85. 2 *Gordon's History*, 150.

(2.) 1 *Belknap*.

(1.) 3 *Farmer's and Moore's Hist. Coll.*, 5.

(2.) 2 *N. H. Hist. Coll.*, 39.

(3.) 3 *Farmer's and Moore's Hist. Coll.*, 5.

(4.) 1 *Belknap*, 416.

(1.) This oration was printed.

(2.) This same is found in Winthrop's Journal, both in its present usual orthography and in other forms, as applied to an early settlement on the Nashua river, now Lancaster, Massachusetts.

In 1648, "Others of the same town (Watertown) began also a plantation at Nashaway, some 15 miles N. W. from Sudbury."

In 1644, "Many of Watertown and other towns joined in the plantation of Nashaway," &c. *Winthrop's Journal, Vol. II., pages* 152, 161.

In a note to the passage last quoted, the editor, Hon. James Savage, says: – "From our Col. Rec. II. 57, I find 'the petition of Mr. Nathaniel Norcross, Robert Chide, Stephen Day, John Fisher and others for a plantation at Nashawake is granted, provided that there shall not be more land allotted to the town, or particular men, (notwithstanding their purchase of land of the Indians,) than the General Court shall allow.'"

In the following entries by Winthrop, in 1648, the name appears to have been spelt as usual at present:

"This year a new way was found out to Connecticut, by Nashua, which avoided much of the hilly way.

"The magistrates, being informed at a court of assistants that four or five Indians who lived upon the spoil of their neighbours, had murdered some Indians of Nipnett, who were subject to this government, and robbed their wigwam, sent twenty men to Nashua, to enquire the truth of the matter," &c. *Journal, Vol. II.* page 325.

In the Appendix to the same volume, page 394, the editor gives the former name of Lancaster as *Nashoway.*

(1.) See history of the Post Office in Appendix.

(1.) This sermon was printed.

(1.) This discourse was also published, and appended to it is a short sketch of the Ecclesiastical history of the town, drawn by up Rev. Mr. Sperry.

(2.) My authority for this statement, is his grand-daughter, Mrs. Brinley.

CHAPTER XV.
NOTICES OF TOWNS INCLUDED IN OLD DUNSTABLE

HISTORICAL SKETCH OF HUDSON

WE have seen that this town was included in the original grant of Dunstable, and was set off into a separate township by the General Assembly of Massachusetts in 1732, by the name of Nottingham. After the establishment of the boundary line, by which it fell within the limits and jurisdiction of New Hampshire, it received a new act of incorporation, July 5, 1746, and its name was changed to Nottingham West, there being already a Nottingham in the eastern section of the state. A small addition was made to its territory, by annexing a part of Londonderry, March 6, 1778, and the township now contains 17,379 acres. July 1, 1830, its name was changed by the Legislature to Hudson.

Hudson was not settled until after 1710, although several tracts of land within its bounds were granted before 1660. The names of some of the early settlers were Blodgett, Colburn, Cross, (taken captive at Dunstable, in 1724,) Cummings, Greeley, Hill, Lovewell, Marsh, Merrill, Pollard, and Winn. The first settlements were made on the banks of the Merrimac where the Indians had cleared fields for cultivating corn. The first settlers lived in garrisons, but there is no record that any depredations were ever committed by the Indians in this town. – Near the Indian cornfields have been found cinders, like those of a blacksmith's forge, which have led to the conjecture that they employed a smith to manufacture their implements of war and agriculture.

November 30, 1737, a Congregational church was formed, and on the same day Rev. Nathaniel Merrill was ordained its pastor. His relation as pastor to the church continued until his death in 1796, although his civil contract with the town was dissolved in 1774. Rev. Jabez Pond Fisher succeeded Mr. Merrill, and was ordained Feb. 24, 1796, but was dismissed in 1801. July 3, 1774, Rev. John Strickland was ordained, but after a few years was dismissed by the town. In 1805 a Baptist church was organized, over which Rev. Daniel Merrill officiated from 1814 to 1819. In 1816 the Congregational church changed their form of government and united with the Presbyterians. In 1842 a new house of worship was erected by this society; Rev. William Page is the present pastor. In 1840, a society was formed and a meeting house erected by the Methodists; Rev. Matthew Newhall is the officiating minister. In 1841 a meeting House was erected by the Baptist society, and Rev. Joseph Storer was settled as pastor.

Hudson contains no lawyer and but one physician, Dr. Henry M. Hooke. There are ten district schools, for the support of which in 1845 $700 were expended. Of this sum $430 were raised by the town, $156 given by the inhabitants in boarding teachers, $84 were derived from interest of the surplus revenue, and $30 from the Literary Fund.

In April 1776, before the Declaration of Independence, the following Test Oath was sent out to each town in the state: "We the subscribers do hereby solemnly engage and promise that we will to the utmost of our power, at the risque of our lives and fortunes, with arms oppose the Hostile Proceedings of the British Fleets and Armies against the United American Colonies." Every person was required to sign this Test, or he looked upon as an enemy to his country. These Test Oaths were returned to the Convention then in session, and a large portion of them still exist. – In Hudson 119 signed the pledge, and one only, Capt. Joseph Kelley, refused to sign. (I.)

In the old French war of 1756. two soldiers from Hudson, Amos Pollard and Asa Worcester, were in the army, in Canada. During the Revolutionary war a large number of soldiers from Hudson were in the army. Jacob Blodgett, Stephen Chase, Joshua Severance, Joseph Greeley, who was wounded, and Nehemiah Winn, were in Capt. Walker's Company at Bunker Hill. In 1777, Hudson contained 124 males from sixteen to fifty years of age, and was hound to furnish fifteen soldiers for every draft made for the army.

The following is a list of the Representatives to the General Court from Hudson, from 1775 to 1783, and since 1793:

Capt. Abraham Paige, 1775, 1776.

Asa Davis, for Hudson and Litchfield, 1777, 1779.

(1778, 1780, see Litchfield.)

William Burns, 1781, 1782.

Asa Davis, 1793, 1794, 1800, 1801, 1802, 1803, 1804, 1805, 1806, 1807, 1808.

Col. Joseph Greeley, 1795, 1796, 1797, 1811, 1815, 1816.

Robert Patterson, 1809, 1810.

Isaac Colburn, 1812.

Isaac Merrill, 1813, 1814, 1817.

Noah Robinson, 1818, 1820, 1821.

Thomas B. Mason, 1819, 1828, 1830, 1831, 1833, 1835, 1836.

Caleb S. Ford, 1822, 1823, 1824, 1825, 1826, 1827.

Reuben Greeley, 1829.

Joseph Greeley, 1837.

David Burns, 1838, 1839.

Jabez P. F. Cross, 1840, 1841, 1842.

William Hadley, 1843, 1844.

The proportionate amount which the town has paid of every thousand dollars of the State tax, has been as follows: 1789, $7.51; 1794, $6.30; 1804, $5.31; 1808, $5.04; 1812, $4.73; 1816, $4.22; 1820, $4.90; 1836, $4.78; 1840, $4.31; 1844, $4.33.

The population of the town at various periods has been as follows: 1775, 649; 1790, 1064; 1800, 1267; 1810, 1376; 1820, 1227; 1830, 1282; 1840, 1144.

In 1820, Hudson contained two meeting houses, 10 school districts, 10 school houses, 1 tavern, 3 stores, 4 saw mills, 4 grain mills, 2 clothing mills, and 1 carding machine.

The following is the return of the resources and products of Hudson in 1840, as certified by the Marshal who took the census of the town: 135 horses, 1241 neat cattle, 1403 sheep, 585 swine. There were raised 173 bushels of wheat, 377 bushels of barley, 6453 bushels of oats, 3419 bushels of rye, 1219 bushels of buckwheat, 8341 bushels of corn, 18,090 bushels of potatoes, 2398 pounds of wool, 2698 tons of hay, and 10 pounds of maple sugar. The annual value of the products of the dairy was $6,987. There are three stores with a capital of $2,600. There are also two grist mills and three saw mills.

The number of polls in Hudson in 1839 was 218; in 1840, 236.

The valuation of the town in 1839 was $386,-277; in 1840, $380,614.

HISTORICAL SKETCH OF LITCHFIELD

THE greater part of the township of Litchfield was granted, as we have seen, as early as 1656, to William Brenton, and called "Brenton's Farm." Its Indian name was Naticook, and the intervale portions of the town, as well as of Merrimac, Hudson, and Nashua, were inhabited and cultivated by a branch of the Penacooks, called sometimes, the Naticooks. It was settled about 1720, but when and by whom is unknown. Of the early settlers some were from Billerica, and some from Chelmsford, and among them were the names of Underwood, Chase, Bixby, Tufts, and Parker. It was set off from Dunstable, and incorporated by Massachusetts as a township, extending on both sides of Merrimac river, July 5, 1734. The charter was afterwards confirmed by New Hampshire, June 5, 1749, the Merrimac being established as its western boundary. It contains 8,426 acres.

In the petition for incorporation, signed by Aquila Underwood in behalf of the town, dated May, 1734, it is said "that they have supported a minister for some time." This was probably Rev. Joshua Tafts, who was settled in 1736, and dismissed in 1744. January 2, 1765, Rev. Samuel Cotton, of Newton, was ordained, – dismissed in 1784, and died at Claremont in 1819. A Presbyterian church was formed 1819, and Rev. Nathaniel Kenedy ordained April 12, 1809. He was dismissed April, 1812. Rev. Enoch Pills- bury was ordained October 25, 1815, and died February 15, 1818, aged 34. In 1825, Rev. John Shirer was minister. Rev. Mr. Porter was ordained as pastor in 1845.

In the French war of 1756, Litchfield had two soldiers at least in the army, Timothy Barron and William Barron. During the Revolutionary war also, Litchfield furnished its proportion of soldiers for the army. It contained 57 males between sixteen and fifty years of age, and its annual proportion of soldiers furnished was seven.

December 4, 1784, died Hon. Wiseman Claggett. He was born at Bristol, England, in 1721, and his father was a wealthy barrister at law. – He was educated at the Inns of Court and admitted a barrister of the King's Bench. In 1748, he went to Antigua, in the West Indies, to seek his fortune, where he remained about ten years. In 1758, he emigrated to New England, and established himself at Portsmouth, N. H. In 1775, he was appointed Attorney General of the Province by the royal commission, which he held until 1769, having been superseded by Samuel Livermore, on account of his attachment to the cause of the people. In 1772, he purchased a farm at Litchfield, and removed there with his family.

On the adoption of the Constitution of January 5, 1776, Mr. Claggett was appointed solicitor general of the State, an office which he held until his death. He was chosen a member of the Council for 1776, and appointed soon after a member of the Committee of Safety. He often represented Litchfield in the General Court, and was once chosen for Merrimac and Bedford, the law not requiring the representative to be an inhabitant of the town for which he is elected. – He was a classical scholar, a good lawyer, a wit and a poet. A full and most interesting biography, drawn up by Hon. Charles H. Atherton, is published in the third volume of the Collections of the New Hampshire Historical Society.

Dr. Jonathan Parker was also a resident of Litchfield. He graduated at Harvard College in 1762, and was a physician of considerable eminence.

Hon. James Underwood was for several years, about 1793, a Judge of the Court of Common Pleas for this County.

The following is a list of the representatives to the General Court from Litchfield, from 1775 to 1780, and since 1793:

Wiseman Claggett and Lt. Samuel Chase, April, 1775.

Capt. John Parker, May, 1775.

Wiseman Claggett, December, 1775 and 1776.

James Underwood, for Litchfield and Hudson, 1775. (See Hudson for 1779.)

Samuel Chase, for Litchfield and Hudson, 1780.

John Webster, 1793.

Robert Parker, 1794, 1806.

Jsaac Huse, 1795, 1807.

Clifton Claggett, 1800, 1802.

Samuel Chase, jr., 1804.

S. P. Kidder, 1805.

Simeon Kendall, 1808, 1810.

Joseph Moor, 1809.

Samuel Moor, 1811, 1813, 1815.

Thomas Bixby, 1812, 1814.

Joseph Chase, jr., 1816, 1817, 1818, 1824, 1825.

Simon McQuesten, 1819, 1820.

Jonathan Abbot, 1821, 1822, 1823.

Moses Chase, 1826, 1827, 1832, 1833.

Joseph Richardson, 182S, 1829, 1830, 1831.

Samuel Corning, jr., 1835, 1836.

Abel G. Quigg, 1837, 1838.

Joshua Marsh, 1839, 1840.

Parker Bixby, 1841, 1842.

Moses Chase, 1843.

Isaac McQuesten, 1844, 1845.

The proportional amount paid by Litchfield, at various periods, in every thousand dollars of the State tax, has been as follows: 1789, $3.02; 1794, $2.43; 1804, $2.04; 1808, $2.14; 1812, $1.97; 1816, $1.86; 1820, $1.90; 1836.$2.26; 1840; $2.27; 1844, $2.28.

The populaton of the town at various periods has been as follows: 1775, 284; 1790, 357; – 1800, 372; 1810, 382; 1820, 465; 1830, 505; – 1840, 481.

In 1820, Litchfield contained 1 meeting house, 3 school houses, 1 tavern, 4 saw mills, and 2 grain mills.

By the census of 1840, its resources and products were as follows: 50 horses, 423 neat cattle, 779 sheep, 265 swine, 14 bushels of wheat, 18 bushels of barley, 5349 bushels of oats, 1342 bushels of rye, 669 bushels of buckwheat, 4072 bushels of corn, 7315 bushels of potatoes, 1236 pounds of wool, 664 tons of hay. The value of the products of the dairy was $1410.00. – There were 2 stores with a capital invested of $15,000.00.

The number of polls in Litchfield was in 1839, 114; in 1840, 103.

The valuation of the town in 1839. was $175,- 615; in 1840, $178,920.

HISTORICAL SKETCH OF MERRIMAC

ALL that part of Merrimac which lies south of the Souhegan river, was included in the Dunstable grant. Its Indian name was Naticook. In July, 1729, the lands lying north of the Souhegan, three miles in width, were granted to Capt. Joseph Blanchard and others. In 1733, all these grants lying north of Penichuck Brook, and including a part of Narragansett No. 5, or Amherst, (granted to the soldiers of Philip's war) were incorporated into a township, at first called Souhegan East; then Rumford, and afterwards Merrimac. April 2, 1746, it was chartered anew by the Legislature of New Hampshire, and contains 19,361 acres.

Merrimac was settled about 1722, and among its earliest inhabitants were the names of Usher, Hassell, and Chamberlain. A daughter of Hassell is said have been the first person born in the town. About 1670, John Cromwell built a trading house at Cromwell's Falls, but was soon driven away by the Indians. His house was standing in 1679. The account of Cromwell with the Indian history of the town, is incorporated with that of Dunstable.

September 5, 1772, a Congregational Church was formed, and October 14, 1772, Rev. Jacob Burnap, D. D., from Reading, Mass., who graduated at Harvard College in 1770, was ordained. He died December 27, 1821, having admitted to the church 194 members. He was eminently distinguished for his superior knowledge of the original languages, in which the scriptures were written, and was much esteemed for his piety, integrity, patience, and all the social virtues. – His son, Rev. George W. Burnap, is now a distinguished clergyman in Baltimore, Md. Since the death of Dr. Burnap, there have been various ministers. At present Rev. Mr. Allen is their pastor.

At the mouth of the Souhegan is a valuable water privilege, upon which a factory was erected many years ago, by Isaac Riddle and Sons. It was consumed by fire June 10, 1818, with a loss of $6,000. Another factory, called "the Souhegan Cotton, Woollen, and Nail Factory," was afterwards erected, and shared the same fate. – There are other privileges upon the river, and it is a matter of regret that they should remain so long unimproved.

"This town claims the first discovery in this region of the art of making what are called ' Leghorn Bonnets,' and other grass work. They were first made by the Misses Burnap, before 1820, who are deserving of much credit for their skill and enterprise in this species of manufacture. Some of their bonnets have been sold in Boston as high as $50.00.

Hon. Matthew Thornton, one of the signers of the Declaration of Independence, resided in this town for many years previous to his death. He was a native of Ireland, but emigrated to this country at an early age. He first settled in the eastern part of the State, from which he removed to Londonderry, and afterwards to Merrimac in 1780. Before the Revolution he was eminent as a physician. He was also a Colonel in the militia, and in 1775 was President of the Convention which met at Exeter, and assumed the Government of the Colony in the name of the

People. He was chosen a delegate to the Congress which met at Philadelphia in 1776, and as such affixed his name to the Declaration of Independence.

He held the office of Chief Justice of the Court of Common Pleas for the County, and afterwards was a Judge of the Supreme Court of the State until 1782. Subsequently he was a member of the House of Representatives, and also of the Senate, and in 1775 was a member of the Coun- cil. He died while on a visit to Newburyport, Mass., June 24, 1803, aged 88.

Edward Goldstone Lutwyche, Esq., an English gentleman of education and property, resided in Merrimac before 1776, at Thornton's, then called Lutwyche's Ferry. He was Colonel of the regiment in 1775, but on the Declaration of Independence he joined the English, left the country, to which he never returned, and at the close of the war his estate was confiscated by the State.

Hon. James B. Thornton, a grandson of Hon. Matthew Thornton, died at Callao, Peru, January 25, 1838. At the time of his death he was Charge des Affaires of the United States, within that Province. For several years he represented Merrimac in the Legislature, and was Speaker of the House in 1829. In 1830, he was appointed Second Comptroller of the Treasury in the United States. In this situation he remained at Washington until 1836, when he was sent abroad to Lima. He died, greatly lamented, at the early age of 38.

The following information relative to the history of the church in Merrimac was furnished by Rev. Mr. Allen:

"The first church in Merrimac was gathered September 5, 1771, and at that time consisted of ten male and three female members. On the 9th of January following, they voted to call Mr. Jacob Burnap, a native of Reading, Mass., and a graduate of Harvard College, to be their pastor. He accepted the call, and was ordained October 14, of the same year. He continued in this relation to them more than forty-nine years, when he was removed by death in December, 1821. Dr. Burnap was a man of sound mind and mature scholarship. He won the confidence and affection of his people by his amiable and pacific character. The whole town was united in one religious society up to the time of his death.

The old meeting house, the first and only one ever built by the town, still remains a relic of olden time. It was erected in 1756, and is unoccupied except as a town house for secular purposes. The religious society which formerly worshipped in it, built a neat and commodious house of worship in 1837, which is located on the river road, a mile and a half to the northeast of the old house. The corporate name of this society is 'The Merrimac Religious Society.' Their first pastor, after the death of Dr. Burnap, was Rev. Stephen Morse, a graduate of Dartmouth College, in 1820, and a native of Bradford, Mass." Rev. Stephen T. Allen, the present pastor, succeeded Mr. Morse, and was installed May 22, 1839.

There is one other religious society in Merrimac, which was formed October 21, 1829. It is composed of persons residing in Merrimac, Amherst, Hollis, Nashville and Milford. The name of their church is the "Union Evangelical Church in Merrimac." Their house of worship was built in the summer of 1829. It is situated on the road from Nashville to Amherst, within the limits of Merrimac, about 20 rods from Amherst line, and not much farther from the line of Hollis. Their pastor is Rev. John W. Shepard.

James U; Parker is the only lawyer in Merrimac.

The physicians are Harrison Eaton, M. D., and William V. Magoon.

The Representatives to the General Court from Merrimac, from 1775 to 1783, and since 1793, have been as follows:

Capt. John Chamberlain, April, 1775.

Jacob McGaw, May, 1775.

Wiseman Claggett, (of Litchfield) 1777, 1780.

Capt. Samuel Patten, (of Bedford,) for Merrimac and Bedford, 1778, 1781.

John Orr, (of Bedford,) for Merrimac and Bedford, 1779.

Jacob McGaw, 1782.

Timothy Taylor, 1793, 1794.

James Thornton, 1796, 1806, 1808, 1809, 1810, 1812.

Simeon Cummings, 1797.

Samuel Foster, 1800, 1801, 1802, 1803, 1804, 1805.

Samuel McConihe, 3d., 1807.

Daniel Ingalls, 1811, 1815, 1816.

Henry Fields, 1813, 1814.

Aaron Gage, jr., 1817, 1818, 1819, 1820, 1821, 1822, 1823, 1824.

Henry T. Ingalls, 1825, 1826.

James B. Thornton, 1827, 1828, 1829, 1830.

Joseph Litchfield, 1831, 1832.

Samuel McConihe, 1833, 1834.

Samuel Barron, jr., 1835, 1836.

Oliver Spalding, jr., 1837, 1838.

Francis Odell, 1839, 1840.

Robert McGaw, 1841.

Leonard Walker, 1842, 1843.

James U. Parker, 1844, 1845.

The proportion of every thousand dollars of the State tax paid by the town of Merrimac at various periods has been as follows: 1789, $5.62; 1794, $5.24; 1804, $4.74; 1808, $4.20; 1812, $3.83; 1816, $4.20; 1820, $4.33; 1836, $4.29; 1840, $4.30; 1844, $4.79.

The population of the town at various periods has been as follows: 1775, 606; 1790, 819; 1800, 926; 1810, 1048; 1820, 1162; 1830, 1191; 1840, 1113.

In 1820, Merrimac contained 1 meeting house, 9 school districts and school houses, 5 taverns, 5 stores, 8 saw mills, 5 grain mills, 2 clothing mills, 2 carding machines, 2 tanneries.

The resources and products of the town as returned by the census of 1840, were as follows: 174 horses, 968 neat cattle, 844 sheep, 551 swine, 213 bushels of wheat, 147 bushels of barley, 7150 bushels of oats, 4772 bushels of rye, 908 bushels of buckwheat, 6463 bushels of corn, 14,969 bushels of potatoes, 1532 pounds of wool, 1480 tons of hay. The estimated value of the products of the dairy was $5,784. There were 4 retail stores, with a capital invested of $12,400. There were six grist mills, and 6 saw mills.

The number of polls in 1839 was 255; in 1840, 241. The valuation of the town in 1839 was $432,072; in 1840, $430,574.

HISTORICAL SKETCH OF HOLLIS

THE township of Hollis was entirely included within the Dunstable grant, and continued to form a part of Dunstable until December 28, 1739, when it was set off as the "West Parish of Dunstable," and soon after was incorporated into a separate township by the name of Hollis. Its Indian name was Nisitisset. It was incorporated by the Legislature of New Hampshire, April 3, 1746.

The earliest settlement in Hollis was made in 1730, by Capt. Peter Powers, who was born in Littleton, Mass., in 1707. In 1728, he married Anna Rogers, of Chelmsford, who was born in 1708. He had been a soldier in 1725, under Capt. Lovewell, and on his return settled at Dunstable. Here he brought his wife upon his marriage, and resided about two years. In the fall of 1730, he crossed the Nashua, – built him cabin in the forest, and in January, 1731, with his wife and two small children, took up his abode in Hollis. The remains of his dwelling were visible in 1830, "a little southwest of the dwelling house of Thomas Cummings." (1.)

"In the summer of 1732, Eleazer Flagg came into the town, and located himself in the southwest part of it, on or near the place now (1830) owned or improved by his descendant, Capt. Reuben Flagg. The house of Mr. Flagg, was subsequently improved as a guard house, and was fortified against an attack of the Indians. The same season, March 9, 1732, Anna Powers, daughter of Peter Powers, was born, and was the first English child born in Hollis. She married Benjamin Hopkins, Esq., of Milford, and died at an advanced age. Thomas Dinsmore, who was the third family in the settlement, came in and located himself on the place now (1830) owned or occupied by Amos Eastman, Esq., and in 1736, the little Colony was augmented to the number of nine families."

In 1741, a meeting house was erected upon the spot now occupied by the Congregational meeting, which for a century has been improved for sacred purposes. Rev. Daniel Emerson, who was bom at Reading, Mass., May 20, 1716, and graduated at Harvard College 1739, was ordained as pastor 20th. April, 1743. At this time there were thirty families in town.

Hollis never sustained any injury from the Indians, although at one time considerable alarm was excited, since May 20, 1746, they "Voted to Petition the General Court of Massachusetts Bay for some soldiers for a Guard for us, being in great danger of the enemy."

In the old French war of 1775, Capt. Peter Powers, of Hollis, commanded a company which was made up from Hollis, Nashua and the vicinity. The following is the muster roll: Captain, Peter Powers; Lieutenant, Benjamin Abbot; Ensign, William Cummings; Ebenezer Lyon, David Hubbard, Samuel Cummings, Sergeants; James Colburn, Clerk; Jonathan Powers, Enoch Noyes, Stephen Hoseltine, James Brown, Corporals; Samuel Brown, Drummer; James Hill, Peter Wheeler, John Martin, John Martin, Jr., James Wheeler, Daniel Wheeler, John Goodhue, Ebenezer Ball, Nathaniel Blanchard, Timothy Farley, Samuel Barrett, Josiah French, Moses Emerson, John Willoby, Christopher Lovejoy, Isaac Sterns, Jacob Abbot, Timothy Richardson, Levi Powers, Philip Ollereck, Richard Adams, Whitcomb Powers, Samuel Sampson, Micah Perkins, Luther Richardson, Thomas Williams, David Hartshorn, John Everden, Jabez Davis, Samuel Perham, Jonathan Fowler, John Secomb, Samuel Fisk, Nathaniel Townsend, Stephen Powers, George Leslie, Benjamin Hildreth, Ephraim Kellogg, David Turner, Robert Gordon, John Flagg, Samuel Skinner. Rev. Daniel Emerson, was Chaplain of the regiment. Dr. John Hall, Surgeon, and Samuel Hobart, all of Hollis, Adjutant.

In 1760, Hollis contained sixty taxable persons. In 1767, it had 81 unmarried males from sixteen to sixty years of age, and 117 married males from sixteen to sixty. August 25, 1775, it had 306 males under sixteen years of age; 174 males from sixteen to fifty; 71 over fifty. There were 60 men in the army, of whom 10 died. The whole number of males capable of bearing arms was 223.

A company of 70 men from Hollis, was in the battle of Bunker Hill, under Capt. Reuben Dow. John Cross was

Lieutenant, and John Cummings, Ensign. This company, as well as the other soldiers from this vicinity, were under the command of Col. Stark and Col. Prescott, and were in the thickest of the fight. Seven were killed, viz: Nathan Blood, Jacob Boynton, Isaac Hobart, Phineas Nevers, Peter Poor, Thomas Wheeler, and Ebenezer Youngman. Six more were wounded, among whom was Capt. Dow. "Caleb Eastman lost his life the second day after by the accidental discharge of a gun while on parade." "In December, 1775, Capt. Noah Worcester marched at the head of a company, about thirty of whom were Hollis men." "July, 1776, Capt. Daniel Emerson marched at the head of a company to Ticonderoga; about half of his company were Hollis men. In August, 1776, Capt. William Reed (of Litchfield) marched with a company to New York, about 20 of whom belonged to this town. In 1777, Capt. John Goss marched to Bennington with a company, of which about thirty were from Hollis." This was the quota of this town during the war. The town had in the army at various times during the war about two hundred and fifty men, of whom thirty died in the service.

Of the Royalist refugees three resided in Hollis, viz: Samuel Cummings, Esq., Benjamin Whiting, Esq., and Thomas Cummings. They were included in the Outlawry Act, and the estates of the two first were confiscated.

November 27, 1793, Rev. Eli Smith, (born at Belcherton, Mass., 1759; graduated Brown University, 1792,) was ordained as a colleague of Rev. Mr. Emerson. Mr.

Emerson died 30th September, 1801, aged 85. His wife, Hannah, daughter of Rev. Joseph Emerson, of Malden, died 25th. February, 1812, aged 90. Rev. David Perry succeeded Rev. Mr. Smith in the ministry of Hollis. There are now (1846) two religious societies in town, an Orthodox Congregationalist, and a Baptist society. Rev. James Aikin is settled over the former, and Rev. Phineas Richardson over the latter. The meeting house now occupied by the Congregational society, was erected in 1804, and the Baptist house in 1837.

The physicians now residing in Hollis, are Wm. Hale, Oliver Scripture, Noah Hardy, John L. Colby, and O. M. Cooper.

Benjamin M. Farley is the only lawyer in town.

A large number of natives of this town have enjoyed a collegiate education. Up to 1823 they were as follows:

At Harvard College. – Rev. Peter Powers, 1754; Rev. Josiah Goodhue, 1755; Rev. Henry Cummings, D. D., 1760; Joseph Emerson, 1774; Dr. Samuel Emerson, 1785; Josiah Burge, 1787; Rev. Daniel Emerson, 1794; Rev. Joseph Emerson, 1798; Benjamin M. Farley, 1804; Dr. Benjamin Burge, 1805; John Proctor, 1813; Rev. William P. Kendrick, 1815; George F. Farley, 1816; Taylor G. Worcester, 1823.

Dartmouth College. – Rev. Samuel Worcester, D. D., 1795; Rev. Abel Farley, 1798; Rev, Mighill Blood, 1800; Rev. David Jewett, 1801; Rev. Caleb J. Tenney, 1801; Jonathan Eastman, 1803; Dr. Noah Hardy, 1803; Rev. Stephen Farley, 1804; Rev. Eli Smith, 1809; Rev. Grant Powers, 1810; Rev. Leonard Jewett, 1810; Dr. Noah Hardy, 1812; Luke Eastman, 1812.

Yale College. – Joseph E. Worcester, 1811; Rev. Ralph Emerson, 1811.

Brown University. – Rev. Daniel Kendrick, 1809; Luther Smith.

Middlebury College. – William Tenney, 1808; – Rev. Fifield Holt, and Solomon Hardy.

Tennessee College. – Eli Sawtell.

Since 1823, a large number have been educated at various Colleges, among whom are Jonathan Sanderson, Benjamin F. Emerson, Joseph Emerson, Henry Sanderson. John G. Worcester, Benjamin F. Farley. In 1830, Hollis had raised and educated 30 ministers, 8 lawyers, and 11 physicians.

Rev. Noah Worcester, D. D., was also a native of Hollis.

The number of deaths for 25 years, ending 1818, was 567. One in nine of this number, lived to the age of SO years or upwards. Mrs. Elizabeth French, died in 1749, aged 103. Mrs. Ulrich, a native of Ireland, died here in 1789, at the age of 104, and was active until she was more than a hundred years old. She lived for many years in Nashua, where the family is called Ollerick upon the records of the town. Capt. Caleb Farley died in 1830, aged 100. In 1830, there were 70 persons in town over 70 years of age, of whom 27 were over 80; and one, Mrs. Elizabeth Hale, was 98!

The Representatives of Hollis in the General Court, from 1775 to 1782, and since 1793, have been as follows:

Samuel Hobart, April, 1775.

Capt. John Hale, May, 1775.

Stephen Ames, December. 1775, 1776, 1777, 1778.

Reuben Dow, 1779.

John Hale, 1780.

Capt. Daniel Emerson, 1781.

Jeremiah Ames, 1793, 1794, 1796, 1798, 1800.

Daniel Emerson, 1801, 1802, 1803, 1809, 1810, 1811.

Benjamin Poole, 1804, 1805, 1806, 1807, 1808.

Nathan Thayer, 1812, 1819, 1820, 1821.

Daniel Bailey, 1813.

Beniamin M. Farley, 1814, 1815, 1816, 1817, 1818, 1824, 1825, 1826, 1827, 1828, 1829.

Ralph W. Jewett, 1822, 1823.

Jonathan T. Wright, 1830, 1831.

Ralph E. Tenney, 1832, 1833, 1834.

Moses Proctor, 1835, 1836, 1837.

Joseph E. Smith, 1838, 1839.

Leonard Farley, 1840, 1841, 1842.

William Merrill, 1843, 1844.

Ralph E. Tenney, 1845.

The proportion of every thousand dollars of the State tax paid by the town of Hollis, at various periods, has been as follows: 1794, $7.77; 1804, $6.57: 1808, $5.62; 1812, $5.32; 1816, $5.13; 1820, $5.52; 1836, $5.50; 1840, $5.79; 1844, $5.69.

The population of the town at various periods, has been as follows: 1775, 1255; 1790, 1441; 1800, 1557; 1810, 1529; 1820, 1543; 1830, 1501; 1840, 1333.

In 1820, Hollis contained 1 meeting house, 12 school houses, 2 taverns, 4 stores, 6 saw mills, 5 grain mills, 1 clothing mill, 1 carding machine, 1 tannery.

The resources and products of Hollis, in 1840, as returned by the United States census, were as follows: 190 horses, 1530 neat cattle, 1055 sheep, 358 swine, 1815 bushels of wheat, 447 bushels of barley, 3988 bushels of oats, 3983 bushels of rye, 578 bushels of buckwheat, 7648 bushels of corn, 17,935 bushels of potatoes, 2G25 pounds of wool, 1806 tons of hay. The value of the products of the dairy was $3,575. There were 2 stores with a capital of $8,000 invested; 3 grain mills, and 3 saw mills.

NOTES:

(1.) The Test Returns from Dunstable, Hollis, Merrimac, and Litchfield are not to be found.

(1.) The Centennial Anniversary was celebrated 15th September, 1830, and an address delivered by a descendant, Rev. Grant Powers. I am indebted to his address for many of the above facts.

APPENDIX NO. I.
GENEALOGY OF THE EARLY SETTLERS OF DUNSTABLE

THERE is a natural desire in every man to know something of his ancestry, and to the descendants of the early settlers of Dunstable it must be interesting to trace back their families to their origin. The materials for this purpose exist, to a great extent, in the ancient records of Marriages, Births and Deaths among the town papers, a large part of which were collected, compared, and arranged by John Farmer, Esq. His deserved reputation as an antiquarian is a guarantee of its accuracy. The list is not generally brought down to a period later than 1750; to have extended it would have required too much time and space.

ACRES, JOHN. – He was of Boston in 1656; settled in Dunstable before 1680; and bad children, *Mary*, born 26th. May, 1682, and *Joanna*, born 10th. Jan., 1684.

ADAMS, THOMAS. – Born 1675: died 18th. Feb., 1746, aged 71. His wife, *Judy*, born 1680: died loth. April, 1754, aged 74. Had children, *Phinehas*, born 1724: died 4th. Dec., 1747, aged 23.

BLANCHARD, DEA. JOHN. – One of the founders of the church in 1685; freeman 1649; son of Thomas Blanchard, who came to New England in the ship Jonathan, in 1639. Settled in Charlestown, and died there 21st. May, 1654. He left children, *Joseph* and *Thomas*.

BLANCHARD, CAPT. JOSEPH. – Son of preceding; married *Abiah Hassell*, daughter of Joseph Hassell, Sen., 25th. May, 1696. She died 8th. Dec., 1746, aged 70. He died in 1727. His children were, 1. *Elizabeth*, born 15th. April, 1697: married *Jona. Cummings*; 2. *Esther*, born 24th. July, 1699; 3. *Hannah*, born 28th. Oct., 1701; 4. *Joseph*, born 11th. Feb., 1704; 5. *Rachel*, born 23rd. March, 1705: died in infancy; 6. *Susanna*, born 29th. March, 1707; 7. *Jane*, born 19th. March, 1709: married *Rev. Josiah Swan*; 8. *Rachel*, born 23rd. March, 1712; 9. *Eleazer*, born 1st. Dec., 1715: died 29th. April 1717.

BLANCHARD, COL. JOSEPH. – Son of the preceding; born 11th. Feb., 1704: married *Rebecca Hubbard*; died 7th. April, 1758: she died 17th. April, 1774. His children were, 1. *Sarah*, born 1706: died 30th. Nov., 1726; 2. *Joseph*, born 28th. April, 1729; 3 and 4. *Eleazer* and *Susanna*, born 15th. Nov., 1730: Eleazer died 19th. March, 1753, aged 22; 5. *Rebecca*, born 20th. July, 1732; 6, *Sarah*, born 7th. Oct., 1734: died in infancy; 7. *Catherine*, born 11th. Nov., 1736; 8. *Jonathan*, born 18th. Sept., 1738: died 18th. July, 1788; 9. *Sarah*, born 2d. Aug., 1740; 10. *James*, born 20th. Sept., 1742: in army; 11. *Augustus*, born 29th. July, 1746: died at Milford, 1809; 12. *Caleb*, born 15th. Aug., 1549; 13. *Hannah*, born 21st. Oct., 1751: married *Dr. Ebenezer Starr*, of D., 21st. April, 1776: died 22d. March, 1794, aged 42.

BLANCHARD, HON. JONATHAN. – Son of the preceding; born 18th. Sept., 1738: married *Rebecca Farwell*, of this town, who died 20th. Aug., 1811, aged 72. He died 10th. July, 1788, aged 50. His children were, 1.

Rebecca, born 4th. May, 1766: married *Dr. Augustus Starr:* died 19th. Oct., 1810, aged 45; 2. *Grace,* who married *Frederick French, Esq.;* 3. *Sophia:* married *Oliver Farwell,* and still living; 4. *Charles,* born 14th. March, 1776: died at Batavia, New York, 16th. March, 1811; 5. *Abigail:* married *Dr. Joseph F. Eastman,* of Hollis, and still living. *Eliza* married *Thomas French Esq.:* died 1843.

BLANCHARD, THOMAS. – Son of *Dea. John;* born about 1670: married *Tabitha——,* who died 29th. Nov., 1696: married *Ruth Adams,* of Chelmsford, 4th. Oct., 1698: died 9th. March, 1727. His children were, 1, *Abigail,* born 5th. May, 1694; 2. *John,* born 20th. May, 1696; 3. *Thomas,* born 12th. Aug., 1799: taken captive by the Indians in September, 1724; 4. *William,* born 1701; 5. *Ruth,* born 1st. April, 1703.

BLANCHARD, THOMAS, Jr., and *Elizabeth,* his wife; – son of the preceding. Had a son *Thomas,* 3d., born 20th. Oct., 1724.

BLANCHARD, JOHN. – Son of *Thomas, Sen.,* born 20th. May, 1696: wife's name, *Mary.* Had a son *William.*

BLANCHARD, NATHANIEL, and *Lydia,* his wife; – killed by the Indians, 3d. July, 1706. Had a son, *Nathaniel, 2d.,* born 12th. Sept., 1705.

BLANCHARD, WILLIAM. – Son of *Thomas,* born 1701: married *Deliverance,* daughter of *Samuel Searles.* Had children, *Olive,* horn 4th. November, 1733; *Nathaniel* born 25th. Dec., 1735.

BEALE, WILLIAM. – Had children, *William,* born 12th. March, 1685, and *Elizabeth* born 16th. Nov., 1686.

BEALE, SAMUEL. – Had children, *Samuel,* born 3d. July, 1685, and *Ebenezer,* born 30th. Jan., 1688.

BANCROFT, LIEUT. TIMOTHY. – Came from ———; born in 1709: died 21st. Nov., 1772, aged 63. He had children, *Col. Ebenezer,* born 1737: an officer in the French and Revolutionary wars, and in the battle of Bunker Hill: died 22d. Sept., 1827, aged 90; *Dea. Jonathan,* born 1750: died 11th. July, 1815, aged 65.

COLBURN, THOMAS. – Probably from Chelmsford, and a son of *Edward Colburn;* born about 1675: died 2d. Nov., 1770, aged 96; his wife died 7th. Sept., 1739, aged 59. His children were, 1. *Elizabeth,* born 29th. Sept., 1700; 2. *Thomas,* born 28th. April, 1702: died 18th. April, 1724; 3. *Hannah,* born 21st. Jan., 1704: died 8th. March, 1718; 4. *Edward,* born 14th. Dec., 1705: died 18th. April, 1724; 5. a *daughter,* born 2Sth. Nov., 1707; 6. a *son,* born April, 1709; 7. *Sarah;* 8. *Bridget,* born 20th. Aug., 1717; 9. *Louisa,* born 1718; 10. *Rachel,* born 18th. Sept., 1721.

COLBURN, THOMAS, and *Elizabeth,* his wife. Had a son *Isaac,* born 28th. Dec., 1811.

CUMMINGS, JOHN, SEN. – His wife was *Sarah* ———, who died 7th. Dec., 1700; he died 1st. Dec., 1700. – His children were, *John, Nathaniel, Sarah, Thomas, Abraham, Isaac,* and *Ebenezer.* The two latter were either killed by the Indians, or were drowned, as they "died Nov. 2, 1688," and were not buried for many days after.

CUMMINGS, JOHN, JR. – Son of preceding; married *Elizabeth*———, 13th. Sept., 1680. She was killed by the

Indians, 3d. July, 1706. His children were, 1. *John*, born 7th. July, 1682; 2. *Samuel*, born 6th. Oct., 1684; 3. *Elizabeth*, born 5th. Jan., 1687; 4. *Anna*, born 14th. Sept., 1698; 5. *Lydia*, born 24th. March, 1701: died April, 1701; 6. *William*, born 24th. April, 1702.

CUMMINGS, NATHANIEL. – Son of *John, Sen.* His children were, 1. *John*, born 14th. Jan., 1698; 2. *Nathaniel*, born 8th. Sept., 1699; 3. *Eliezer*, born 19th. Oct., 1701; 4. *Joseph*, born 26th. May, 1704.

CUMMINGS, ABRAHAM. – Son of *John, Sen.* Had a son *Josiah*, born 12th. July, 1698.

CUMMINGS, THOMAS. – Son of *John, Sen.;* born in 1659: married *Priscilla Wamer*, sister of *Samuel W.,* of D., 19th. Dec., 1688: died 20th. Jan., 1723. His children were, 1. *Priscilla*, born 1st. Oct., 1689; 2. *Mary*, born 25th. April, 1692; 3. *Anna*, born 6th. Feb., 1699; 4. *Thomas*, born 10th. April, 1701; 5. *Jonathan*, born 3d. July, 1703: married *Elizabeth*, daughter of *Capt. Joseph Blanchard;* 6. *Ephraim*, born 10th. March, 1706: 7. *Samuel*, born 12th. April, 1708.

CUMMINGS, DEA. WILLIAM. – Son of *John, Jr.;* born 24th. April, 1702: married *Sarah*, daughter of *William Harwood:* died 9th. Sept., 1758. His children were, 1. *Sarah*, born 10th. Nov., 1728; 2. *Ebenezer*, born 29th. Jan., 1730; 3. *John Harwood*, bom 24th. April, 1733; 4. *Dorcas*, born 18th. Dec., 1737.

CUMMINGS, JONATHAN. – Son of *Thomas;* born 3d. July, 1703: married *Elizabeth*, daughter of *Capt. Joseph Blanchard*, and had a son, *Benjamin Blanchard*, born 15th. Aug., 1732.

CUMMINGS, SAMUEL, (and *Prudence*, his wife,) son of *Thomas*; born 12th. April, 1708. Had daughters *Sybil*, born 1st. Nov., 1736; *Prudence*, born 26th. Nov., 1740.

CUMMINGS, NATHANIEL, JR. – Son of *Nathaniel*; – born 8th. Sept., 1699: married *Elizabeth* ——. His children were, 1. *Nathaniel*, born 7th. July, 1724; 2. *Jeremiah*, born 27th. Dec., 1726: 3. *Oliver*, born 10th. April, 1728; 4. *Elizabeth*, born 30th. Dec., 1730; 5. *Abigail*, born 12th. Feb., 1732.

CUMMINGS, ELEAZER. – Son of *Nathaniel, Sen.*; born 19th. Oct., 1701: married *Rachel* —— Had a son *Eleazer*, born 15th. Dec., 1730.

COOK, ANDREW. – His children were *Lydia*, born 26th. July, 1686; and *Andrew, Alice*, and *Elizabeth*, born afterwards.

COFFIN, REV. ENOCH. – From Newbury, Mass. Had a daughter, *Mehitable*, born 5th. Nov., 1719. Settled in Concord, N. H.

DARBYSHIRE, JOHN. – His children were, 1. *William*, born 14th. Aug., 1698; 2. *James*, born 30th. April, 1702.

DANFORTH, JOSEPH. – Died in Tyngsborough, 30th. March, 1795, aged 75.

FARWELL, HENRY. – From Chelmsford; a son of *Henry Farwell, of* Concord. His children were, 1. *Henry*; 2. *Oliver*, born 1691: killed by the Indians at Naticook, 5th. Sept., 1724; 3. *Josiah*, the only survivor of that fight: was a lieutenant under Lovewell, and killed at Pigwacket, 8th. May, 1725; 4. *Jonathan*, born 24th. July, 1700; 5. *Susanna*, born 19th. Feb., 1703; 6. *Isaac*, born 4th. Dec., 1704; 7. *Sarah*, born 4th. Dec., 1706.

FARWELL, HENRY, JR. – Son of the preceding; married *Esther Blanchard,* daughter of *Capt. Joseph Blanchard.* His children were, 1. *Eleazer,* born 7th. Oct., 1726; 2. *Esther,* born 16th. May, 1730; 3. *Olive,* born 19th. July, 1732.

FARWELL, JONATHAN. – Son of *Henry, Sen.;* born 24th. July, 1700: married *Susanna*——. His children were, 1. *Susanna,* born 17th. Jan., 1724; 2. *Rachel,* born 19th. Feb., 1728; 3. *Jonathan,* born 28th. Aug., 1729.

FARWELL, OLIVER. – Son of *Henry, Sen.;* born 1691: married *Mary Cummings,* daughter of *Thomas Cummings:* killed by the Indians, 5th. Sept., 1724, aged 33. His children were, 1. *Mary,* born 8th. May, 1716; 2, *Oliver,* born 19th. Nov., 1717: married *Abigail* ——. who died 18th. Aug., 1789, aged *68:* he died 12th. Oct., 1808, in this town, aged 91; 3. *Benjamin,* born 14th. May, 1720: died 20th. March, 1772; 4. *Sarah,* born 8th. May, 1724.

FARWELL, LT. JOSIAH. – Son of *Henry, Sen.;* married *Hannah Lovewell.* Had a daughter *Hannah,* born 27th. Jan., 1723.

FARWELL, ISAAC. – Son of *Henry, Sen,;* born 4th. Dec., 1704. His children were, 1. *Elizabeth;* 2. *Josiah,* born 19th. Aug., 1728; 3. *Relief;* 4. *Bunker,* born 28th. Jan., 1732; 5. *Abigail; 6. Isaac,* born 18th. Feb., 1736.

FLETCHER, ROBERT. – Came from Chelmsford. His children were, 1. *Sarah,* born 1st. March, 1724; 2. *Robert,* born 1727: died 9th. Sept., 1792, aged 65; 3. *Elizabeth;* 4. *Mary.* '

FLETCHER, ROBERT. – Son of the preceding; born 1727: died 9th. Sept., 1792, aged 65. Had children, *Robert,* born 1st. Aug., 1762; *Hannah.*

FRENCH, SAMUEL. – Son of *Lt. William French;* bom at Cambridge, 3d. Dec., 1645: removed to Billerica, and thence to Dunstable: married *Sarah,* daughter of *John Cummings, Sen.,* 24th. Dec., 1682. His children were 1. *Sarah,* born Feb., 1684; 2. *Samuel,* born 10th. Sept., 1685, died 4th. Nov. 1727; 3. *Joseph,* born 10th. March, 1687; 4. *John,* born May, 1691; 5. *Ebenezer,* born 7th. April, 1693: killed by Indians 5th. Sept., 1724; 6. *Richard,* born 8th. April, 1695; 7. *Alice,* born 20th. Nov., 1699; 8. *Jonathan,* born 1st. Feb., 1704: a deacon: – died 17th. Nov., 1757.

FRENCH, JOSEPH. – Son of preceding; born 10th. March, 1687: married *Elizabeth,* daughter of *John Cummings, Jr.* His children were, 1. *Joseph,* born 28th. July, 1713; 2. *Sampson,* born 28th. July, 1717; 3. *Jo- siah,* born 24th. Feb., 1723; 4. *Thomas,* born 29th. June, 1724; 5. *Benjamin,* born 6th. July, 1726; 6. *Samuel,* born 10th. Aug., 1730.

FRENCH, SAMUEL. – Perhaps a brother of *Henry French;* born about 1665. His children were, *John,* born 6th. May, 1691; and *Ebenezer,* born 7th. April, 1693.

FRENCH, JOHN. – Son of *Samuel;* born 6th. May, 1691. His children *were, John,* born 1st. March, 1719; *William,* born 18th. Oct., 1721; and *Hannah, Eleazer* and *Elizabeth, Ebenezer,* and *Sarah,* born from 1723 to 1733.

FRENCH, EBENEZER. – Son *of Samuel;* born 7th. April, 1693: killed by the Indians at Naticook Brook, 5th. Sept., 1724. Had a son, *Ebenezer,* born 27th. Oct., 1723.

FRENCH, JOSEPH, JR. – Son of *Joseph;* born 28th. July, 1713: died 21st. April, 1776. His first wife, Bridget

——, died 29th. Oct., 1735, aged 29: childless; his second wife, *Elizabeth* ——, died 20th. Jan., 1753, aged 44. Had a son, *Joseph,* born 1st. Nov., 1739: was a Colonel, and died 1770: married *Sybil Richardson,* who died 3d. March, 1768.

FRENCH, THEODORE.-Son of *Joseph 3d.;* born 6th. Jan., 1759 married *Rhoda Danforth,* 4th. Oct., 1781. – His children were, 1. *Joseph,* born 22d. Nov., 1783; 2. *Theodore,* born 19th. Dec., 1786: married *Lydia Allds,* of D., now of Concord, N. H.; 3. *Jacob,* born 24th. Oct., 3789: of Stoddard.

FRENCH, BENJAMIN. – Son of *Joseph, Sen.;* born 6th. July, 1726: married *Molly,* daughter of *Col. Zaccheus Lovewell,* 28th. Jan., 3751, who died 17th. Dec., 1774; and for a *second* wife, *Mrs. Mary Cummings,* 1st. Feb., 1776. He died 15th. Dec., 1799, aged 74. His children were, *Benjamin,* born 4th. Dec., 1752: died 29th. Oct., 1776, aged 23; *Esther; Augustus; Betty; Charlotte; Frederic,* born 26th. Sept., 1766; *Thomas,* born 7th. May, 1768; *Lucy,* married *James Cummings,* 5th. July, 1787: and *Bridget.*

FRENCH, FREDERIC. – Son of the preceding; born 26th. Sept., 1766: married *Grace,* daughter of *Hon. Jonathan Blanchard,* 30th. Dec., 1790: died at Amherst, N. H. His children were, *Benjamin Frederic, born 2d. Oct., 1791; Charles; Arthur; Rebecca; and Edward.*

FRENCH, THOMAS. – Son of *Capt. Benjamin;* born 7th. May, 1768: married *Elizabeth Blanchard,* 7th. Jan., 1796; he died 3d. May, 1846, aged 78: she died 4th. May, 1843. Their children were, *Jonathan Blanchard,* born 16th. Oct., 1796; *Mary; Elizabeth; Caroline; Thomas; Benjamin;* and *Charles.*

HARWOOD, WILLIAM. – Born in 1665: married *Esther ——* –; he died 17th. Sept., 1740, aged 75: she died 8th. Oct., 1737, aged 72. His children were, *John,* killed in the Pigwacket Fight, 8th. May, 1725; *Thomas,* born 9th. Jan., 1702; *Mary; Sarah; Abigail; Rachel; Dorcas;* and *Lydia.*

HASSELL, JOSEPH, SEN. – Of Cambridge: freeman 1647: his wife was *Joanna——*; both killed by the Indians, Sept., 1791. His children were, 1. *Joseph, born* at Cambridge, 1645; 2. *Esther,* born at Cambridge, 1648: married *Obadiah Perry;* 3. *Richard,* taken prisoner by the Indians; 4. *Abiah,* married *Capt Joseph Blanchard.*

HASSELL, JOSEPH, JR. – Son of the preceding; born in 1645. His children were, *Joseph; Benjamin; Hannah; Esther; Dinah; Abiah; Betsy; Rachel;* and *Sarah,* born from 1700 to 1721.

HASSELL, BENJAMIN. – Son of *Joseph, Jr.;* born 19th. Aug., 1701. Had a daughter, *Adah,* born 27th. April, 1734.

HOWARD, SAMUEL. – Born in 1684; died 7th. Feb., 1769, aged 85.

JOHNSON, NOAH. – Probably from Woburn; born in 1698: survivor of Lovewell's Fight: died at Pembroke, 13th. Aug., 1798, in the *one hundredth* year of his age. His children were, *Elizabeth,* born 3d. Oct., 1728; *Noah,* born 27th. May, 1730; and *Edward,* killed in the old French war.

KENDALL, JOHN. – Probably from Woburn; married *Deborah ——*, who died 3d. March, 1739, aged 45. –

His children were, 1. *Sarah,* born 23d. May, 1727; 2. *Jacob,* born 9th. Aug., 1729; 3. *Temple,* born 10th. Aug., 1731. He was the ancestor of Hon. Amos Kendall, and lived in that part of the town which is now Dunstable, Mass.

LOVEWELL, JOHN. – Probably from Weymouth; born in England before 1650: married *Hannah* ——: died about 1754 – said to have been aged 120. His children were, 1. *John,* a Captain, the hero of Pig- wacket, born 14th. Oct., 1691; killed by the Indians at Pigwacket, 8th. May, 1725; 2. *Hannah:* married *Ccpt. Joseph Baker,* of Roxbury; 3. *Zaccheus,* a Colonel in the French war, born 22d. July, 1701; 4. *Jonathan,* bom 14th. May, 1713: a judge: died about 1792, unmarried.

LOVEWELL, CAPT. JOHN. – Son of the preceding; born 14th. Oct., 1691: killed 8th. May, 1725. His widow, *Hannah,* died 5th. Jan., 1754. His children were,1. *John,* born 30th. June, 1718: died 2d. July, 1763; – left children, *John, Jonathan, Rachel,* and *Mary;* 2. *Hannah,* born 24th. July, 1721; 3. *Nehemiah,* born 9th. Jan., 1726: married *Rachel,* daughter of *Jonathan Farwell,* 24th. Nov., 1748: removed to Corinth, Vt., where he died, leaving a numerous family.

LOVEWELL, COL. ZACCHEUS. – Son of *John, Sen.;* born 22d. July, 1701: married *Esther* ——: died 12th. April, 1772, aged 72. His children were, 1. *Zaccheus,* born 19th. Feb., 1726; 2. *Esther,* born 10th. Nov., 1728; 3. *Lucy,* born 12th. Jan., 1730; 4. *Molly,* born 26th. May, 1732, who married *Capt. Benjamin French,* and died 17th. Dec., 1774; 5. *Bridget,* who married *Augustus*

Blanchard, and died 25th. Nov., 1836, aged *88;* and 6. *Noah,* born 1741, and died in D., 29th. May, 1820, aged 79.

LOVEWELL, GEN. NOAH. – Son of *Col. Zaccheus;* born 1741; married *Mary Farwell,* 17th. Dec., 1767. He died 29th. May, 1820; she died 24th. Nov., 1835, aged 93. His children were, *Betsy,* who married H*on. Jesse Bowers; Mary,* who married *Luther Taylor,* of D.; and *Moody D.,* still living.

LUND, THOMAS. – Born about 1660. His children were, 1. *Thomas,* born 9th. Sept., 1682; 2. *Elizabeth,* born 29th. Sept., 1684; 3. *William,* born 25th. Jan., 1686.

LUND, THOMAS, 2d. – Son of the preceding; born 9th. Sept., 1682: killed by the Indians, 5th. Sept., 1724. – His children were, 1. *Thomas,* born 31st. Oct., 1712; 2. *Elizabeth,* born 14th. May, 1715; 3. *William,* born 12th. Oct., 1717; 4. *Ephraim,* born 3d. Aug., 1720; 5. *Phinehas,* born 3d. April, 1723.

LUND, WILLIAM. – Son of *Thomas, Sen.;* born 25th Jan., 1686: married *Rachel* ——: died in 1768, aged 81. His children were, 1. *William,* born 18th. July, 1717; 2. *Rachel;* 3. *Charity,* (a son) born 16th. Feb., 1731; 4. *Mary.*

LUND, THOMAS. – Son of *Thomas, 2d.;* born 31st. Oct., 1712: a Deacon: married *Mary* ——: died 4th. Feb., 1790. He had a son, *Thomas,* born 12th. March, 1739.

LUND, EPHRAIM. – Son of *Thomas, 2d.;* born 3d. Aug., 1720: married *Rachel* ——. Had a daughter, *Rachel,* born 29th. Aug., 1743.

PERRY, OBADIAH. – Married *Esther,* daughter of *Joseph Hassell.* His children were, *John,* born 31st. Jan., 1682;

and *Elizabeth,* born 7th. April, 1683. He was killed by the Indians, 28th. Sept., 1691.

POLLARD, THOMAS. – The family came from Coventry, Eng. He married *Mary*——. His children were, 1. *John,* born 20th. Sept., 1727; 2. *Ebenezer,* born 4th. Dec., 1728; 3. *Thomas,* born 17th. Sept., 1730.

PRENTICE, REV. NATHANIEL. – His children were, 1. *Mary,* born 2d. Jan., 1725; 2. *William Henry,* born 2d. Dec., 1726; 3. *Nathaniel,* born 29th. May, 1729.

PATTERSON, JAMES, and *Mary,* his wife. Had a son, *John,* born 10th. April, 1711.

POWERS, CAPT. PETER, and *Anna Keyes,* his wife; the first settlers of Hollis. He died 27th. Aug., 1757; his widow died 21st. Sept., 1798, aged 90. His children were, 1. *Peter,* born 29th. Nov., 1728: graduated at Harvard, 1758: was a minister 40 years, and died at Deer Island, Me., in 1800, aged 72; 2. *Stephen,* born 28th. Oct., 1729; 3. *Anna,* born 9th. March, 1731: married *Benjamin Hopkins,* of Milford. For a farther account see Powers' Centennial Address at Hollis.

ROBBINS, LT. JONATHAN. – Probably came from Concord, Mass.: married *Margaret Goold;* was Lieutenant under Lovewell, and killed in the fight, *8*th. May, 1725. His children were, *Jane,* born 26th. Dec., 1712; *Margaret,* born 29th. Feb. 1716; *Jonathan,* born 4th. Nov., 1718; *Elvira,* and *Elizabeth.*

RICHARDSON, JOSIAH, and *Phebe,* his wife. Had children, *Phebe,* born 19th. Jan., 1728; *Josiah,* born 28th. Sept., 1729; *Lucy,* born 5th. Oct., 1731; *Eunice,* born 13th. Oct., 1733.

SEARLES, SAMUEL, and *Sarah,* his wife. His children were, *Sarah,* born 20th. Oct., 1700; *Deliverance; Samuel,* born 1st. March, 1707; *Mary; Daniel,* born 17th. July, 1715; *John,* born 11th. Oct., 1717; *Jonathan,* born 21st. Sept., 1720.

SEARLES, SAMUEL, *2d.* – Son of the preceding; born 1st. March, 1707. His children were, *Samuel,* horn 4th. Sept., 173S; *Benjamin,* born 6th. Sept., 1740.

SEARLES, DANIEL. – Son of *Samuel, 1st.:* born 17th. July, 1715. His children were, *Oliver,* born 20th. Aug., 1736; and *James,* born 17th. Nov., 1738.

SOLLENDINE, JOHN. – Married 2d. Aug., 1680. His children were, *Sarah,* born April, 1682; *John,* born May, 1683; *Alice,* born Jan., 1686.

SMITH, DEA. BENJAMIN. – Born 1736: died 29th. March, 1821, aged 85.

SWAN, REV. JOSIAH. – Married *Jane,* daughter of *Capt. Josiah Blanchard.* Had a son, *Josiah,* born 25th. Aug., 1740.

TAYLOR, ABRAHAM, and *Mary,* his wife. Born about 1690; from Concord, Mass. His children were, 1. *Abraham;* 2. *Samuel;* 3. *Timothy,* born 1st. Sept., 1718; 4. *Alice;* 5. *Amos,* born 10th. Sept., 1725.

TAYLOR, JONATHAN, and *Hannah,* his wife. His children were, *David,* born 1st. Jan., 1723; *Jonathan* and *Ephraim,* born 8th. Sept., 1725; *Hannah; Esther; Sarah; Nathan,* born 9th. Oct., 1734; *Oliver,* born 6th. April, 1737; *Sampson,* born 6th. Dec., 1739.

TAYLOR, SAMUEL. – Son of *Abraham*. His children were, *Reuben*, born 8th. March, 1733; *Samuel*, born 13th. Oct., 1734; *Susannah*.

TEMPLE, CHRISTOPHER. – Phobably from Concord, Mass.; married *Alice*, daughter of *Joseph Hassell*, 3d. Dec., 1685: killed by the Indians, 28th. Sept., 1691. His children were, *Jeremiah*, born 6th. Oct., 1686; *Alice*, born 3d. Jan., 1689; *Christopher*, born 3d. Oct., 1690.

TYNG, HON. EDWARD. – From Boston, where he was Rep. Assistant, and Major General; removed to Dunstable in 1679, and died 28th. December, 1681, aged 81. His children were, *Jonathan*, born 15th. Dec., 1642; *Edward*, Governor of Annapolis, &c.; *Hannah*, who married Habijah Savage, and for a second husband, Rev. Thomas Weld; *Eunice*, wife of Rev. Samuel Willard, President of Harvard College; *Rebecca*, wife of Gov. Joseph Dudley; and another daughter who married a Searle.

TYNG, HON. JONATHAN. – Son of *Hon. Edward*; married *Sarah*, daughter of *Hezekiah Usher*: died 9th. Jan., 1724. His children were, *John*, born about 1680; graduated Harvard College, 1690: killed by Indians in Aug., 1710; *William*, born 22d. April, 1679; *Jonathan*, born 29th. Sept., 1686; *Eleazer*, born 30th. April, 1690: graduated Harvard College, 1712; *Bersheba*, (a son) born 5th. Feb., 1694; *Mary*.

TYNG, ELEAZER. – Son of *Jonathan*; born 3d. April, 1690: graduated Harvard College 1712. His children were, *Jonathan*, born 10th. Sept. 1717; *Sarah*, born 22d. April, 1720, who married *John Winslow*; *Benjamin*, born 26th.

January, 1722; *John Alford,* [Judge Tyng,] born 29th. August, 1729; *James,* born 6th. March, 1731.

USHER, ROBERT. – Son or relative of *Hezekiah Usher;* from Charlestown, Mass. His children were, *John,* born 31st. May, 1696; *Robert,* born June 1700; killed in Pigwacket fight.

USHER, JOHN. – Son of the preceding: born 31st. May, 1696; his children were, *John,* born 2d. May, 1728; *Robert,* born 9th. April, 1730; *Rachel; Habijah,* born 8th. August, 1734.

WALDO, JOHN. – From Chelmsford: son of *Dea. Cornelius Waldo;* removed to D. His children were, *John,* born about 1682; *Catharine; Rebecca.*

WALDO, DANIEL. – Son of Dea. *Cornelius.* He had two daughters, born 1684, and 1687.

WARNER, SAMUEL. – Married *Mary Swallow* 4th. May, 1684. His children were, *Eliezer,* born 27th. Jan. 1686; *Priscilla.*

WELD, REV. THOMAS. – First minister of Dunstable: son *of Thomas Weld* of Roxbury, Mass.; married *Elizabeth,* daughter of Rev. *John Wilson of* Medfield, 9th. November, 1681, who died 29th. July, 1687; his second wife was widow *Hannah Savage,* daughter of Hon. *Edward Tyng.* He died in 1702; she died at the residence of her son, Rev. *Habijah S. Weld,* in Attleboro', Mass., in 1731. His children were, *Elizabeth,* born 13th. October, 1682; *Thomas,* born 7th. February, 1684; by his first wife: and *Samuel,* born 4th. March, 1701; and *Habijah Savage,* born in September, 1702, by his second wife; ordained at Attleborough, Mass., 1727, and died there in 1782, aged 80. (1.)

WHITING, SAMUEL. – Probably a sou of Rev. *Samuel Whiting,* of Billerica; born 19th. January, 1662; died 14th. March, 1715, aged 51. His children were, *Samuel,* born 22d. October, 1687; who was in the Pigwacket Fight; *Elizabeth; Catharine; Leonard,* born 12th. Aug. 1693; *Joseph,* born 14th. Dec. 1695; *Mary; Dorcas; John,* born 11th. March, 1706.

WHITING, JOSEPH. – Born about 1735; grandson of preceding; married *Abigail Chamberlain,* 11th. June, 1761; she died 19th. April, 1779. His children were, 1. *Joseph,* born 13th. November, 1761; died 21st. August, 1778; 2. *Samuel,* born 30th. June, 1763; died at Amherst in March, 1805, aged 42; 3. *Susanna,* born 20th. March, 1765; 4. *Leonard,* born 16th. January, 1767; 5. *Oliver,* born 29th. January, 1769; 6. *William,* born 28th. September, 1770; died in Merrimac; 7. *Elizabeth,* born 16th. July, 1772; 8. *Thomas,* born 20th. Oct., 1774; died at Amherst; 9. *Abigail,* born 18th. August, 1776; 10. *Jonathan,* born 14th. February, 1778; died at Amherst,

NOTE:

(1.) Of Mr. Weld it is said, that he "was distinguished for his usefulness in the ministry, and highly respected as a man, both at home and abroad. He united to an uncommon degree the affections of his people for a period of fifty-five years, during which he was their pastor." – White's Early History of N. E., 271.

APPENDIX NO. II.
LIST OF SOLDIERS
IN THE ARMY

LIST of soldiers *from* that part of Dunstable which is now in New Hampshire, in the Army of the Revolution, from 1775 to 1783: (1.)

David Adams,* David Adams, Jr.,* Richard Adams,* Henry Adams, Silas Adams,† Isaac Adams,† John Alld, David Alld, Jacob Adams,† James Blanchard,† Quartermaster of Scammel's regiment; Josiah Butterfield, Abel Butterfield, Simeon Butterfield,* Thomas Butterfield, Chas. Butterfield, Benjamin Bayley,* Oliver Blodgett, Daniel Blood,† James Brown,* a Lieutenant; Samuel Butterfield,† John Butler,† killed at Hubberton, Vt., July 7th., 1777; Ebenezer Bancroft, (2.) Jonathan Bancroft, Ephraim Blood,† Reuben Blood,† Simeon Blood,† John Blanchard,† Nathaniel Blanchard, Jonathan Butterfield,† Timothy Blood,† Eliphalet Bayley,* Eleazer Blanchard,* William Butterfield,* Paul Clogstone,* died at Cambridge, 1775; John Cockle,† Stephen Conery,† John Conery,† Medad Combs,* Joseph Combs, died in the army; William Cox, Thomas Clark, John Clogstone, Samuel Conery, William Dandley, James Dandley, Joseph Dix, Jonathan Danforth,* Noah Downs,† Castor Dickinson, [colored;] Jonathan Emerson,* a lieutenant under Cilley; Ebenezer Fosdick,* Benjamin French, Jr., killed in the army; John Fletcher, Joseph Farrar, Eleazer Fisk, [living;] David Fisk,

Nathan Fisk, Richard Francis, Isaac Foot, [living;] Theodore French, John French, Archibald Gibson,* James Gibson,* William Gibbs,† David Gilson,† David Gilson, Jr.,†
Peter Honey,* Peter Honey, Jr., died in the army; William
Harris,* died in the army; William Harris, Jr.,* Jonathan
Harris,* Abraham Hale, William Hunt, John Honey, Jr.,
died in the army; Thomas Harwood, James Harwood.*
killed at Hubberton, Vt., July 7th., 1777; Ebenezer Har-
ris, Jr., [living:] William Honey, Abijah Honey, Calvin
Honey,† Archibald Harrod, James Harrod,† died Decem-
ber, 1777, in army; John Honey, John Harwood, Joseph
Honey,† Calvin Honey,† died in the army; Israel Ingalls,
James Jewell, [living;] Nathaniel Jewell, Nathaniel Kemp,
Jeremiah Keith,† Reuben Killicut, Charity Killicut, Wil-
liam Lund,* killed at Bunker Hill; Joel Lund,† an Ensign;
John Lund,* Jonathan Lund, Thomas Lund, Jonathan
Lovewell, Jr., Jonathan Lovewell,† Ichabod Lovewell,*
John Lovewell,* Nehemiah Lovewell,* Henry Lovewell,*
Asa Lovejoy, Noah Lovewell,† Quarter-master of Col.
Gilman's regiment; Joseph Lamson, Jr.,† William Lancey,
Richard Lovewell, Stephen Lovewell, [colored;] Thomas
Lancey, Levi Lund, William Mann,† killed in the army;
John Manning,† taken prisoner at Ticonderoga, and af-
terwards retaken; Eliphalet Manning,† Jonathan Powers,
Thomas Perry,† Ebenezer Perry, William Powell, ——
Pike, William Quinton,† William Roby,* an Ensign, and
died in the army; Samuel Roby, John Robbins, Jr., Abijah
Reed,* Abbot Roby,* Benjamin Robbins, David Reed,†
Thomas Roby, John Searles. Benjamin Smith, John Snow,
Jr.,* Joseph Swallow,* Joel Stewart,* Daniel Shed,† Joseph

Snow, died in the army; Daniel Searles, David Smiley,†-James Seal,† Silas Swallow,† Benjamin Taylor, Jacob Taylor, Benjamin Temple, Levi Temple, Benjamin Taylor, Jr.,† William Walker,* a Captain and Major; Daniel Warner,* Quarter-master; Joseph Whiting, Wenioll Wright, Oliver Woods,* died at Cambridge; Oliver Woods, Jr., John Wright, Jr.,† Benjamin Whitney,* Sylvanus Whitney, Phinehas Whitney* Paul Woods,* Daniel Wood,† Nehemiah Wright* Oliver Wright,† Jonathan Wright,† Samuel Whiting,† Oliver Whiting.†

NOTES:

(1.) Those persons to whose name (*) is appended, were in the Battle of Bunker Hill; those with (†) appear from the records to have belonged to this town; the others are derived from the recoltions of the survivors who are still living.

(2.) They resided on the southern border of the town, and were called of Dunstable, though afterwards living in Tyngsborough.

APPENDIX NO. III.
DESCRIPTION OF TOWN HOUSE, AND CEMETERY

THE following description of the Nashua Town House, and Cemetery, is taken from the Directory of 1843. The Town House was completed in the spring of 1843: –

At the annual meeting of the Town of Nashua, March, 1842, it was voted to erect a Town House. The committee appointed to receive proposals for a site on which it should be erected, purchased of Aaron F. Sawyer, Esq., the land on which stood his house and office, a lot about 95 by 133 feet. The building committee were Leonard W. Noyes, Israel Hunt, Jr., Thomas Chase, Franklin Fletcher, and Samuel Shepherd, Esqs. Samuel Shepherd, Esq., was chosen Architect; and under his superintendence, the edifice, for taste in its design and utility in its construction, is not surpassed by any other structure of the kind in New England. It is constructed of brick on a very durable foundation of stone, with a basement of fine hammered granite. The ornaments, lamp stands, and balconies, mostly from Grecian patterns, are of cast iron. The portico, 7 feet by 18, is of iron on a base of granite.

The building is 66 by 90 feet, and consists of the basement, first and second stones, and the attic.

One half of the basement is used for a cellar; the other half is occupied as a market, it being 9 feet high, 4 feet of which are above ground. It is well lighted, and there is good access from the north, south and west sides.

The first story contains two large rooms, the entrances to which are on Main street, each 18 by 24 feet and 13 1-2 feet high, one on each side of the front entrance; occupied as stores. In the rear of these rooms are two smaller ones, each 18 by 14 feet, occupying nearly one half of the first story; and in the rear of the above rooms, is the lower hall, a fine room 17 feet high and 38 by 63 feet. It is lighted by seven windows, and contains a gallery – thus giving room for an audience of about five hundred persons. The entries in this story are very spacions. The front entry is 38 feet in length and 8 in width. Entering this from the portico on Main street, we observe first two spacious stairways for the ascent to the third story. On our right and left, beyond the stairs, are entrances to the rooms fronting on Main street. Following the entry to its end, we find the door, opening into the lower hall. Crossing at right angles the eastern end of the entry we have described, is another entry, leading from the north to the south side of the building, 66 feet long and 10 wide. – These of couse give three doors for entrance or exit. On this second entry are the two smaller rooms. Ascending the stairs into the second story, we find the Town Hall, 70 feet long, 63 feet wide, 24 feet high, with moveable seats, arranged so as to form a centre aisle and two side aisles. With the gallery, there is sufficient room for 1300 persons to be comfortably seated. It is lighted by eleven large windows. There are also, in this story, two small rooms, one on each side of the stairway, each 14 by 12 feet, and occupied as offices. The attic, 70 by 20 feet, is finished for the use of military companies.

The height of the building, from the ground to the top of the cupola, is about 100 feet The cost was nearly $23,000.

NASHUA CEMETERY

MARCH 19, 1835, the proprietors of the real estate of the First Unitarian Congregational Society in Dunstable passed a vote appropriating their grounds contiguous to the meeting-house for a burial place, under the designation of the Nashua Cemetery. In addition to which, a piece of land, owned by Daniel Abbot, Esq., lying north of the premises above described, containing about *8,000* feet, was purchased and appropriated to the same use. After having disposed of 29 lots by subscription, at $25 per lot, the proprietors enclosed the ground with a substantial fence, – made the several paths and avenues, and divided the whole into 85 lots of 20 by 17 feet each. Five lots were reserved as ministerial lots for the then religious societies in Dunstable. Four only were accepted. The first was accepted by the First Congregational Society in Dunstable, the second by the First Congregational Society in Nashua, the third by the First Methodist Episcopal Society, the fourth by the Unitarian Society.

In August, 1835, an addition to the Cemetery was made by the purchase of a piece of land of Mr. Christopher Paige, lying east of the same, containing about 35,000 feet, by an association of individuals for that purpose, to be known by the name of *The Nashua Cemetery Additional,* and which was divided into 104 lots, two of which were appropriated by the proprietors for the use and benefit of strangers. Of the 85 lots in the original Cemetery, 22 remain unsold, leaving 26 lots unsold out of 189 in both Cemeteries.

The price of lots is $26, with interest from June 15, 1835. The officers of the Cemetery consist of a Committee of three, a Secretary and a Treasurer. The present *officers* are, Daniel Abbot, Joseph Greeley, and Moses Tyler, Committee. John A. Baldwin, Secretary. Alfred Greeley, Treasurer.

APPENDIX NO. IV.
POPULATION OF NASHUA

The population of the town at various periods has been as follows:—

1680:	30 families, or about 120	inhabitants.
1701:	25 " " " 180	"
1711:	13 " " " 86	"
1730:	50 " " " 250	"
1756:	about 100 rateable polls, " " 450 (1.)	"
1767:	262 males; 258 females, 520 (2.)	"
1775:	376 males; 329 females, 705	"
1783:	578 (3.)	"
1790:	632	"
1800:	862	"
1810:	1049	"
1820:	1142	"
1830:	2417	"
1836:	2105 males; 2960 females, 5065	"
1837:	2138 " 3472 " 5610	"
1838:	2167 " 3524 " 5691	"

1840:	2285 males; 3675 females,	5960(4)inhabitants.
1840:	August U. S. Census,	6054 "
1841:	2389 males; 3770 females,	6159 "
1842:(5)	2608 " 3828 "	6436 "
1843:	Nashua, 3779 } Nashville, 2354 }	6133 "
1844:	Nashua, 4128 } Nashville, 2427 }	6555 "
1845:	Nashua, 4429 } Nashville, 2432 }	6861 "

NOTES:

(1.) This included a part of Hollis. Of these rateable polls, "not above forty were able to bear town charges." So says *a* petition of the day.

(2.) There were 32 unmarried males between 16 and 60 years of age; 69 married males of the same age; males under 16 years, 151; males over 60 years, 10.

(3.) In 1783 there were *in* Nashua *88* dwelling-houses, and *74 barns.*

(4.) Th*e number of polls in* 1839 *was* 1082; in 1840, 114C (5.) *The town* was divided *June* 23, 1842.

APPENDIX NO. V.
LAWYERS AND PHYSICIANS

ATTORNEYS AT LAW. – Previous to 1800 there was no regular bred attorney in town. Judge Lovewell and Judge Blanchard acted in that capacity whenever necessity required. In 1802, Hon. Daniel Abbot opened an office a little south of the old South Meeting House, but in 1803 he removed to the spot where Nashua village now stands, which was then an almost unbroken forest. About 1812, Samuel Abbot, Esq., of Wilton, opened an office also, but remained a short time only. In 1816, Benjamin F. French, Esq. opened an office, and practised in partnership with Mr. Abbot until he was appointed agent of the Jackson Company, in 1831. At present there are, arranged in the order of their residence in town: Hon. Daniel Abbot,* Hon. Charles G. Atherton,* Aaron F. Sawyer, George Y. Sawyer, Benjamin F. Emerson,* A. P. Dudley, B. B. Whitte- more, A. F. Stevens, A. W. Sawyer, Charles B. Fletcher, Benjamin M. Farley.

Hon. Charles F. Gove – Judge of the Court of Common Pleas – also resides in Nashville.

Physicians and Surgeons. – During the Revolutionary war and for many years previous, Dr. Nathan Cutler was the only physician in town. After the war, Dr. Ebenezer Starr, of Dedham, who married Hannah, daughter Hon. Joseph Blanchard, removed here, and died September, 1798, aged 52. After his death, his son, Dr. Augustus

Starr, who married Rebecca, daughter of Hon. Jonathan Blanchard, resided and practised in town for some years. Dr. Maynard resided here in 1803; he afterwards removed to Boston, where be died. About this time, Dr. Peter Howe practised here for a number of years, until Dr. Ebenezer Dearborn removed here, who still resides in town. There are now *nine* physicians in Nashua, who are named according to the length of their residence in town. Ebenezer Dearborn, Elijah Colburn, Micah Eldridge, Josiah G. Graves,* Edward Spalding, Josiah Kittredge, Evan B. Hammond, J. H. Graves.* J. F. Whittle.

J. & S. Ball, Surgeon Dentists.

NOTES:

* Now reside in Nashville.
* Now reside in Nashville.

APPENDIX NO. VI.
LIST OF THE REPRESENTATIVES TO THE GENERAL COURT

1689, May session, John Waldo.

June session, Cornelius Waldo.

December session, Robert Parris.

1692, Hon. Jonathan Tyng and Maj. Thomas Henchman.

From this time, until annexed to New Hampshire, it was too poor and feeble to be able to send a Representative. After its annexation to New Hampshire, the Royal Governor refused the town the *privilege* of representation. In 1768, it was classed with Hollis, and Dr. John Hale elected.

1774, September, Jonathan Lovewell, delegate to the Revolutionary Convention at Exeter.

1775, April, Joseph Ayers, delegate to the Revolutionary Convention at Exeter.

1775, May, Joseph Ayers and Noah Lovewell, delegates to the Revolutionary Convention at Exeter.

1776, December, Jonathan Blanchard, delegate to the Revolutionary Convention at Exeter.

1776, Jonathan Blanchard.

Jonathan Lovewell, 1777, 1778.

Noah Lovewell, 1779, 1780.

William Hunt, 1781.

Benjamin French, 1782.

[Names of Representatives from 1782 to 1793, not preserved.]

Frederick French, 1793, 1795, 1797, 1803, 1805, 1806.

Noah Lovewell, 1794, 1796, 1802.

Theodore French, 1801, 1804.

Zaccheus Lovewell, 1807.

Thomas French, 1809, 1813, 1814.

Daniel Abbot, 1810, 1811, 1812, 1821, 1838, 1839.

Timothy Taylor, 1815.

Jesse Bowers, 1816, 1817, 1818, 1819, 1820, 1822, 1823, 1824.

Benjamin F. French, 1825, 1826, 1829.

1826, Benjamin F. French, Eleazer F. Ingalls.

1827, Eleazer F. Ingalls, William Boardman.

1828, Israel Hunt, Jr., Moody D. Lovewell.

1829, Benjamin F. French, James Osgood.

1830, Moody D. Lovewell, Charles G. Atherton.

1831, James Osgood, Josiah Fletcher, (died before taking his seat.)

1832, Eleazer F. Ingalls, Robert Anderson.

1833, Charles G. Atherton, Moody D. Lovewell.

1834, Moody D. Lovewell, Charles G. Atherton, Zebediah Shattuck.

1835, same as 1834.

1836, Charles G. Atherton, Benjamin L. Jones, Zebediah Shattuck.

1837, Benjamin L. Jones, George W. Bagley, Hugh Jameson, Charles J. Fox.

1838, Daniel Abbot, Stephen Kendrick, George Y. Sawyer, Silas Butterfield.

1839, same as 1838.

1840, George Y. Sawyer, Isaac Spalding, Albin Beard, Josephus Baldwin.

1841, same as 1840.

1842, Leonard W. Noyes, Abner Andrews, Anthony *Gage*.

1843, Josephus Baldwin.

1844, no election.

1845, Thomas Chase, William F. Lawrence, Josephus Baldwin.

1846, Thomas Chase, William F. Lawrence, Isaac Spalding, Aaron F. Sawyer.

REPRESENTATIVES OF NASHVILLE

1843, William Boardman, Albert McKean.

1844, E. T. Merrill, Albert McKean.

1845, William Wetherbee, Ziba Gay.

1486, Ziba Gay, Albin Beard.

APPENDIX NO. VII.
PROPORTION OF THE PUBLIC TAXES AT VARIOUS PERIODS

The wealth of the town as compared with that of the whole State may be learned from the following apportionments required tu be paid by the town at different periods out of every *thousand* dollars raised by the State.

In 1700 silver was worth about 10 shillings per ounce.

1775: the proportion was			$5.15
1794:	"	"	"	4.14
1803:	"	"	"	3.43
1808:	"	"	"	3.80
1812:	"	"	"	3.47
1816:	"	"	"	4.46
1820:	"	"	"	4.20
1824:	"	"	"	4.83
1828:	"	"	"	10.00
1832:	"	"	"	11.99
1836:	"	"	"	29.19
1840:	"	"	"	28.50
1844:	"	"	"	20.42
Nashville's proportion in 1844, was			14.98

APPENDIX NO. VIII.
VALUE OF SILVER AT DIFFERENT PERIODS

In order to compare the value of sums of money as used at different periods, the fluctuation of which, as compared with paper, has been very great, I subjoin the following table prepared by Dr. Belknap, 5 N. H. Hist. Coll., 258. The value of silver is now fixed at six shillings eight pence ($1.08) per ounce. In 1750, it was worth 56 shillings per ounce. The common currency had depreciated therefore in 1750, *88* per cent., or a dollar in paper was worth hut *12* cents in silver.

In 1700 silver was worth about 10 shillings per ounce.

1704	"	"	"	7	"	"	"
1705	"	"	"	10	"	"	"
1710	"	"	"	8	"	"	"
1715	"	"	"	10	"	"	"
1720	"	"	"	12	"	"	"
1725	"	"	"	15 (1.)	"	"	"
1730	"	"	"	21	"	"	"
1735	"	"	"	27	"	"	"
1740	"	"	"	29	"	"	"
1745	"	"	"	36	"	"	"
1750	"	"	"	56	"	"	"

NOTE:

(1.) In 1721 the colony issued 50,000l. bills of credit, and in 1727, 60,000l. more. Other issues were made about 1745, to defray the expenses of the Louisburg Expedition. From these periods the rise in the value of silver as compared with paper is very striking.

APPENDIX NO. IX.
HISTORY OF THE POST OFFICE IN NASHUA (1.)

THE Post Office in this town was established sometime between April 1st., and July 1st., 1803, and Gen.
Noah Lovewell appointed Postmaster. The office was
opened in the tavern of Mr. Cummings Pollard, who was
appointed Assistant Postmaster, and had the charge of
the office until 1811. Up to that time it was located in the
tavern lately owned and occupied by Mr. Silas Gibson.

In 1811, the office was removed to the *"Harbour,"* so
called, and placed under the charge of Israel Hunt, who
was appointed Assistant Postmaster, and in whose dwelling house it was stationed. After its removal to the latter
place, it being located near the residence of Gen. Lovewell, he continued to superintend the duties of the office
personally until his death, which took place in May, 1820.
Upon his death, John M. Hunt, Esq., was appointed and
commissioned in June, 1820. He established the office in
the office of I. and J. M. Hunt, (at the Harbour,) where
it remained until 1826, when it was removed to Nashua
Village, soon after the erection of the cotton mills. Since
its establishment in 1803, the receipts of the office have increased to an astonishing, and almost incredible degree.

The *receipt* for the first quarterly balance of postage,
for the quarter ending June 30, 1803, is still on file in the
office, and acknowledges the sum of *twenty cents!!* For

the quarter ending September 30, 1805, the receipts of the office had increased to the sum of *two dollars, eighty-seven cents,* yielding a commission as compensation for discharging the various duties of the office of *eighty-six cents* per quarter, or *three dollars, forty-four cents* per annum.

But a glance at the finances of the office at periods of ten years will best show its rapid advancement.

In 1810 the net rec'ts to the Gen. P. O. were $31.86: gross $46.00

1830 " " " " " " " " " "	55.95: "	80.00
1830 " " " " " " " " " "	356.64: "	510.00
1840 " " " " " " " " " "	1715.53: "	2450.00
1845 " " " " " " " " " "	1902.30: "	2679.02
First 6 m'ths of '45 under the old postage law,	997.18: "	1406.61
Last G months under the new law,	905.12: "	1272.41
Difference,	$ 92.06 $	134.20

The present facilities for travelling, when compared with those of by-gone days, have placed the expedition of the mails on a par with their advancement in amount of business and increase of revenue. In former times, Wheat's old mail stage occupied two days in travelling from Amherst to Boston, and "put up" regularly for the night in Billerica. Now by the aid of steam power and railroad accommodation, we can receive a mail from Boston in less than two hours!

Forty years ago there was not a single letter or newspaper brought into this town by mail conveyance. For the quarter ending September 30, 1840, the amount of postage collected on letters was five hundred and twenty-three dollars, and on newspapers and pamphlets one hundred and thirteen dollars, eighty cents.

NOTE:

(1.) This sketch was prepared for the Nashua Directory, by John M. Hunt, Esq.

APPENDIX NO. X.
INVENTORY AND EXPENSES
OF NASHUA

THE Inventory of the town in 1839 was $2,511,501. –
In 1840 it was $2,467,822, which is thus made up:
Real estate, including factory buildings and
machinery, mills, locks and canals, and toll

bridge,	$2,102,272
285 horses valued at	14,656
115 pairs of oxen valued at	4,250
376 cows " "	9,373
144 other neat stock, " "	2,437
503 sheep " "	1,509
Stock in trade	143,750
Bank stock and money at interest	112,900
Other stocks	70,400
Carriages	6,275
	$2,467,822

EXPENSES OF THE TOWN FOR THE YEAR
ENDING MARCH, 1841

For repairs of highways,	$1,933.88
For building new roads	2,928.22
For the support of schools and school houses	4,000.95
For military expenses	331.50
Amount carried up,	$9194.55

Amount brought up,	$9194.55
For town and county paupers	1,385.81
For police expenses	84.36
For services of town officers and incidental expenses	950.21
For bounties	11.25
For State tax for the year 1840	1,167.60
For county tax	768.61
For collection of taxes	223.69
For old bills and orders	1,518.33
	$15,304.41

Of this amount the sum of $11,555.72 was raised by the assessment of taxes, and the balance principally defrayed from the surplus revenue.

In 1740, a century ago, the whole amount of money raised for all the "town charges," exclusive of the minister tax, was about *fifty dollars* !

The following tables will show the expenses of the towns of Nashua and Nashville, for the year 1845:

EXPENSES OF NASHUA

Repairs of highways and bridges	$1816.88
Support of schools	2223.37
Military expenses	141.00
Balance of alms house expenses	451.58
Pauper expenses other than alms house	95.35
County paupers	300.65
Town house	77.50

Fire department	553.29
Burial grounds, hearse, &c.	62.81
Police expenses	119.61
Amount carried up,	$5,842.04
Amount brought up,	$5,842.04
Printing and stationery	79.50
Miscellaneous	61.00
Old bills and interest	7374.03
Services of town officers	375.08
State and county tax	2775.79
Collection of taxes	153.16
	$16,660.60

EXPENSES OF NASHVILLE

Repairs of highways and bridges	1097.46
Schools and school houses	2332.61
Military	115.50
Printing and stationery	35.06
Alms house	934.70
Paupers other than alms house	325.60
County paupers	134.00
Town officers	288.10
Miscellaneous	485.25
State tax	898.80
County tax	1137.50
Paid old orders	400.00
Tax outstanding	137.40
Paid collector and constatble.	104.97
	$8,462.95

APPENDIX NO. XI.
STATISTICS OF THE DISTRICT SCHOOLS

THE town was first divided into school districts, five in number, and school houses erected, in 1775. Previously *one* teacher had been employed by the town to "keep school" in different places alternately. The sum raised never exceeded and rarely equalled *one hundred dollars*. – There are now *eleven* districts, and the whole amount of money raised and expended during the fiscal year 1840, for schools and school houses, was $4,000.95; of which $263.93 only were expended for the latter. The amount required by law to be raised by the town was only $2,627.10.

From the following table we learn that there were 11 districts, 17 schools, and 26 teachers. The amount of money expended for the support of teachers and for fuel, was $3,411.00. The whole number of scholars in all the districts was 1452. Of these 1268, (viz: 613 males and 655 females,) attended school in summer; and 1188, (viz: 696 males and 492 females,) attended school in winter. The average attendance in summer was only 722, however, and in winter only 788; shewing that almost *one half* of all the children in town were constantly absent from school.

STATISTICS OF THE SCHOOLS IN NASHUA, FOR 1840

(Previous to the division of the Town.)

No. of District.	Terms.	No. of Schools.	Number of Teachers.	Wages per month including board.	Length sch. in weeks.	Whole No. scholars attending school.	Whole No. Males.	Whole No. Females.	Average Attendance.	Census of Scholars.	Amount of money appropriated.
1	Sum.	1.	One female teacher, $	10.33	16	27	13	14	18	40	131.00
	Win.	1.	One male.	26.00	12	49	27	13	35		
2	Sum.	1.	One female.	11.00	16	45	28	17	25	45	131.00
	Win.	1.	One male.	25.00	9	36	25	11	28		
3	Sum.	3.	4 females; 17, 14, 14 & $13.		21	292	111	151	185	358	758.16
	Win.	3.	1 m. & 3 fe.; 29, 17, 14 & $14.		19	288	164	124	183		
4	Sum.	1.	One female.	11.60	14	24	12	12	16	29	131.00
	Win.	1.	One male.	23.00	8	26	21	5	20		
5	Sum.	1.	One female.	11.32	9	20	10	10	18	22	88.77
	Win.	1.	One male.	20.00	10	20	13	7	14		
6	Sum.	1.	One female.	10.00	16	22	13	9	18	36	131.00
	Win.	1.	One male.	21.68	14	33	23	10	26		
7	Sum.	1.	One female.	12.00	14	40	17	23	23	47	131.70
	Win.	1.	One male.	24.00	13	47	26	21	32		
8	Sum.	1.	One female.	12.00	29	31	14	17	13	30	88.77
	Win.	1.	One female.	12.00							
9	Sum.	3.	1 male $42; 6 fem. $13 each.		23	411	227	214	275	556	1177.47
	Win.	3.	1 male $42; 6 fem. $13 each.		12	415	250	165	274		
10	Sum.	2.	2 females; wages, 14 & $13.		26	169	66	103	90	135	316.69
	Win.	2.	1 male, $26; 1 female, $14.		12	114	53	61	80		
11	Sum.	2.	2 females; wages, $14 each.		20	157	72	85	91	154	326.14
	Win.	2.	1 male, $27; 1 female, $14.		13	138	60	58	83		
11		17	22 Teachers.	Summer	1265	613	655	772		1452	3411.00
				Winter	1168	696	492	788			

Of the scholars in all the schools, 1000 attended to reading, 949 to spelling, 831 to arithmetic, 273 to geography, 152 to grammar, 54 to history, 17 to moral philosophy, 16 to natural philosophy, 8 to chemistry, and 7 to algebra.

STATISTICS OF THE SCHOOLS IN NASHUA, FOR 1845

Table of Teachers, Scholars, Attendance, &c.

District.	Term.	Room.	No. of Teachers.	Wages and Board per month.	Number of Weeks.	Number of Scholars.	Males.	Females.	Average Attendance.	Money Expended.
1	1st		1 female.	$10.12	14	19	09	10	15	101 34
	2d		1 male.	26.00	9	31	20	11	25	
2	1st		1 female.	10.00	12	35			25	90 19
	2d		1 male.	21.00	10	35	20	15	25	
3	1st	1	1 female.	12.00	16	47	19	28	24	302 31
		2	1 female.	12.00	16	61	30	31	38	
	2d	1	1 male.	26.00	14	50	26	24	35	
		2	1 female.	13.00	12	57	35	22	39	
4	1st	1	1 male & 2 females.	68.00	26	188	90	98	80	1416 97
		2	2 females.	26.00	26	136	58	78	60	
		3	2 females.	26.00	26	157	75	82	81	
		4	1 female.	14.00	26	74	28	46	40	
	2d	1	1 male & 2 females.	68.00	11	126	61	65	93	
		2	2 females.	26.00	11	98	46	52	71	
		3	2 females.	26.00	11	97	59	38	68	
		4	1 female.	14.00	11	46	19	29	33	
5	1st	1	1 female.	10.00	10	20	9	11	10	25 00
6	1st		1 female.	10.00	12	18	10	8	14	98 34
	2d		1 male.	22.67	8	29	19	10	23	
7	1st		1 female.	11.00	17	29	15	14	22	107 34
	2d		1 male.	23.00	12	36	18	18	30	

STATISTICS OF THE SCHOOLS IN NASHUA, FOR 1845

Table of Teachers, Scholars, Attendance, &c.

District.	Term.	Room.	No. of Teachers.	Wages and Board per month.	Number of Weeks.	Number of Scholars.	Males.	Females.	Average Attendance.	Census of Scholars.	Money Expended.
1	1st	1	1 female.	$14.00	20	44	20	24	26		
		2	1 female.	14.00	20	54	24	30	37	160	$336 38
	2d	1	1 male.	30.00	16	65	27	36	52		
		2	1 female.	14.00	16	56	30	26	40		
2	1st	1	1 male.	35.00	25	90	42	48	50		
		2	1 female.	16.00	25	65	30	35	42		
		3	1 female.	16.00	25	70	36	34	55		
		4	1 female.	16.00	25	85	39	46	52	442	1032 95
	2d	1	1 male & female.	49.00	17	86	45	41	59		
		2	1 female.	16.00	17	59	27	32	45		
		3	1 female.	16.00	17	60	33	27	47		
		4	1 female.	16.00	17	77	35	42	56		
3	1st		1 female.	10.80	11	22	16	6	16	20	91 75
	2d		1 male.	21.00	10	18	16	2	12		
4	1st		1 female.	12.00	15	16	7	9	12	19	139 39
	2d		1 female.	13.25	12	22	10	12	17		

There are *two* academies in Nashua. "The Nashua Literary Institution," David Crosby, A. M., and Mrs. Louisa S. H. Crosby, Principals; and "The Nashua Academy," Zuinglius Grover, A, M., and Miss Caroline Wood, Principals, These academies were both incorporated in 1840.

"Abbot's High School," in Nashville, is under the charge of Mr. Charles Abbot. Beside the usual branches taught in high schools, daily instruction is given in vocal and instrumental music.

There arc also numerous private schools in the village, for small scholars.

ERRATA. In a work abounding like this with names and dates and published without the last revision and superintendence of the author, occasional mistakes will, it is hoped, be regarded as excusable. The following list comprises all of importance which have been detected:

Page.	Line.		Page.	Line.	
11,	7,	for Dramcap read Dram-cup.	167,	5, from bottom, for 1818 read 1813.
15,	3,	for othordox read orthodox.	180,	note, line 6, for Kindee read Raby
29,	21,	for 1678 read 1675.	181,	7, from top, for voted read vested.
66,	6,	for sagamon read sagamore.	207,	12, from top, for $15,000 read 1500
		note 1, for supra read infra.	205,	2, from bottom, for 1848 read 1843
74,	10, & 20,	for Magnolia read Magnalia.	221,	24, from top, for 1775 read 1765.
86,	9,	for sure read sore.	225,	last line, for 1775 read 1765.
97,	3,	from bottom, for Shate read Shute.	238,	15, for 1706 read 1726.
108,	3,	for Satwych's read Lutwyche's.	241,	8, for Wamer read Warner.
136,	19,	for 1631 read 1731.	246,	1, for 1791 read 1691.
140,	31,	for The bridge read No bridge.	251,	7, for 1680 read 1670.
	33,	for effected read affected.		8, for 1690 read 1691.
156,	5,	from bottom, for 1746 read 1764.	251,	4, for 150 read 100.
161,	12,	from top, for even read ever.	271,	last line, for 8,162.95 read 8,125.95.
166,	6,	from bottom, for 1758 read 1759.		

The name spelt "Lollendine" in the body of the work, is given as "Sollendine" in the Appendix, which, on examination of the ancient records, appears to be correct.

2   LOWELL

The Lowell Daily Courier.

MONDAY, APRIL 4, 1881.

TYNGSBORO'.

An Interesting Letter.

The following letter from a distinguished graduate of Harvard university, published in the Harvard Register, will probably prove interesting to many of our readers:

TYNGSBORO', February, 1881.
Editor of the Harvard Register:

This little town, delightfully situated on both sides of the Merrimack river, in the northerly part of Middlesex county, bordering on Nashua, N. H., with which it was formerly connected, as were many other towns, under the name of Dunstable, has been much identified by its citizens with Harvard college and Harvard graduates. By the town we mean the territory from its earliest settlement, while it was part of the old township of Dunstable as well as after its incorporation as a parish or district, and subsequently as a town. It never contained many more than eight hundred inhabitants, and most of the time the number has been far less than that. The facts which we have found, in the course of our historical resources of a more general character, and which we will endeavor correctly to relate, show to a marked degree the influence which individuals exert in the neighborhood of their residence, and among relatives and friends everywhere, in respect to the college.

Edward Tyng, who came to this country from London before 1640, settled in Boston, but subsequently acquired a large landed estate here, came to reside upon it, and died here in 1681. It is understood that his wife, Mary Sears, was born in Dunstable, England, from which place the old township took its name in honor of her. Mr. Tyng was a benefactor of the college, to a small extent, as early as 1658, according to President Quincy's History of Harvard University; and Mr. Quincy refers to him as of "one of the earliest, wealthiest, and most influential families in the colony." His second daughter, Rebecca, married Joseph Dudley (1665), who was the colonial governor of Massachusetts and New Hampshire, and chief justice of the supreme court of New York. His third daughter, Hannah, married two Harvard graduates: first, Abijah Savage (1659); second, Rev. Thomas Weld (1671), and the Rev. Abijah Weld (1723), who was for fifty years the minister in Attleboro', where he died, was his son. His fourth daughter, Eunice,

Higginson Tyng (1817), the elder of the two distinguished Episcopal clergymen of that name in New York, to whom the college gave the honorary degree of S. T. D. in 1851.

Rev. Nathaniel Laurence (1787) was the first minister of the town after its incorporation, and remained here until his death in 1843.

Dr. Samuel L. Dana (1813), LL. D., distinguished as a physician, chemist, and author, passed the latter years of his life here, upon the estate of Rev. Mr. Laurence, which he purchased. He married the youngest daughter of President Willard (1765) and Samuel Dana Kittredge (1876) is their grandson.

Rev. Horatio Wood (1827), now of Lowell, succeeded Rev. Mr. Laurence as pastor of the First parish; his son is Horatio Wood, jr. (1857).

Rebecca Bancroft, a daughter of Col. Timothy Bancroft, a life-long citizen, married Rev. Ebenezer Hill (1786), the minister of Hollis, N. H. Their two only children, twins, both graduated at the college:— Rev. Joseph B. Hill (1821), and John B. Hill (1821), who has published in pamphlet form his "Reminiscences of Old Dunstable," including the town of Tyngsboro', where he passed much time in the family of his grandfather during the years 1824, '25, '26 and '27.

William Bancroft Hill (1879), who was the class day orator, is a son of the Rev. Joseph B. Hill.

Francis Brinley (1818), although born in Boston, and now living in Newport, R. I., lived here several years, was town clerk, took a conspicuous interest in town affairs, and did good service in matters relating to schools and education.

Charles Butterfield (1820) was born and lived here continuously until his death. He was one of the founders of the once famous "Med. Fac. Society," as stated in the "Harvard Book," and as we have often heard him relate.

Dr. Augustus Peirce (1820) was the only practising physician here for many years immediately preceding the time of his death, which occurred here in 1849. He was the author of the "Rebelliad," which was delivered before the Engine club in 1819. It is a remarkable production in some respects, for a boy, then only about sixteen years of age, and the youngest member of his class. The college library has long had a valuable printed copy of it, and has recently received the original manuscript, carefully written out by the author from notes which he used at the time of its delivery. His son, Dr. Warren Peirce (m. 1869), is a successful physician in West Boylston, Mass.

Dr. Calvin Thomas (M. D. 1824), the im-

HISTORY OF THE OLD TOWNSHIP OF DUNSTABLE

www.ingramcontent.com/pod-product-compliance
Lightning Source LLC
Chambersburg PA
CBHW071406090426
42737CB00011B/1371